THE SPICE PORTS

The

SPICE
PORTS

NICHOLAS NUGENT

MAPPING THE
ORIGINS OF GLOBAL
SEA TRADE

BRANDEIS UNIVERSITY PRESS,
WALTHAM, MASSACHUSETTS

CONTENTS

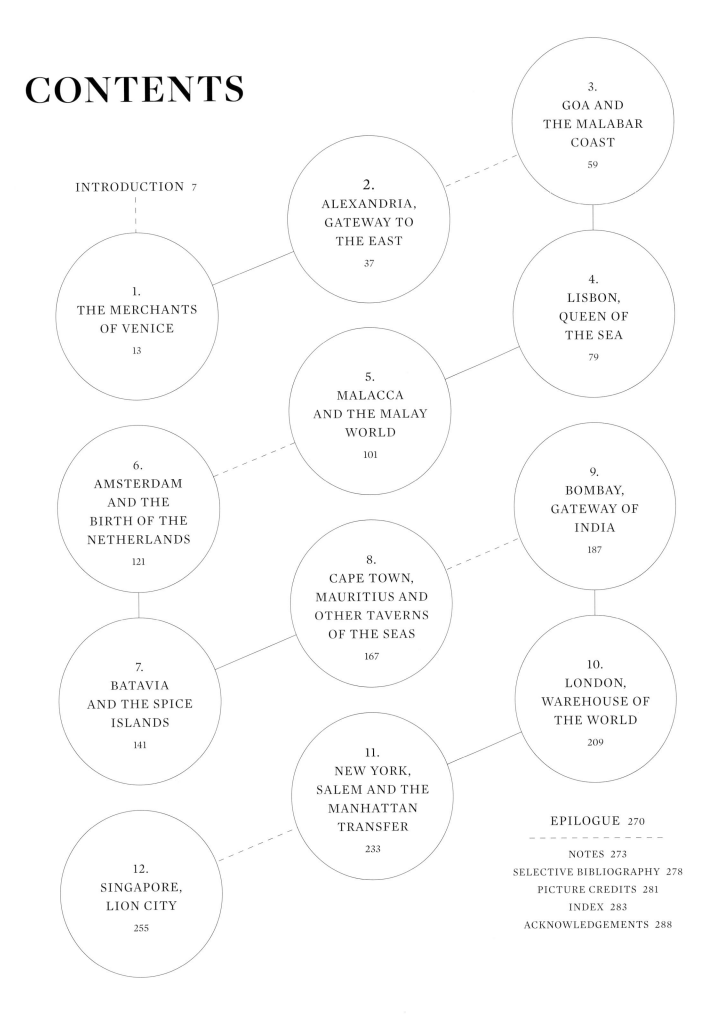

'Geography is the eye of history.'

ABRAHAM ORTELIUS, CREATOR OF *THEATRUM ORBIS TERRARUM*,
THE FIRST ATLAS, 1570

*'To read a map we need to understand why
it was drawn in the first place.'*

EXHIBITION OF MAPS AND THE 20TH CENTURY,
BRITISH LIBRARY, 2016–17

INTRODUCTION

*Watercolour of a branch of
a clove tree from a series
commissioned around 1824
from a Chinese artist in
Bencoolen by Stamford Raffles.*

The idea for this book came during a visit I made many years ago to the Banda Islands of Indonesia. Hard to find on a map, these eight islands are the original home of the nutmeg and its fellow spice, mace, which is part of the same fruit. Until the early seventeenth century nutmeg and mace grew nowhere else, so once Europeans developed a taste for these spices there was fierce competition to bring their flavours to European markets, and rich profit for those who had control of the source.

The Banda Islands are part of the fabled Spice Islands, properly known as the Moluccas or, in the Indonesian language, *Maluku*. While the Dutch controlled the southern Banda archipelago from the early seventeenth century, the Portuguese competed with the Spanish for control of Ternate in the northern Moluccas, and the Dutch and English fought each other for dominion over the central island of Ambon. Here the prize was access to the clove, another spice which enabled European households to make bland cuisine more appetising in an age when cooking was much less exciting than we expect today. For pepper, cinnamon and ginger, European traders did not have so far to sail to the spice gardens of southern India, Ceylon and Sumatra.

7

The fortunes of the European nations competing for spices rose and fell according to their successes or failures in this trade. First Venice became wealthy, giving rise to an extraordinary flowering of both art and science. Then, successively, Lisbon, Amsterdam and London dominated the Indian Ocean and its trade, prospering as a consequence of their control over the sea routes and earning the port cities their epithets: Lisbon, Queen of the Sea; Amsterdam the Golden; London, Warehouse of the World. Much of this advantage for Western ports came as a result of their technological innovation in compasses and mapping, and enterprise in exploiting their commercial advantage.

At the other end of what today we would call a 'supply chain' we see how Asian ports like Goa, Bombay, Malacca and Batavia (or Jakarta) grew around the trade in spices – initially to China and the Arab world, and subsequently to Europe where strong demand gave impetus to seaborne trade generally. Europe's lust for spices had its impact further afield as well – on the fortunes of New York, and in helping to make Singapore the trading entrepôt it is today. The individual chapters of this book interweave to give an account of each port's rise and fall: how they fought to control the markets in cloves, nutmeg and mace and subsequently for sugar, tea, coffee, cotton, rubber and tulips, all of which were then propagated through transplantation.

There is a darker side to this history, in that each of the European nations who were engaged in the trade then attempted to maximise their profits, first by enslaving local people, and later by transporting labourers between continents to work as 'slaves'; this has resulted in a legacy that the descendants of those who suffered find hard to forgive, and the descendants of the perpetrators find shameful to remember. This was not on the scale of the later transatlantic 'slave trade' in which, from the sixteenth to nineteenth centuries, powerful European nations bought captured individuals on the west African coast and shipped them to work the cotton estates of North America or the sugar plantations of the Caribbean. Our narrative details the localised enslavement – by the Venetians to row their galleys, by the Portuguese, Dutch and English as domestic servants or estate workers – though it also includes the capture and transhipment of people from Africa. Some examples might be regarded today as 'indentured' or 'bonded' labour, which became commonplace after the trade in enslaved people was abolished, and has in turn given way in modern times to 'economic migration'. Some of the colonial practices – notably those in fifteenth-century Banda – were indeed horrific.

This is inevitably mainly a story of men: male mariners and traders as well as kings, princes, *zamorins*, sultans and village headmen. However,

The nutmeg tree showing the core 'nut' as well as mace, the red outer skin, from a collection commissioned around 1824 by Stamford Raffles.

The known world as perceived by Claudius Ptolemy in the second century and portrayed by German cartographer Sebastian Münster in 1540. India barely features, China and south-east Asia are depicted as 'India Extra' while the Indian Ocean is enclosed by land.

two powerful women, Queen Isabella of Spain and Queen Elizabeth I of England, were personally responsible for sponsoring and funding the pioneering long-distance explorers Vasco da Gama and Francis Drake respectively, each of whom furthered the trade in spice. And European sailors were surprised at how frequently they dealt with women as the most active traders; the non-Muslim south-east Asian countries still top the world's tables for female participation in trade and marketing (see Chapter 7).

This book requires us to take a leap backwards to an age when the spices we now take for granted were a novelty to most households. Only then can we understand the significance of the innovative discoveries that brought them to European and American markets: the technology of building and powering ships, the navigational skills needed to harness wind power and tackle the seas, maps and the cartographical skills to draw them, knowledge of astronomy and time and their role in navigation, and the development of the telescope.

The search for spices was enabled by practical and scientific developments of the age, but also by theoretical and cultural advances such as early formulations of laws of the sea and the economic theories of supply and demand and of monopoly power. This was some centuries before the father of economics, Scotland-born Adam Smith, wrote in his book *The Wealth of Nations* that 'monopoly of one kind or another seems to be the sole engine of the mercantile system'. With Smith's help we note the effect on profit of cutting out the middleman. We also drop in on evolutionary theory in the footsteps of Charles Darwin and Alfred Russel Wallace.

In the process of telling the spice story we encounter key figures of history such as Alexander of Macedonia, Marco Polo, Napoleon Bonaparte, Horatio Nelson and Stamford Raffles, each of whom played a key part in the unfolding of events. Alexander and Raffles actually founded 'spice ports'. Others like the Greek Hippalus, the Egyptian Claudius Ptolemy, Portugal's Henry the Navigator and Dutch mariner-cum-map-maker Jan Huygen van Linschoten played vital roles in advancing navigation and cartography, while pioneer scientists like Eratosthenes of Cyrene, Galileo Galilei and John Harrison also contributed to the story.

Maps are indeed 'the eye of history', literally charting how each port played a role in extending geographical knowledge. Claudius Ptolemy, described as 'the Prince of Geographers' by map-publisher Abraham Ortelius, created the first maps in the second century, but not until the fifteenth century did they become widely available through the invention of printing. In 1570 Ortelius published the first atlas, *Theatrum Orbis Terrarum,* disseminating the work of cartographers whose maps, he tells us, are like 'glasses before our eyes [which] will longer be kept in memory, and make the deeper impression on us ... that now we do seem to perceive some fruit of that which we have read'. Ortelius is also credited with introducing an early form of copyright by pledging to include the names of the map-makers and to follow their 'faithfulness and diligence'.[1]

Early nineteenth-century painting of a spice seller, in the Benares style.

Early maps were notoriously inaccurate, so not very helpful to mariners. Christopher Columbus and Vasco da Gama did not use maps, just the stars. But by the late sixteenth century map-makers had become pioneers in a third dimension by imagining what a city looked like from above long before we developed the means to rise into the air and gain a bird's-eye view. The evolution of mapping is a powerful indication of traders' increasing mastery of their environment.

So too are words written at the time, early accounts and descriptions, though like maps they cannot necessarily be relied upon for their accuracy. I have drawn on contemporary sources, including *The Periplus of the Erythræan Sea* by a first-century author, Jan Huygen van Linschoten's *Itinerario*, Antonio Pigafetta's account of Ferdinand Magellan's round the world voyage and the *Colloquies* of the botanist Garcia da Orta, each of which gives a fascinating insight into their times.

I have also drawn from literature on the grounds that, as has been claimed, you have to read historical fiction to understand what *really* happened. Writers like William Shakespeare and Bertolt Brecht had their own vantage point on events described, while the books of two writers of fiction, Eduard Douwes Dekker (known by the pseudonym Multatuli) and Jacques-Henri Bernardin de Saint-Pierre, give us contemporary stories of Java (Chapter 7) and Mauritius (Chapter 8) respectively. Dekker's novel *Max Havelaar* paved the way for the end of the Dutch Republic's dictatorial system of crop cultivation in Indonesia, while de Saint-Pierre's novel *Paul et Virginie* encouraged eighteenth-century France to end enslavement in the territories it controlled in the Indian Ocean.

Who is to say whether contemporary accounts or novels written later – or indeed maps – give the most accurate representation of those times? After all, Marco Polo was given the nickname *Emilione*, teller of a million stories, because nobody could be sure how much truth there was in his tales.

I have focused on the main ports involved in the oriental spice trade, though inland cities also played a vital part. Nicolaus Copernicus' book *On the Revolution of the Celestial Spheres* and the fifteenth-century world maps of Hartmann Schedel were first published in Nuremberg, a pioneer city in printing. This book is made up of self-contained histories of each port city in the order in which they rose to prominence in long-distant trade and prospered. Together the chapters build a history of the trade in oriental spices which inaugurated the basis of the pattern of global maritime trade that we know today.

1/

THE MERCHANTS OF VENICE

The eighteenth-century artist Canaletto here depicts the entrance to Venice's arsenale, c.1740.

To tell the story of the international trade in spices, we need to put the ports involved in historical context. Imagine yourself in the late Middle Ages, around 1450, when any form of international travel or trade was exceedingly limited. In Europe travel by land was on horseback or in a horse-drawn carriage and further east by donkey, mule or camel. Travel across water required ships which, over long distances, needed to be hardy enough to withstand strong winds and large waves, though wind was essential to enable vessels to move. Early travel was not comfortable, so there was not much movement between the kingdoms and principalities of Europe let alone further afield to Africa and Asia. Australia and the Americas were unknown to Europeans, 'not yet discovered' in the patronising language suggesting that anything not known to Europe did not exist.

Of course these continents existed and were inhabited by people who were self-sufficient in their own way. What was missing was the means for people and goods to travel between continents, which was why the pioneer voyages westwards in 1492 by Christopher Columbus and eastwards in 1498 by Vasco da Gama had such an impact. A Genoese seafarer sailing under a Spanish flag 'discovered' the Americas, specifically the islands of the Caribbean, while a Portuguese mariner set foot in Asia, in south-western India, after a journey entirely by sea. The Venetian Marco Polo and his family members had taken a land route to Asia visiting India, Mongolia and China two hundred years earlier, but the tales he told on his return were not at first believed. Until the invention of the steamship in the 1830s, all sea travel was powered by wind, or in the Mediterranean Sea by oarsmen.

FOOD CULTIVATION AND TRANSPORTATION

These pioneers had a mixture of motives for their journeys: to prove the world was round, to extend human geographical knowledge, or to proselytise on behalf of the Christian religion; also, a desire to find the source of foodstuffs and other goods which were reaching Europe from Asia. These included spices from 'the Indies' – a loose term for India and the islands beyond – and silk and fine porcelain from China. Potatoes, tobacco and rubber were among products which grew only in the Americas and were brought to Europe following Columbus' pioneering voyage.

Consider for a moment the dietary fare of the average European in the fifteenth century. They were cultivators of vegetables and grain growers, bread being their staple food. The inhabitants of what we now know as Italy probably developed the idea of turning grain into pasta from Marco Polo who encountered noodles in China, though pasta consumption did not become widespread in Italy until the nineteenth century. Rice was first brought overland from China to Spain in the tenth century but only widely cultivated in the Venetian hinterland in the fifteenth century, after the city authorities exempted it from tax. The potato did not arrive from America until the turn of the seventeenth century, at first to Ireland and then Spain. There was limited farming of livestock for consumption by the wealthy. Venetians brought salt from the mainland to make their vegetables more palatable and to preserve meat and fish, since fresh stocks were not readily available.

Europeans were even worse off for drink. Water was not very tasty and often impure, so early Europeans developed the art of turning it into ale, the brewing process helping to purify the water and adding taste. Wine, first fermented in the Middle East around 3000 BC, was brought to Europe by the Phoenicians and Romans though Venetian mariners played their part as well. Tea and coffee did not reach Europe until around 1650 – at similar times, albeit it from different points of origin in the East. Before that, ale was the standard drink for young and old alike.

Then there were spices, initially pepper which improved the taste of cooked dishes. More exotic spices – ginger, cinnamon, cloves, nutmeg and mace – arrived in due course from the East. By modern standards European cuisine was bland, so it is understandable that once a new flavour was tasted there arose a demand for whatever produced that flavour, sending the price up. Some spices were credited with medicinal properties, while cinnamon was used in ancient Rome to embalm the dead. An advantage of spices is that they are easily transportable; after being dried they last for years.

EARLY MAP-MAKING

With so little long-distance travel, there was almost no understanding of the world beyond the horizon; maybe a slight grasp of the next village and the one beyond, less of the nation further afield and almost none of nations and continents which could only be reached by a long land journey or sea voyage. Hence the tales told of Asia by Marco Polo, after he was captured by Venice's rival seafarers, the Genoese, were both awe-inspiring and highly inaccurate. Christopher Columbus thought he was sailing to India, a land little understood before Vasco da Gama found the direct route. Even further in the future was the circumnavigation of the world by Ferdinand Magellan (1519–22), which proved once and for all that the world was indeed a sphere.

European knowledge of the world was largely 'Ptolemaic', based on the book *Geographia* written in Alexandria by Claudius Ptolemy in AD 150, which portrayed the known world around two oceans, Mediterranean and Indian, both of which he believed to be landlocked and therefore unconnected. Ptolemy's maps were not widely circulated, since the invention of printing was still several centuries in the future. Even after Vasco da Gama had rounded the Cape of Good Hope, Ruscelli's *Ptolemaic Cognita*, published in Venice in 1574, continued to represent the Indian Ocean as surrounded by land, like the Mediterranean Sea. It took time for new geographical information to spread. Map-making was the natural corollary of travel and trade, so it is not surprising that it began in Venice before spreading to European cities like Amsterdam, Antwerp, Nuremberg

Europe and Asia by Italian Girolamo Ruscelli in 1574, based on Ptolemy's calculations. The Indian Ocean is enclosed by land; India hardly features; but Ceylon, known to Greeks as Taprobana, is prominent.

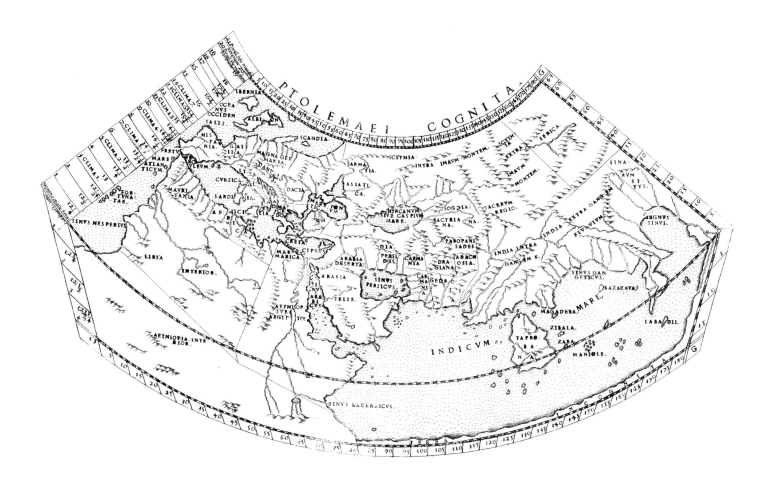

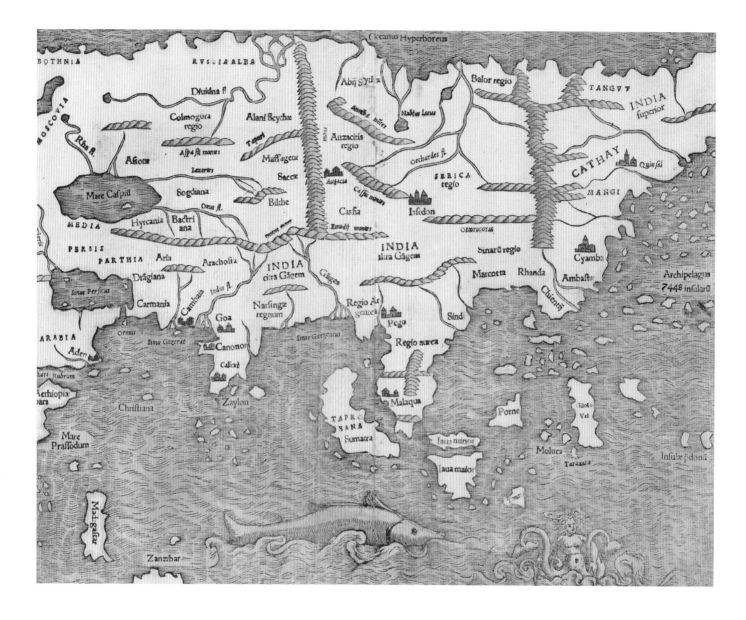

and Cologne, gaining in accuracy over time. Early maps were created by draughtsmen from the accounts of sailors.

In Basel in the mid-sixteenth century the German theologian Sebastian Münster revised Ptolemy's *Geographia* as an 'atlas' of world maps, making use of mariners' tales to produce a map of Asia which demonstrated that the Indian Ocean was not enclosed and could be reached by sailing around the southernmost point of Africa. Münster is known for his early 'upside-down' representation of Europe of 1550 which departed from the convention set by Ptolemy of putting north at the top. He was instead following a lead set by Venice's own pioneering map-maker, Fra Mauro, who beavered away at the monastery of San Michele on the glass-famous Venetian island of Murano to create a world map, or *mappa mundi,* which was also based on the tales of returning travellers. He had been commissioned by two interested parties: in Venice the *signoria* or supreme city authority was keen to learn just where it sat in relation to other known lands, while in Portugal King Afonso V was already set on upstaging the island republic in trading ventures but needed

more cartographic information than was available from maps based on
Ptolemy's calculations.

The result, completed around 1450, was one of the greatest maps of its
time showing the known world – Europe, Africa and Asia, and their oceans
and seas – on a single piece of circular parchment 2.4 metres in diameter,
together with notes. Of vessels traversing the Indian Ocean, Fra Mauro
wrote: 'The ships called junks that navigate these seas carry four masts
or more, some of which can be raised or lowered, and have forty or sixty
cabins for the merchants and only one tiller. They can navigate without a
compass because they have an astrologer who stands on the side and, with
an astrolabe in hand, gives orders to the navigator.' Fra Mauro also made a
remarkably accurate estimate of the circumference of the world. There is
some uncertainty as to who received his map first, though little doubt about
their impact. The one commissioned by the city enabled Venetian merchants
to retain their trading advantage for another fifty years, while that provided
to Portugal ultimately helped Lisbon gain ascendancy over Venice.

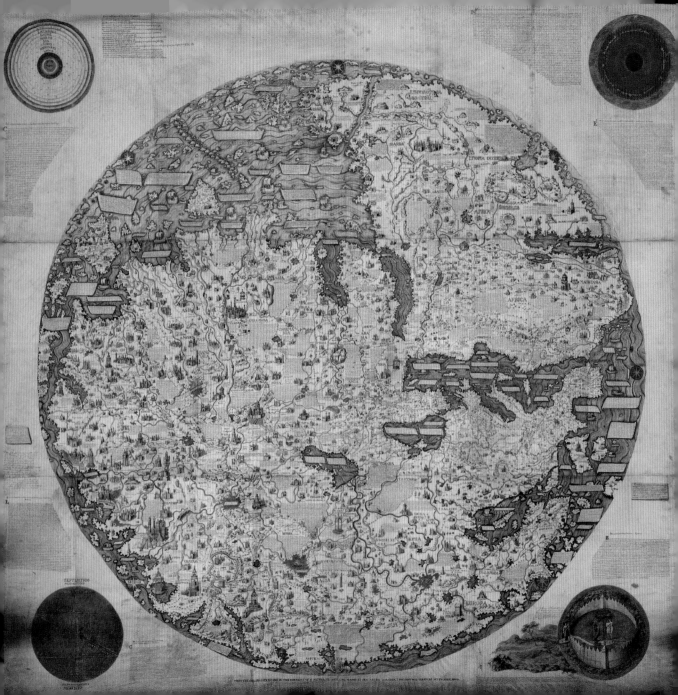

(right) This detail from the British Library's Mappa Mundi shows the islands of Java and Banda, claiming falsely that the latter was 'where cloves are born'. The Banda Islands are actually the natural home of nutmeg and mace.

(opposite) The British Library's 1804 reproduction of the Mappa Mundi, probably the earliest world map, produced on the Venetian island of Murano around 1450 by the monk Fra Mauro.

THE FOUNDATIONS OF VENICE

The islands that constitute Venice were first inhabited when migrants from the adjacent district of Lombardy fled the mainland when the Goths under Alaric conquered territory which had been under the control of Rome, in around AD 400. Migrants from the mainland were known as *Veneti*, though whether they brought that name with them or adapted it from the Latin verb 'to come', *venire*, is a matter of conjecture. As early as 446 BC the Greek writer Herodotus, known as 'the father of history' (who also knew something of geography), wrote that the borders of the region of Thrace 'reach almost to the Veneti on the Adriatic' suggesting that the people brought the name with them.[2] An alternative theory suggests that the city's name comes from the Latin *venetus* meaning 'sea-blue', a colour still associated with Venice as in 'Venetian blue'.

Venice was originally an archipelago of separate islands, gradually becoming linked by bridges or causeways to assume the shape and reputation of a single island, proud of its separateness from the mainland. Venice had nowhere to grow grain or other crops and barely any space on which to keep animals, so Venetians built boats to bring essential sustenance from the mainland. A desire for more appetising foodstuffs encouraged them to sail farther afield; gradually they progressed from building boats to reach the mainland to establishing an industry producing larger vessels. Venice's superior shipbuilding and seamanship enabled it to provide for the food needs of its own citizens as well as those of the hinterland of Lombardy and the rival city state on Italy's western coast, Genoa.

Venice was founded in AD 421 when three consuls from Padua established a trading post on what were then known as the Rialto Islands. Its population grew after another marauder, Attila the Hun, followed

Alaric's pillaging invasion of northern Italy. Rome was in decline before Venice was founded, though Rome's eastern empire based in Constantinople (now Istanbul) remained strong and Venice fell within its dominion. Island status allowed Venice to emerge as a separate nation untroubled by rivalry for territory on the mainland. As one historian of the city put it, Venice's greatness 'was built upon her geography'.[3]

From early times Venetian sailors enjoyed a monopoly in the transportation of salt which they brought from the Po valley on rafts or *zattera*, giving that name to the city's main quay near the southern entrance to the Grand Canal. When supplies from the Po ran short, they turned to Dalmatia and as far afield as Cyprus. Grain was brought from Sicily, Anatolia and the Black Sea. Less heroically, Venetian vessels played a role in transporting people from Black Sea ports to be traded on the Rialto alongside the Grand Canal. Venetians are among the earliest recorded users of 'forced' labourers, mainly as oarsmen on their galleys, a case of a strong power imposing its will on poorer peoples who may have had little choice but to work in return for being fed. They were rarely chained, but by the late fifteenth century formed 'a veritable underclass . . . debt slaves to the captains'.[4]

In AD 726 the Byzantine empire based in Constantinople lost control over Venice, causing the city to make a bid for self-government. A noble of Eraclea on the mainland assumed the title *dux*, or 'duke'. In the Venetian dialect he was known as the *doge*, which is more usually translated as magistrate. He was first of a line of 118 *doges* who successively presided over what became the Republic of Venice, self-governing if not fully independent. Christian nation that it was, Venice paid homage to the pope in Rome, whose strictures against trading with Muslim cities slowed the growth of the Venetian empire.

Venice developed a trading empire across the eastern Mediterranean. As vessels came under threat, it developed more heavily armed war galleys, the basis of a navy, also used to defend the home port. Its 'overseas' trading ports were also its naval bases – places like Beirut, Tyre, Crete and Alexandria and smaller ports on the Mediterranean littoral. As the power of the Byzantine empire of Constantinople declined, so that of Venice grew. Full trading access to Constantinople was granted to Venice in 1082.

Venice's founding myth is that early seafarers brought the body of St Mark the evangelist from Alexandria and reburied it at the cathedral church of San Marco. This is alleged to have taken place in 828, the year the papal ban on trade with Muslim countries was imposed, suggesting that Venetians were trading with Alexandria before then. The story of St Mark's journey by boat to Alexandria is told in mosaics in a chapel of Venice's Basilica San Marco.

FROM REPUBLIC TO *STATO DA MÀR*

Venice's rise from an island settlement sustaining itself with imported foodstuffs owed everything to its prowess in shipbuilding, which in turn depended on obtaining wood from the European mainland. The city became a pivot of trade, shipping Baltic amber, Cornish tin and Flemish cloth as well as timber, wool, copper and armaments from various European lands to Venice and thence to ports of the eastern Mediterranean. They returned with Indian pepper and Chinese porcelain and silk, among other exotic goods. Later ginger, cinnamon, nutmeg and cloves as well as Egyptian cotton and Russian furs arrived in Venice to be shipped onwards. By the year 1000 Venice was the main European market place for exotic oriental goods. Pirates were a major impediment to Mediterranean shipping, as were fierce winds such as the *bora* from the north and *sirocco* from the south. These hazards and the seamanship they demanded may have prevented less experienced seafarers from gaining a share of the trade.

Venice established the maritime empire that Rome never managed, with trading posts in Alexandria, the Levant, Constantinople, the Black Sea and along the Barbary coast of north Africa. Most commercially successful were Alexandria, Tyre and Acre because they had onward connections by land to the East, the fabled 'Indies', a loose term meaning anywhere beyond Arabia, and the exotic sounding Spice Islands whose exact location was unknown. Venetian merchants were not always sure where goods originated. As far as they knew they came from the *souks* (markets) of Cairo, Constantinople or Damascus.

Venice's opportunity to progress from trading republic to empire came at the turn of the thirteenth century when Jerusalem, symbolically important to Christians and Muslims, was captured by the Muslim warrior Saladin. Pope Innocent III called for a Fourth Crusade to win back the Holy City and – to nobody's surprise – Venice won the contract to provide ships. It also won a concession from the pope to trade with Muslim nations, provided it did not sell them arms. The Fourth Crusade would establish Venice as the greatest trading power in the Mediterranean, eclipsing its Italianate rivals, Genoa, Pisa and Amalfi. The Treaty of Venice of 1201 which launched the Fourth Crusade was the most important commercial contract of the Middle Ages, and a triumph for the blind *doge* Enrico Dandolo. He commissioned the republic's state-owned arsenal, the *arsenale*, to fulfil the 'supply' contract and to build fifty extra warships at the city's expense. As many as a quarter of the city's estimated 60,000 inhabitants were engaged in shipbuilding or providing supplies. The *arsenalotti,* as shipyard labourers were called, worked round the clock to complete the vessels, using timber from Germany and pioneering a new method of 'mass production'. At its busiest the *arsenale* was producing a ship a day, dominating activity on the island for more than a year to produce 450 transporter vessels and 50 warships.

Fewer crusaders than expected responded to the papal summons, which meant that they paid little more than half the contracted amount, giving Venice an upper hand in determining their route. Venice's priority was to recover strategic ports along the Dalmatian coast under the control of the King of Hungary and Croatia, which threatened Venetian trade and its access to Dalmatian pine with which to build more ships. Its next target was its own 'mother city' of Constantinople, capital of Rome's eastern empire, Byzantium, another Christian land. A much larger city than Venice, Constantinople held sway over the eastern Mediterranean. The pope turned a blind eye to this further deviation from the fleet's objective in the hope that the Eastern Orthodox Christian church would fall under his control, though that did not happen.

Venice's capture of Constantinople had a far greater impact in changing the balance of power in the region than the subsequent rather weak assault on the Holy Land by a severely depleted crusader army. By sacking a Christian-ruled city, Venice demonstrated that its trading business was more important than religion. 'At a stroke, the city was changed from a merchant state into a colonial power, whose writ would run from the top of the Adriatic to the Black Sea, across the Aegean and the seas of Crete … whose power would be felt, in its own proud formulation, wherever water runs', according to a leading historian of the city. Venice knew that 'wealth lay not in exploiting an impoverished Greek peasantry, but in the control of sea-lanes along which the merchandise of the East could be channelled into the warehouses of the grand canal'.[5]

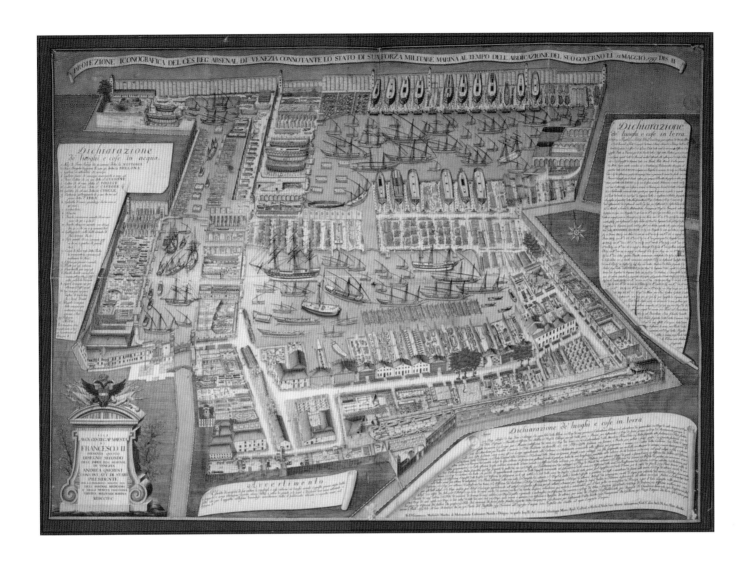

PROIEZIONE ICONOGRAFICA DEL CES REG ARSENAL DI VENEZIA CONNOTANTE LO STATO DI SUA FORZA MILITARE MARINA AL TEMPO DELL ABDICAZIONE DEL SUO GOVERNO LI 11 MAGGIO 1797 DIS II

An engraving by Gian Maria Maffioletti of the Venice arsenale at the time of the Napoleonic occupation of the city in 1797.

Venice called its loose network of trading posts its *Stato da Màr* or maritime empire: not an empire like those of later European powers occupying distant territories and their peoples, but one which controlled the sea lanes connecting its port to the spice markets of the eastern Mediterranean, 'the portal to another world'.[6] The city's commercial principle was 'for the honour and profit of Venice'. It had a strict code of ethics to prevent individual seamen enriching themselves, as all trade was considered to be on behalf of the republic. Venetian traders understood the power of monopoly, though the term was not in common use until much later. Having sole access to something in high demand enabled its possessor to benefit by setting a high price. Hence it was important to deny access by the Genoese and Pisans to the spice markets of the Levant. As long as Venice had sole access to the spices of the Orient that were in heavy demand in Europe it stood to make money, an economic theory that Lisbon, Amsterdam and London in their turn would try to exploit.

Venice's maritime supremacy was not unchallenged: for much of the fourteenth century the republic battled the Genoese, who were trying to restore the pre-eminent position they had held before the fall of Constantinople. Northern Italian regions like Lombardy depended on either Genoa or Venice for their food supplies, so their maritime rivalry reached close to home. It was in Italian waters that the 'battle royal' took place when Genoa attempted to throttle Venice's food supplies just down the Adriatic coast at Chioggia. Venice eventually emerged triumphant, but with considerably depleted naval power.

By 1400 Venice was the most admired and beautiful city in Europe and already the most favoured tourist destination: the Piazza San Marco was a mingling place for visitors from many lands. This was the start of Venice's Golden Age when the city's population may have reached 100,000. They gave their city the name *La Serenissima,* the most serene, and used its dominant position to shore up its advantage over other maritime states in trade with the East. This was still a century before a pope signed the Treaty of Tordesillas of 1494 dividing the newly discovered world beyond Europe between Portugal and Castile, forerunner of Spain.

Venice's trade brought great wealth to the republic. Its Rialto market place was the leading centre of exchange for all Europe. Ships from western and northern Europe reached the city to meet the Venetian convoys, known as *muda,* returning from Alexandria and the Levant, where they had collected spices brought by the Indian Ocean seasonal winds to these Middle Eastern market places.

Entrance to the arsenale *at Venice in 1741, drawn by Michele Marieschi.*

The arrival of the spice convoys in Venice signalled the start of a major trading festival, like an early version of the modern 'just in time' supply chain theory. By the fifteenth century Venice's biggest trade in volume and profit was in pepper, followed some way behind by ginger. Early European trading practices originated in Venice, so it is fitting that the word 'company' was adapted from the Italian *compagnia*, which originated in the practice of sharing bread, *cum panis*.

THE COMING OF THE OTTOMANS

Soon after the turn of the fifteenth century, Venice had 3,300 ships manned by 36,000 mariners trading on behalf of the republic; there was hardly a commodity that was not transported in Venetian ships. When necessary, merchantmen trading vessels were transformed into men-of-war to fight off predator nations or Mediterranean pirates. Continuing threats from Genoa may have distracted Venice from taking notice of another challenge to its pre-eminence in the eastern Mediterranean in the form of the Ottomans, Muslims from Central Asia. First engaging with the Venetians at Gallipoli in 1416, they threatened Venice's trade with Black Sea ports as they advanced on Constantinople. When an Ottoman fleet arrived in the Adriatic within striking distance of Venice, this appeared as a stand-off between the forces of Christianity and Islam.

The pope called for another crusade against this new Muslim threat, but Venice was reluctant having felt let down financially by its previous involvement. In any case, some Italian states – like Florence and Naples – considered that siding with the advancing Ottomans was the best way of challenging Venice's control of the sea lanes. The Ottomans needed little help and in 1453 took Constantinople, displacing Venice. Rome's former eastern capital, so important to Venice's extended empire, was now in the hands of Muslims. Victory by the Ottomans in a sea battle for the Greek island of Negroponte gave them control of the Aegean, a further humiliation for the once great Venetian empire. Henceforth Venice had to pay a tax to trade with Ottoman-ruled territories.

Venice's trade with Alexandria, which was ruled by Egypt's Muslim Mamluk dynasty from 1250, continued and was highly profitable, making the close of the fifteenth century a golden age for both cities. According to the economist Adam Smith writing three centuries later, the shared interest between the Mamluks and Venetians, both enemies of the Ottomans, 'gave the Venetians almost a monopoly of the [spice] trade'.[7] Sea battles between Venice and Ottomans off the coast of the Peloponnese ended with Venice signing a humiliating treaty with the Ottoman ruler in 1503. Its maritime empire, the *Stato da Màr*, was over; reduced to the status of any other trading nation, Venice would never recover control of the eastern Mediterranean.

While at battle, Venice received disturbing news from Alexandria that Portuguese ships had reached the Indian port of Calicut by sailing around the south of Africa. First reports suggested that the vessels were captained by the Genoese Christopher Columbus, though it later became clear that they were under the command of the Portuguese Vasco da Gama. Even so, it was a blow

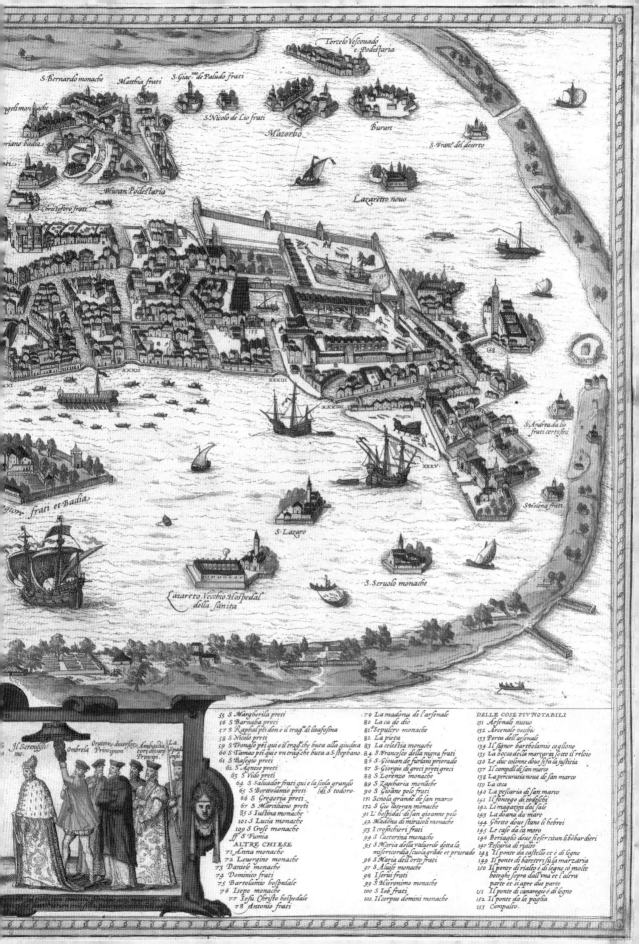

to Venice and its near monopoly of the spice trade. A contemporary diarist, Girolamo Priuli, wrote that for Venice to lose the spice trade 'would be like the loss of milk and nourishment to an infant'.[8] In a reflection of what would become modern economic theory, the writer argued that by cutting out the middlemen of Egypt and the Levant, the Portuguese would be able to sell Indian spices to Germans, Hungarians, Flemish and French at much lower prices than prevailed in Venice. As Venice was considering how to respond to setbacks at the hands of the Ottomans and the Portuguese, the Florentine polymath Leonardo da Vinci arrived in the city to take up employment as a military architect. The man who would later conceptualise flying machines and other inventions drew up plans for what would have been, had it been built, the world's first submarine.

The city state remained a self-governing republic, falling under the sway of Austria and briefly of Napoleon-ruled France before in 1866 becoming part of the newly created kingdom of Italy, later to become the Italian republic. In 1846 a causeway brought a road and railway into the city, ending forever its 'water-locked' status. Venice had been the centre of the largest and most significant empire since the Romans, ruling much of the Mediterranean littoral, and could claim to have been the first Renaissance city with the birth there of Titian (in 1490) and Tintoretto (1518). It has been called 'a medieval Singapore' where business was the state ideology and the government's main role was 'to keep the wheels of commerce primed and tuned'.[9] Both islands emerged from little to become great trading emporia, though Venice was in decline well before Singapore emerged, as we shall see in later chapters.

VENICE FROM THE AIR

The map of Venice in 1572 (pages 26–7) comes from *Civitates Orbis Terrarum* or Cities of the World, an atlas published in Cologne by map-makers Georg Braun and Franz Hogenberg, pioneers of the art of mapping cities.[10] They collected information from accounts and drawings of returning travellers, imagined the city from the air and engraved the images on copperplate, centuries before techniques of surveying and photography made the map-maker's art more scientific. Such maps provided an A-Z guide of how to reach a particular place in the city, valuable to seafarers visiting a port for the first time, and gave insight into the urban life of each city in the late sixteenth century. Such bird's-eye views were created two centuries before the invention of the hot air balloon in 1783 gave us the ability to rise into the air,[11] providing a perspective that nobody had ever seen, but a vantage point that visionaries like Leonardo da Vinci had dreamed of reaching. This image shows a city with a population of about 170,000.

The Customs House (*Dogana da Mar*) stands on the promontory at the southern entrance to the Grand Canal with its adjacent warehouses. (It remains there today, though no longer with its original function.) Ships unloaded there to pay the city's tax or import duty before making their way to the market area nearby. The city's seat of power, the blue-roofed Doge's Palace and Basilica San Marco, pillars of justice and Campanile (bell-tower) next to the Piazza San Marco lie at the centre on the island's southern shore.

(previous spread) German cartographers Georg Braun and Franz Hogenberg produced this 'aerial view' of Venice in 1572. The arsenale *is prominent at the eastern end of the island.*

Turkish traders living in Venice around the time the map was drawn are credited with having introduced the coffee drinking habit.

Leading north from Piazza San Marco by the clock tower is the Merceria or Market Street, a trading area running towards the Rialto Bridge over the Grand Canal, which a fifteenth-century visitor from France described as 'the loveliest thoroughfare, I believe, in the whole world'. The map legend tells us that the Rialto Bridge was made of wood, had shops on both sides, and could open up into two parts to let tall vessels pass. The spice market was at Campo San Bartolomeu close to the bridge. The *arsenale*, once the largest shipyard in the world and the source of the city's strength, occupied an extensive area at the eastern end of the island. It was said to be admired by monarchs including Peter 'the Great' of Russia and Henry VIII of England, and was mentioned by Dante in his *Divine*

Venice by Daniel Meisner pictured in 1637 during the port city's golden age. The Basilica San Marco and towering campanile are at the centre.

Comedy.[12] At top right of this image is the old *arsenale,* while the larger compound below houses the 'new' *arsenale* (built in the 1570s) with access to the sea via the Arsenal Canal.

The image below the map shows the 'Most Serene Doge' or magistrate – under the parasol – escorted by courtiers bearing symbols of his authority including a ceremonial chair, while the doge's ceremonial rowing barge, the *Bucintoro* (from *buzino d'oro,* vessel of gold) with its gilded roof, can be seen on the water. It was used only on Ascension Day when 168 oarsmen rowed it from the Venice lagoon into the Adriatic Sea for the doge to cast a ring into the water, symbolising Venice's 'marriage' to the sea. This ceremony of thanksgiving for Venice's prosperity, known as the *sensa,* took place from 1100 until Venice fell to Napoleon's army in 1797, marking the end of the independent republic. The last *Bucintoro* was broken up in 1824. It features in several paintings by the artist Canaletto.

MARCO POLO'S *TRAVELS*

Not far from the Rialto Bridge was the house of the Polo family. In 1271, the teenage Marco Polo accompanied his father Matteo and uncle Nicolò along the land route to Cathay (China), travelling north of the Caspian Sea through Central Asia on what came to be known later as the Silk Road.[13] They passed through the Mongol capital of Saray and thence to Cathay, source of the silks and porcelain which would later be sold at the Rialto market. Matteo and Nicolò had met the Mongol ruler Kublai Khan on an earlier visit. Marco would tell the story of their journey in his *Travels*, originally titled *Il Milione*[14] and later *Le Livre des Merveilles du Monde* (Book of the Marvels of the World). It is a book that nearly did not get written.

Returning from Cathay after a 24-year absence, Marco served on a Venetian warship engaging the Genoese in the Adriatic in one of their periodic wars; his ship was captured and he was incarcerated in jail in Genoa. There he told stories of the wonders he had seen in the East, possibly in an embellished form, to a Pisan fellow-prisoner, Rusticiano, who wrote them down, ensuring they reached a wider readership in those pre-printing press days. He may have intended them to be a guidebook for other travellers.

When Marco Polo's *Travels* appeared in manuscript form in around 1300, fellow Venetians learned there was an 'abundance' of pepper and ginger in Malabar, southern India, as well as in Gujarat and Delhi, and that pepper, nutmeg and cloves could all be found on the island of Java. It is likely that this 'intelligence' also reached the Spanish and Portuguese monarchs, fuelling their own plans to find a direct route to the East. Little is known of Marco Polo after his release from prison. He is thought to have returned to Venice and led a quiet life in business, never returning to the East. Yet by telling his story, he influenced the future course of international trade and travel and marked Venice out as a truly cosmopolitan city.

The British poet John Masefield places Marco Polo alongside Herodotus as one of history's greatest travellers: 'The wonder of Marco Polo is ... that he created Asia for the European mind ... [Before Marco Polo] the popular conception of the East was taken from the Bible.'[15] The Polos were not the first Europeans to reach China, but Marco was the first to tell the story in a way that inspired later travellers, including Christopher Columbus. He encouraged mariners to seek the source of the spices, and doubtless inspired John Masefield's own poem 'Cargoes' (1903) whose first stanza reads: 'Quinquereme of Nineveh from distant Ophir, Rowing home to haven in sunny Palestine, With a cargo of ivory, And apes and peacocks, Sandalwood, cedarwood, and sweet white wine.'

SHAKESPEARE'S *MERCHANT OF VENICE*

The Merchant of Venice, written by the English playwright William Shakespeare in 1600, tells how Bassanio seeks to borrow 3000 *ducats* from his best friend Antonio to woo the lovely Portia whom he wants to marry. It is a play about the value of money – specifically Venetian *ducats* – versus human relationships, against a backcloth of Venice's trading empire: the opening scene refers to silks and spices. Antonio would like to help Bassanio, but all his money is tied up in trading ventures with ships destined

Marco Polo setting sail from Venice, 1271, as depicted in an early fifteenth-century French language edition of the Venetian's travels by artist Johannes.

Ci coumence li liures du grant Caam qui parole de la grannt Ermenie. de perse.
et de tartars et dynde. Et des granz merueille qui p le monde sont ;

Our sauoir la pure verite des
diuerses regions du monde. si
preuez cest liure si trouuerez les
grandsimes merueilles qui sot
escriptes en la grant hermenie
et de prsse. et de tartas. + dynde
et de maintes autres prouinces. si conme nre liures
nous coutera tout par ordre des que nre sires marc. pol
saiges et nobles si toies d'neuer raconte pource que il
les uit. mais auques ilya choses ;

uil ne vit pas. mais il entendi dou
mes certains par uerite. Et pource
metrons nous les choses venes pour
venes. Et lentedue pour entendue
ace que nre liure soit urais et uertu

bles fans nule menconge. Et chascais qui ce liure ona
ou lenale doit croire. pour ce que toutes sont choses ve
ritables. Car ie vous fais asauoir que puis que nre
sire diex fist adam le premier pere ne fu onques de
mil homme generation qui tant seust ne cerchast
des diuerses parties du mode come cestu nre sire mar
pol en ce. et pource pnsa que ce seroit granz maus se
se ne fist mettre en escript ce que il auoit veu + oi par le
rite. A ce que lautre gent que ne sont vraue oi le sa
chent par cest liure. Et si vous di quil de nosra a ce
sauoir. en ces diuses parties bien. xxvj. ans le quel
liure puis que demoura sut fu en la carcere de gene sa
retraire par ordie par mesire Rasta pisa. Qui en cele
mesimes prison estoit au temps que il courot de
crist. mil. CC. z iiij. et xcij. ans de lincarnacion.

for Tripoli, the East Indies, Mexico and England, so instead he suggests that Bassanio borrow *ducats* from a Jewish moneylender against his (Antonio's) credit and reputation.

Antonio to Bassanio:
Thou know'st that all my fortunes are at sea;
Neither have I money nor commodity
To raise a present sum. Therefore go forth:
Try what my credit can in Venice do;
That shall be racked, even to the uttermost
To furnish thee to Belmont to fair Portia.
Go, presently inquire, and so will I,
Where money is, and I no question make
To have it of my trust, or for my sake.

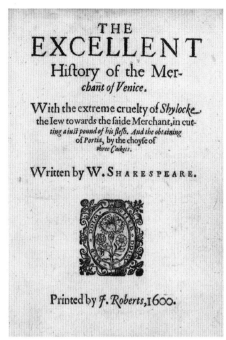

After Bassanio takes the loan, it appears that some of Antonio's ships have been lost at sea, a common occurrence. This prompts the Jewish moneylender, Shylock, to endeavour to collect the 'pound of flesh' promised by Antonio as part of the loan deal, refusing an offer of double the initial loan instead. A court hearing before the Duke of Venice is influenced by a speech made by Portia (disguised as male lawyer Balthazar) which balances the case for mercy against justice, arguing that 'the quality of mercy is not strained … it is twice blest: it blesseth him that gives and him that takes'. The court rules that Shylock may not collect his 'pound of flesh' because the contract does not allow him to spill blood and it would be impossible to cut flesh without spilling blood.[16]

The play is a morality tale written at a time of heightened anti-Semitism in Europe; according to some interpretations, it was an attempt to show Christians as more merciful than Jews. By demanding flesh rather than cash, Shylock seeks to avenge Antonio, who constantly berates him for usury – charging high rates of interest on loans – and Christians in general, since his daughter had eloped with Antonio's friend Lorenzo and converted to Christianity. As part of the court-imposed settlement, Shylock himself was forced to convert to Christianity. In a final touch which gives the whip hand to Christians, it transpires that Antonio's ships are not lost after all.

Shylock would have resided in the ghetto where Venetian law required all Jewish families to live. It was close to an iron foundry – *geto* in the language of the time. The Italian word *ghetto* has come to mean in English an area where a disadvantaged race or community reside. Another word from Venice which gained international usage was *quarantina*, or quarantine, after the practice of ships being held offshore for a required forty days of isolation to avoid spreading infection after the great plague of the 1570s, which killed nearly a third of the city's inhabitants.

GALILEO'S TELESCOPE

In Venice, a significant revolutionary idea and a crucial invention both developed through to maturity, although both originated elsewhere.

The new idea was that the Sun lay at the centre of the universe while the Earth and all the other planets rotated around it. For centuries religious and scientific orthodoxy had held that the Sun and the planets revolved around the Earth, which was the centre of the universe. This notion had been articulated by the Greek philosopher Aristotle in the fourth century BC; supported by another Greek, the astronomer and father of map-making, Claudius Ptolemy, in the second century AD; and backed by the Bible, or so it was said. Hence any attempt to revise this scientific theory risked upsetting the Christian church and its figurehead, the pope.

The first attempt in modern times to challenge this orthodoxy was by the Polish mathematician Nicolaus Copernicus in his book *De revolutionibus orbium coelestium* (On the Revolutions of the Celestial Spheres). Copernicus, a clergyman living in northern Poland, while still a young man suggested the contrary theory of the Sun being the centre of the solar system. His publication was delayed for many years, and by the time it appeared in print he was on his deathbed. Because of the distance from Rome, the reaction from the Catholic church was muted.

The Pisa-born Tuscan Galileo Galilei, who taught mathematics at the University of Padua (which lay within the boundaries of the Venetian Republic), was less fortunate in escaping the church's sanction. Both Copernicus and Galileo had studied medicine as well as mathematics and astronomy, Copernicus at the university in Padua where later Galileo taught. Copernicus died in 1543 while Galileo was born in 1564 – the same year as William Shakespeare. Galileo promoted Copernicus' theory and offered greater evidence by observing the planets through a 'spyglass' containing a set of lenses, a system invented in Flanders. Galileo demonstrated his spyglass to cardinals of the church in Rome, whereupon a Greek mathematician, Giovanni Demisiani, gave it the name by which it is better known: the telescope.

Galileo set up a 'production line', a new industrial concept, using glass from the Venetian island of Murano to grind the lenses before selling the telescopes for a small sum. For his efforts the University of Padua awarded him the unheard of privilege of tenure for life. Galileo's common-law wife Marina – they never married – lived in Venice, where he was a regular visitor. His telescopes were much in demand by sailors, quick to understand their application for astronomical navigation or finding one's way using the stars. In the magnificent painting by Giuseppe Bertini (overleaf) you see Galileo at the Campanile showing the doge how to use the telescope.

Galileo presented evidence that the Sun rather than the Earth was at the centre of the universe, in his theory of heliocentrism or Copernicanism. In studying the planets, he claimed that they revolved around the Sun as well as rotating on their own axes; he observed the phases of Venus, the satellites of Jupiter and the rings of Saturn as well as the phenomenon of sunspots. His university rewarded him, but the church chose instead to make an example of him. Its enforcement division, the Inquisition, called Galileo's ideas blasphemous, an attempt to reinterpret the Bible which (it said) came dangerously close to Protestantism, the challenge to Christian orthodoxy sweeping northern Europe and perceived as a threat to the

Galileo shows the doge how to use the 'telescope' to prove that the Earth circulates around the Sun, painted by Giuseppe Bertini, 1838.

position of the pope. Venice liked to regard itself as beyond the reach of the Inquisition, but by the time Galileo was put on trial he was living in the Tuscan city of Florence so in no position to seek the protection of the Venetian authorities. The charge against him was that he held opinions 'contrary to Holy Scripture' and his writings, and those of Copernicus, were banned. Although a devout Catholic, Galileo was fortunate to be spared the usual sentence of excommunication or worse; a Dominican friar had earlier been burnt at the stake in Rome for claiming the Earth rotated around the Sun.

Galileo was held under house arrest where, despite increasing blindness, he continued his scientific research, publishing his most famous work at Leiden in the more enlightened atmosphere of the Protestant Dutch Republic. He died in 1642, the year another great mathematician and scientist, Isaac Newton, was born in England. Newton would in due course strengthen the view of the universe advanced by Copernicus and Galileo, adding the important ingredient of gravity.

Galileo's clash with the Catholic church is regarded as the most significant milestone in the confrontation between science and the church which would later engulf scientists like Newton and Charles Darwin, though never as critically as in Galileo's case. Galileo has been described as the first 'secular saint' and 'a martyr to science'.[17] Not until three a half centuries later did a commission come close to making a recantation on behalf of the

Catholic church, declaring it the result of 'tragic mutual incomprehension' between the scientist and theologians, leading both to 'transpose a question of factual observation into the realm of faith'.

Also in the twentieth century, the German playwright Bertolt Brecht's *Life of Galileo* portrays the episode as a turning point in relations between the church and science. As told by Brecht, Galileo's sin in the eyes of the church was that he 'got rid of heaven' and 'made God unnecessary'. Brecht was in exile from Nazi-ruled Germany, having been stripped of German citizenship after espousing Marxist ideology, so doubtless felt sympathy for Galileo's treatment at the hands of the church.

In the play's penultimate scene, Brecht depicts Galileo as remorseful towards science rather than religion, declaring himself unworthy to be called a scientist for having publicly recanted in a battle between scientists and rulers. Speaking of the human race 'which shambles around in a pearly haze of superstition', the Galileo figure continues: 'As a scientist I had a unique opportunity ... astronomy [had] emerged into the market place ... Had I stood firm the scientists might have developed something like the doctors' Hippocratic oath, a vow to use their knowledge exclusively for mankind's benefit.' Instead (he goes on) we have become no better than 'inventive dwarfs who can be hired for any purpose'.[18] Not long after the play's first performance in 1943, atomic bombs were dropped on two Japanese cities creating a new ethical test of the social responsibility of science.

Another mathematician from the Tuscan city of Pisa some centuries before Galileo also contributed to the expanding wisdom of the age by introducing to Europe a system of writing numerals which originated in India and was adopted in the Arab world in the ninth century. Leonardo Bonacci, who lived from around 1170, became aware of these numerals while visiting Algeria with his merchant father Guglielmo Bonacci. At his behest the Hindu-Arabic system of numerals, as they are known, replaced the Roman system in use at the time because the former were easier to use in calculations. It subsequently became the most widely used numeric system in the world, another credit for a son of Tuscany growing up at a time when international travel and trade were giving rise to an exchange of learning and wisdom. The system's pioneer is better known to the world as Fibonacci, short for *filius Bonacci*, son of Bonacci.

The new numbers would have been useful for Venetian merchants trading goods in Alexandria, a profitable port on the opposite side of the Mediterranean to which we now turn our attention.

'Science ... was the greatest achievement of the [Ptolemaic] dynasty and makes Alexandria famous until the end of time ... Mathematics, Geography, Astronomy, Medicine, all grew to maturity in the little space of the land between Rue Rosette and the sea.'

E. M. FORSTER, *A HISTORY AND A GUIDE TO ALEXANDRIA*

2/ ALEXANDRIA, GATEWAY TO THE EAST

Detail from Jan Huygen van Linschoten's 1596 map of Asia and the Indian Ocean showing the Nile Delta, the Red Sea and Aden.

Alexandria, one of the Mediterranean's oldest settlements, lies close to the point where the mighty River Nile drains into the sea. It was both a terminus for European ships and a barrier to trade further east until a way was found through the intervening bridge of land, whereupon it became a gateway to the East. That thought spurred the city's founder, the Greek Alexander of Macedonia, to conquer a significant part of Asia in his search for a land route to India, earning him the soubriquet 'the Great'. The idea that Egypt was key to reaching India led Napoleon Bonaparte to try to incorporate the country into his expanding empire. His defeat at the naval battle of Aboukir Bay close to Alexandria prevented him from realising his ambition to conquer the East and gain access to its spices.

Alexander and Napoleon both dreamed of opening up European trade with the East by removing the isthmus of land that separates the Mediterranean and Red Sea, and joins the continents of Asia and Africa. Until the completion of the Suez Canal in 1869, European ships docked at Alexandria to offload cargoes which were then transported by land and water, camel and *felucca*[1] to the Red Sea for their onward journey to the East, while spices, tea, silks, porcelain and other goods made the transit in the opposite direction.

THE FOUNDATION OF ALEXANDRIA

Alexander III of Macedonia founded the port city in 331 BC at a natural anchorage close to one of the outlets of the Nile. Just as Venice was founded after the decline of the Roman empire, Alexandria did not exist when the Pharaohs ruled Egypt. An earlier settlement may have been submerged underwater. Archaeologists believe they have now discovered the lost city of Heracleion, referred to by Herodotus, 32 km (20 miles) north-east of Alexandria in Aboukir Bay. This suggests that the coastline has receded and that Alexander, a student of Aristotle, founded his port city on land created by silt from the River Nile, at a time when Heracleion was already in decline.

Alexander had defeated a Persian army to take Syria and Palestine and then found himself in control of Egypt whose people, we are told, were glad to be free of Persian domination. He arrived at the place that would become Alexandria by sailing down the River Nile from Memphis, then Egypt's capital, landing at a fishing village on the edge of Lake Mariout (or Mareotis). There, aged only 25, he founded the port city which bears his name. He did not stay long enough to see it grow, but pursued his war against the Persians, Greece's traditional enemy, bringing western Asia under his dominion and reaching lands as far distant as Bactria in northern Afghanistan and the valley of the Indus River in northern India, believed to be a source of great riches.

It was not an obvious place to found a new city – a narrow strip of land between the Nile-fed Lake Mariout to the south and the sea to the north. Alexander brought from Rhodes an architect, Dinocrates, who connected the island of Pharos to the mainland by a causeway, the Heptastadion, which was 7 *stades* or about 1,300 metres long. This created two seaports, one on either side of the causeway: the Great or Eastern Harbour, where the royal fleet of the later Ptolemaic dynasty would moor their vessels alongside the Royal Palace, and the Western or *Eunostos* ('safe return') Harbour.

The westernmost or Canopic mouth of the Nile lay some kilometres east of the city on the western headland of Aboukir Bay. The Canopic Way, later renamed Rue Rosette, ran from the river mouth to the Western Harbour. The Nile's Canopic mouth silted up in the Middle Ages leaving the Bolbitic mouth dominated by the port of Rashid or Rosetta[2] as its western outflow, while the town of Damietta guards the eastern Phatnic mouth – as the map from the time of Napoleon shows. The foundation of Alexandria drew sea trade away from Rashid which, like Damietta, continued to play a key part in the river trade. The Greek historian Herodotus, who visited Egypt a century before Alexander, gave the name 'delta' to the region where the Nile fanned out to meet the Mediterranean because it resembled the Greek letter of that name [Δ].

Alexander the Great died in Babylon aged 32. His body was returned to the city he founded seven years earlier and laid to rest where the Canopic Way crosses the north–south Street of the Soma, which links the Eastern Harbour to Lake Mariout.[3] *Soma* is a Greek word meaning 'body'. Alexander's empire was divided among his generals: Egypt became the realm of one named Ptolemy,[4] beginning a dynasty of Greek rulers who took the names Ptolemy or Cleopatra according to gender. Sometimes described as 'the Hellenic Pharaohs', they ruled Egypt for the next three centuries, making Alexandria the foremost city in the Greek world, more Greek than Greece it was said, and a centre of learning that earned the dynasty its place in history.

The word 'museum' comes from Alexandria's *mouseion*, a place dedicated to the nine muses built on the pattern of one in Athens. It included a garden, a zoo and an observatory and the famous *Alexandrina Bybliothece* or library, which held as many as 500,000 scrolls including works by the philosophers Homer, Plato and Socrates. Most of the scrolls were of papyrus, a plant

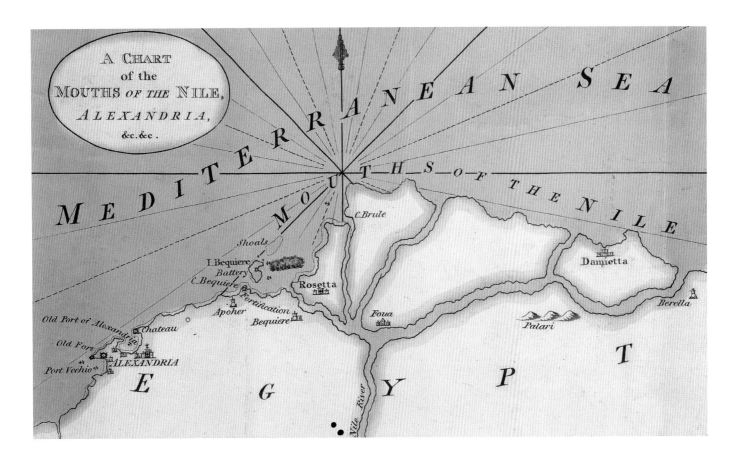

By the time this chart was drawn in 1798 by John Fairburn, the River Nile no longer flowed through the port of Alexandria. Rosetta (Rasheed) lies close to Aboukir (Abu Qir) Bay.

which grew prolifically in swamps along the Nile. At one stage the Ptolemies banned the export of papyrus to preserve Alexandria's pre-eminent position in the world of learning; this caused its rival, the city of Pergamon (in present-day Turkey) with its own library, to experiment with writing on animal skins, thus creating *pergamina* or parchment. As well as a centre of Greek wisdom, Alexandria was a city of Jewish scholarship and many of the scripts in the library were written in – or translated from – Hebrew.

So much was concentrated in the library of Alexandria that it was said that all the knowledge of the world was contained within a single city. Many mathematical, astronomical and geographical developments date from the Ptolemaic era. Euclid, the father of geometry, published his *Elements* which

is considered a standard text. Archimedes of Syracuse, part of the Greek empire in Sicily, visited Alexandria from where he observed the annual rise and fall of the River Nile, measured by various forms of 'Nilometer', and invented the 'screw', a device for lifting water, making him a pioneer of hydrostatics as well as the mathematics of measuring volumes, remembered by his *eureka* moment which gave rise in due course to Calculus. Steam power for pumping water was also first developed in the city.

Eratosthenes of Cyrene (now in Libya), who became chief librarian at Alexandria around 255 BC, is credited with calculating the Earth's circumference by comparing the Sun's midday shadow at Aswan in Upper Egypt with that at Alexandria. From these measurements he calculated the exact length of a year and 'invented' the extra day concept of the 'leap year' adopted in Julius Caesar's Julian calendar. The geographer Strabo (64 BC–AD 21) came to Alexandria as tutor to one of the Ptolemy princes and there wrote his *Geographica*, an early textbook about the world. Strabo wrote that the great Greek philosopher Aristotle 'taught the kings of Egypt how to arrange a library'.[5] The library was founded during the reign of Ptolemy Soter (c.323–283 BC). According to legend it was destroyed in 48 BC when the Roman ruler Julius Caesar, finding himself beleaguered in the Greek city, ordered that ships in the harbour be burned. The fire spread to nearby buildings and engulfed the library. Other accounts suggest that the library was still standing well into the Roman era.

Strabo gave us a contemporary description of another construction that made Alexandria famous, the lighthouse or *pharos* at the eastern end of the island of the same name: it was a three-tiered white tower rising 117 metres into the sky, whose lantern could be seen by ships up to 60 kilometres away. At its summit was a huge statue of one of the Greek gods, Zeus or Poseidon. Twelve years in construction and inaugurated during the reign of Ptolemy II Philadelphus, the *pharos* was a protector of seafarers for seventeen centuries until it was destroyed by an earthquake in 1303.

The view of the *Eunostos* or Western Port in about 1860 with the Eastern Port in the distance shows how Alexandria's harbour commanded access to the River Nile. The Heptastadion, originally a causeway to the island, separates the two ports. Nine years after this image was drawn, the opening of the Suez Canal revived Alexandria's fortunes as a trading port. In his history and guide to Alexandria, the writer E. M. Forster calls the *pharos* 'the greatest practical achievement of the Alexandrian mind and the outward expression of the mathematical studies carried out in the Mouseion'.[6] It was one of the seven wonders of the ancient world.

ROMANS, ARABS AND TURKS

Rome conquered Alexandria and the Egyptian hinterland around 30 BC. One of the city's most famous inhabitants during Roman times was Claudius Ptolemy, whose *Geographia* was written in Greek in the form of a treatise around AD 150. Claudius Ptolemy is credited with devising an early version of longitude and latitude from his celestial observations. These became the basis of maps shown in the previous chapter which helped the Romans to expand their empire eastwards. Ptolemy's maps were not widely disseminated until the mid-fifteenth century, when printing on paper was developed at the German city of Mainz. Ptolemy's depiction of the Mediterranean Sea and Indian Ocean as adjacent, enclosed, seas was the accepted view until the Portuguese 'discovered' the route to Asia around the southern tip of Africa, proving that Africa could be circumnavigated, as both Herodotus and Eratosthenes believed, and that the Indian Ocean was not a closed sea.

Shakespeare, and later Hollywood, remember the last of the Ptolemies, Queen Cleopatra VII, for her dalliance with two Roman generals, Julius Caesar and, after Caesar's assassination, Mark Antony. The latter's defeat by fellow triumvir Octavian led to the suicide of both Antony and Cleopatra and the end of Greek rule in Egypt, which was incorporated as a province into the expanding Roman empire. Romans ruled Egypt till AD 640, twice as long as the Greeks, firstly from Rome and subsequently from their eastern capital, Constantinople. Egypt was a source of grain to feed citizens in Rome and the empire, so a lively trade developed with Alexandria. The Roman Emperor Trajan was one of those who promoted the digging of canals to attempt to link the Mediterranean Sea with the Red Sea via the River Nile to improve access to spices and other goods from the East.

Christianity was introduced into Egypt during Roman times by the evangelist St Mark – not the disciple of Jesus of the same name – who became the first bishop of Alexandria. The famous Septuagint translation of the Old Testament from Hebrew into Greek had been carried out on the island of Pharos during the reign of Ptolemy II Philadelphus (285–247 BC) – according to legend seventy Jewish elders worked on it – and later Alexandria played a role in the adoption of the Nicene Creed in AD 325. Another saint, Catherine, is said to have been martyred in the city and her body was spirited to Sinai where St Catherine's monastery now stands, though there are some doubts whether this saint ever existed. The legendary female mathematician, Hypatia, was murdered in the city in AD 415, giving

A remarkable painting by the Venetian brothers Gentile and Giovanni Bellini from 1504–7 purporting to show St Mark preaching in Alexandria, though the architecture is clearly of Venice, the city to which St Mark's body was brought from Alexandria.

Alexandria in the 1880s by Charles Burckardt, looking north. The view is towards the Mediterranean Sea from Fort Napoleon (also known as Fort Caffarelli) on the hill of el-Nadoura, with the Eastern Harbour on the right.

rise to another layer of mythology. She was a follower of neo-Platonism, a philosophy developed in Alexandria from an idea advanced by Plato six centuries earlier that holds that we live in a poor imitation of an idealised perfect world.

The coming of the Arabs around AD 640, with their own religion of Islam, ended Roman rule and supplanted Christianity as the dominant faith of Egypt, though a significant minority of Egyptians today are Coptic Christians. Before Arab rule was consolidated, Egypt was ruled for several more centuries by outsiders from other corners of the Mediterranean, starting with the Mamluk Turks in 1250. The Ottoman Turks took over from 1517 and remained in power until Napoleon brought France into the game of power politics at the end of the eighteenth century. The British followed with their determination to protect access to – and trade with – India. Napoleon was thwarted in his ambition, but it was a French engineer who finally cut a waterway though the desert isthmus. All its conquerors recognised Egypt's importance as a transit route between Europe and India. We can get an idea of how Alexandria looked soon after the opening of the Suez Canal in the street scene depicted by Charles Burckardt in about 1880 when the camel was still the main beast of burden.

Alexandria played a role in modern Egyptian history from the founding of the Egyptian monarchy there by Mohammed Ali in 1805, after Napoleon ousted the Ottomans, to the overthrow of that same dynasty by Alexandria-born Colonel Abdul Nasser in 1952. Egypt's last king, Farouk, sailed into exile

ALEXANDRIA

MEDITERR ANEVM MARE

from Ras el-Tinn palace on what was once Pharos Island. Today the city has a decidedly European feel about it (described eloquently by Lawrence Durrell in his quartet of novels) because of its past links with Greece and Rome as well as Venice.

THE VENICE CONNECTION

Venetian merchants conducted their business in the city from guest houses known as *fondaci* (from the Arabic *funduq*), which combined the functions of an inn with those of counting house and warehouse. They bought spices – cinnamon, ginger, cloves and nutmeg – as well as silk, linen, precious stones and other oriental goods and locally produced cotton from the city's markets and sold woollen goods and furs, timber and iron. Their purchases were shipped back to Venice to be sold at the Rialto to maritime traders from all parts of Europe.

The oriental spice trade was at its height towards the close of the fifteenth century and Alexandria was the pivot between Asia, 'the Indies' so called, and Europe. Neither Venetian nor Arab traders would have realised how they were about to be eclipsed by mariners from the west of Europe,

Alexandria mapped 'from the air' in 1575 by German cartographers Braun and Hogenberg showing eastern and western ports and inaccurately depicting branches of the River Nile flowing through the city.

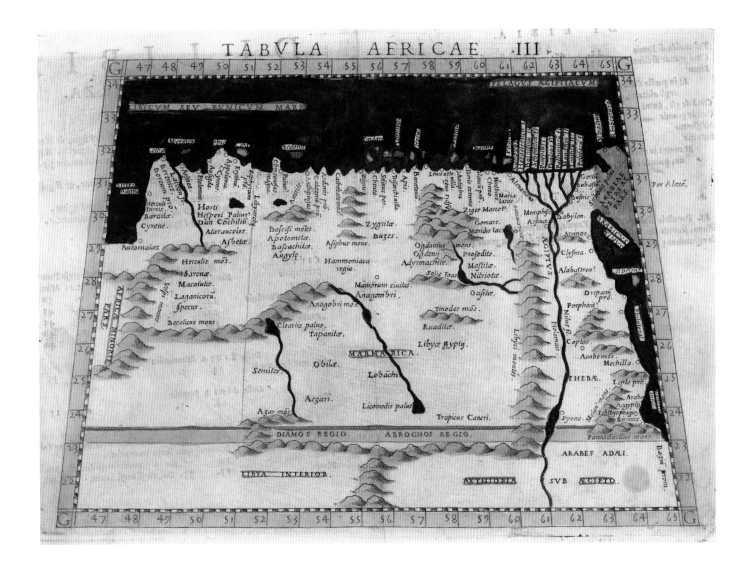

An early view of Egypt, produced in Venice by Girolamo Ruscelli in 1564, showing the Mediterranean and Red Sea coastlines and the River Nile delta.

who were on the way to discovering a route to Asia around the African cape, sending both traditional spice trading cities into decline.

Alexandria made its contribution to lexicography. Besides the word 'delta' which was first applied there, *pharos* or some variant means 'lighthouse' in several European languages and its Arabic name of *el-Manarah* is the origin of the word 'minaret'. The word 'Ptolemaic' refers both to the Graeco-Egyptian dynasty and the map-making system of Claudius Ptolemy which viewed both the Mediterranean Sea and Indian Oceans as enclosed seas. The term 'Alexandrian' is often used to describe the golden age of learning associated with the city. The British novelist E. M. Forster, who worked there during the First World War, suggested in his guide to the city that a memorial be erected to mark Alexandria's scientific achievements; this eventually happened at the start of the twenty-first century with the opening of the *Bibliotheca Alexandrina* on the site of the ancient library of Greek times, suggesting that Alexandria hopes to resume its position as a centre of research and learning.

The bird's-eye view of Alexandria by German map-makers Braun and Hogenberg purports to show the city in 1570 but is wildly inaccurate, as was commonly the case with maps of that time. The only accurate depictions are of the Eastern and Western ports and of 'Pompey's pillar' at the top right, which can still be seen today. This view looks southwards from the Mediterranean towards Upper Egypt, again defying the 'north at the top' convention of the city's most celebrated map-maker. The Latin text tells us that Alexandria was built 'with towers and battlements' around 320 BC by Alexander the Great and was at the time about the size of Paris. It describes it as the oldest trading port in Egypt and says the River Nile flows through the city along several channels – which may have been the case in the sixteenth century – refilling cisterns for the benefit of people the whole year round. A map produced in Venice by Girolamo Ruscelli in 1564 suggests that by then the Nile had changed its course and no longer flowed through the city. The text refers to the stone under which the body of St Mark was found, and from where it was taken to Venice. At the centre bottom we can see the Quat Bey fort built by the Mamluk Turks on the site of the *pharos* lighthouse. Pharos Island was by this time a peninsula jutting out from the mainland.

NAPOLEON'S DREAM

Alexandria lies 30 kilometres east of Aboukir Bay, where Napoleon Bonaparte's French fleet was defeated in 1798 by his British adversary, Horatio Nelson, at the brief but decisive Battle of the Nile. The defeat marked the end of Napoleon's ambition to ride triumphantly into Asia on an elephant (as he later wrote) with a turban on his head and in his hand 'the new Koran that I would have composed to suit my needs'.[7]

Just how much of a setback this was for Napoleon's ambitions is clear from a memoir written twenty years later after his defeat at Waterloo in 1815 and exile to the British-ruled island of St Helena. He told his captors that he would rather have been emperor of the East than of the West, and that the key to becoming so was to have allied with the Mamluk rulers of Egypt. Napoleon told a visitor to St Helena 'If the French had kept possession of Egypt, the English sooner or later would have lost India ... [and I] would have even made the East Indian Company trade with [me]', so it is ironic that he should spend his last years as a prisoner of the British on an island controlled by the East India Company. History is inclined to see the Napoleonic Wars as about the power balance in Europe, but when we take account of Napoleon's Egyptian venture it is clear that they were as much about Asia. Had Horatio Nelson not defeated him in Egypt, destroying the French fleet including its flagship, Napoleon had planned to march to the River Euphrates at the head of an army of 200,000 and thence onwards to India in the manner of his hero, Alexander the Great.

'Had I remained in Egypt, [I] should probably have founded an empire like Alexander, by going on a pilgrimage to Mecca,' he said. Revealing a thorough grasp of Britain's far from secure position in India, he said he would have allied with the Marathas who controlled the area around Bombay and were the chief threat to British rule at the time. In this way Napoleon believed he would have succeeded in driving the British from India. Referring to the capitals of present-day Armenia and Georgia in the Caucasus region of south-east Europe, he said 'I have all the maps and

statistics of population for a march from Erivan [Yerevan] and Tiflis [Tbilisi] to India ... Once touched by a French sword, the scaffolding of [British] mercantile power in India would fall to the ground.'[8]

SUEZ AND ITS CANAL

Suez, at the head of the western branch of the Red Sea, was a fishing and trading port since ancient times and the furthest north and west that goods from Asia could reach by sea. From there Alexandria on the Mediterranean is 285 kilometres distant. The stretch of land that blocked passage between the two seas was tantalisingly narrow, around 120 kilometres, and the wedge of land between Suez and the River Nile at Cairo was of similar width. These distances were nothing beside the thousands of miles which an Arab or Indian vessel would already have travelled across the Arabian Sea.

The earliest attempt to link the Mediterranean Sea to the Indian Ocean was in around 1874 BC when Pharaoh Sesostris III started building a canal to connect the Nile at Memphis, south of Cairo, with what was then known as the Erythræan Sea. Surprisingly for a people who had already constructed the pyramids, the ancient Egyptians seem not to have completed the project. In his book *Meteorology*, Aristotle suggests that the project was halted out of fear that sea water would spoil the fresh water of the Nile.[9]

Later attempts were made to 'pierce the cork' which kept the seas apart: by Pharaoh Necho II in 609 BC, Darius I of Persia in 510 BC, Ptolemy II Philadelphus in 269 BC, the Roman Emperor Trajan in AD 117 and the first of the Arab rulers of Egypt, Amr ibn Elas, in AD 640, when he also built the Mamoudieh canal to connect Alexandria to the western branch of the Nile, making the city the main transit point in East–West trade. Much later Napoleon planned separate canals, 'one from the Red Sea to

Ships on the Suez Canal at Port Said, near its northern, Mediterranean entrance.

MER MÉDITERRANÉE

MER ROUGE

the Nile at Cairo, the other from the Red Sea to the Mediterranean',[10] but was discouraged by his surveyors who calculated that the Red Sea was 10 metres higher than the Mediterranean. This was not the case and probably delayed the start of the project by more than sixty years, until more advanced technology discounted any imbalance in water levels. In any case, Napoleon's canal building ambitions were sunk at the Battle of the Nile.

Eventually in 1869 a channel was cut through the most direct route – from the Red Sea to the Mediterranean Sea – by French engineers with British finance, making Egypt a fully navigable thoroughfare rather than a barrier. To mark the canal's opening the Italian Giuseppe Verdi wrote his Egyptian-themed opera *Aida*, first performed in Cairo, demonstrating what a truly European project it had been to cut a channel through the isthmus to connect two mighty seas. For the first time, ships departing from European ports could dock weeks later at Asian ports without going round the Cape of Good Hope. Following the best tradition of aerial views (and still before powered flying was possible) the panorama of the canal soon after its opening shows the relatively modest challenge that was overcome to link the Mediterranean Sea to the Indian Ocean.

THE PERIPLUS OF THE ERYTHRÆAN SEA

The Periplus of the Erythræan Sea[11] was a handbook written by an unknown merchant based at the Red Sea port of Berenicê in the first century AD, after the Roman Emperor Augustus had taken control of Egypt. The Erythræan Sea, based on the Greek word for 'red', was an early name for the Indian Ocean.[12] No distinction was made between the two-forked gulfs we know as the Red Sea (because of the way it reflects the red hills of the Arabian peninsula) and the vast Indian Ocean to which it leads, as journeys between Egypt and India started or finished in the Red Sea.

The *Periplus* refers to the trade carried on by Arab sailors in everyday items like wood, metals, grain, oil and textiles and the Roman merchants who were importing silver, ivory, tortoiseshell and aromatics from east Africa; myrrh, frankincense and white marble from Arabia; and indigo, agate, turquoise, onyx, lapis lazuli, diamonds, fine clothes and silks from more distant parts of Asia, enabling Egyptian and European nobility to look and smell good. The only mention of edible items being brought to Egypt was of pepper, while grain, olive oil and Arabian wine feature in the list of goods flowing in the opposite direction, together with cosmetics, silver and glassware and people of both genders – girls to join Muslim rulers' harems and boys as servants or musicians.

Much of the *Periplus* is devoted to India, the most important trade destination at the time. Arabian and Indian sailors understood the seasonal winds or monsoons that blow across the Indian Ocean, and the traditional *dhow* sailing boat was built to withstand these strong winds. (The word 'monsoon' in English and Dutch is derived from the Arabic *mawsim*, having been first adopted by the Portuguese as *monção*.) According to the *Periplus*, the ideal month for a vessel to depart from Egypt was July, since this would enable it to use the wind blowing from the north to sail down the Red Sea. Sailing by day and anchoring at night because of dangerous shoals, it would take about a month from the port of Berenicê to reach its mouth. On exiting through the straits of Bab el-Mandeb or 'Gate of Grief', ships turned eastward and made use of the south-westerly wind to sail across open sea to the Gulf of Cambay, the shoreline of Gujarat, or a more southerly Indian port. Because of the severe squalls brought by the south-westerly monsoon, many Indian ports were closed during that season with only anchorages protected from the wind remaining accessible. To reach India before September was to avoid the most dangerous winds. The journey from Red Sea ports to India's west coast was about 3,000 nautical miles or 5,600 km and took up to two months.

The *Periplus* advised that the earliest time for home-bound departure from India was November, when the north-easterly winds started to blow. These were less fierce than the south-westerlies and allowed a longer window of opportunity to depart, up to April, so even a late departing vessel could get back to its home port within a year from the time it set out. Like European sailors centuries later, Arab ship-owners were keen to reap the return from their sizable investment without undue delay. The 1740 map of the Erythæan Sea or Indian Ocean by Dutch map-maker Jan Jansson (which refers to the ocean as Red Sea in both Greek and Latin)[13] shows how

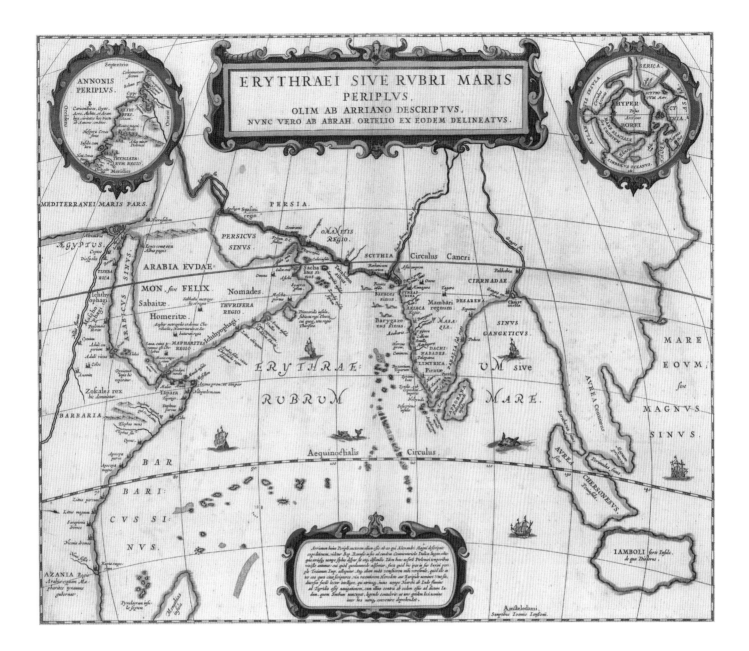

ERYTHRAEI SIVE RVBRI MARIS
PERIPLVS,
OLIM AB ARRIANO DESCRIPTVS,
NVNC VERO AB ABRAH. ORTELIO EX EODEM DELINEATVS.

The Indian Ocean depicted
by Dutch cartographer Jan
Jansson in 1652 (this version
dates from 1740) under the
Greek and Roman names
Erythæan Sive Rubri Maris.
Among ports depicted are
Berenicê in the Red Sea and
Muziris in southern India.

straightforward was the voyage between Egypt, Arabia and western India, provided navigators took account of the seasonal winds or monsoons.

Greek mariners sailing from Egypt were late to acquire this traditional knowledge and could reach no further than the port of Eudaimôn Arabia,[14] known today as Aden, which provided a safe anchorage and thus grew into an early entrepôt where goods were traded and trans-shipped. A first-century Greek explorer called Hippalus[15] is credited with discovering the 'secret' of the monsoon winds. He demonstrated that the fastest way to reach India was by sea using the winds, rather than by following a land route. Hippalus has been rewarded by having a crater on the moon named after him.

By the time the Romans took Egypt into their empire, the principles of navigation to Arabia and India were well understood. The *Periplus* was written to facilitate the trade in luxury goods. An early impetus was the demand for frankincense, the resin of a tree which grew in the otherwise barren wilderness of southern Arabia and was used in aromatherapy. One early map calls the land we now know as Oman 'Frankincense-bearing land'. Even more in demand and hence more costly was another tree resin, myrrh, which was burned at funerals to hide the smell of rotting flesh. These high-value luxury items together with gold had been brought to Bethlehem from the land we know as Yemen by three Arabian kings to pay their respects at the birth of Jesus. In biblical times control of the trade in frankincense and myrrh gave power and wealth, so it is little wonder that the peninsula came to be known as *Arabia Felix*, or Lucky Arabia, by the Romans.

According to the *Periplus*, the Egyptian ports most used for the luxury trade were Myos Hormos (Mussel harbour) and Berenicê, both reachable by journeys by camel across the desert from Coptos, an easy boat ride from Alexandria and the nearest point on the River Nile to the Red Sea. (These locations are shown on the map opposite the chapter opening, though higher up the Red Sea coast than they actually were.) The *Periplus* tells us that Indian ships arriving from the Gulf of Cambay were forbidden by their Arab rivals to pass the Bab el-Mandeb straits into the Red Sea and had to offload their goods at Aden on the Arabian coast or Zeyla (also known as Ocelis) on the African coast. Beyond the straits, only Arab vessels were allowed.

The *Periplus* provides the earliest reference to the practice of trans-shipping goods between the Mediterranean Sea and Indian Ocean with help from the 'ship of the desert', the camel. This technique was as precious a secret to traders as those of the monsoon and the navigational routes, and gave those who knew it monopoly power in transporting sought-after products such as jewels, cosmetics and spices. This is why pioneering travellers like Hippalus, Marco Polo and the Dutchman Jan Huygen van Linschoten (whose story we shall tell later) contributed so much to the rise in power and wealth of their respective nations. Egypt's Roman rulers imposed an import duty of 25 per cent. Goods arriving at Red Sea ports were transferred to customs houses for dues to be collected. Customs houses figure prominently in many of the port city views in this collection as places where goods were assessed and duty collected.

Indeed, whoever controlled the trans-shipment port held a licence to make a profit. Marco Polo told of the importance of Aden – lying just beyond the Red Sea – as a trans-shipment centre. 'Aden ... is the port to which all the ships from India come with their merchandise. It is a great resort of merchants. In this port they transfer their goods to other small ships, which sail for seven days along a river. At the end of this time they unload the goods and pack them on camels and carry them thus for about thirty days, after which they reach the river of Alexandria; and down this river they are easily transported to Alexandria itself.'[16] The 'river' close to Aden is evidently the Red Sea, while the river of Alexandria is the Nile.

Polo tells us this is the shortest route by which pepper and 'precious wares' reach Alexandria, and says there is a lucrative trade in shipping Arabia-bred horses in the opposite direction from Aden to the west coast of India. Many merchant ships sailing east started their voyages from Aden, and Polo says the sultan of Aden is one of the richest rulers in the world as a result of the duties he levies on merchants coming and going in his country, though he goes on to note that the sultan also derives a large income from his monopoly of the trade in frankincense, which he buys for 10 gold *ducats* and sells to merchants for 40.[17] With horses in demand in India and frankincense commanding a high price in Alexandria, it is no wonder that *Arabia Felix* was such a prosperous land.

EUDAIMÔN ARABIA, OR ADEN

Like Alexandria, Aden went into decline after the route around the Cape of Good Hope was discovered, only to be revived by the opening of the Suez Canal in 1869 and the coming of steam-powered vessels. Ships docked there in a sheltered bay off the rocky island of Sira, with its defensive fortress built by the Portuguese. In the first century AD the Himyarites who inhabited the region built a series of large cisterns or tanks on the slopes of Aden's extinct volcano to overcome a shortage of water. They were still in use when the fourteenth-century Moroccan traveller, Ibn Battutah, visited Arabia, though they fell into disuse soon after. Battutah tells us that seafarers came to Aden from Cambay, Quilon, Calicut, Mangalore and Goa in India, as well as from Egypt. He wrote that the merchants of Aden 'have enormous wealth; sometimes a single man may possess a great ship with all it contains, no one sharing in it with him, because of the vast capital at his disposal, and there is ostentation and rivalry between them in this respect'.[18]

A decade or so before the Suez Canal opened, a British engineer, Sir Lambert Playfair, restored thirteen of the ancient cisterns (of which there were originally about fifty) enabling Aden to become a key bunkering post for both cargo and passenger vessels. One of the first vessels to steam through Suez in 1869 carried coal from South Wales to Aden to support its role as a bunkering facility.

The view of Aden in 1575 (overleaf) remains recognisable today, though Sira Island is now connected to the Arabian peninsula as it was in early times. The map-makers Braun and Hogenberg tell us that Aden was a famous trading place to which merchants travelled from India, Ethiopia and Persia in search of myrrh and frankincense: 'The city is magnificent, well fortified by its site and construction, famed for the beauty and large numbers of its buildings, surrounded by a wall and very high hills, on the summits of which blazing torches point out the harbour for sailors.' So Aden had its *pharos* as well. Aden was once in the domain of the famously wealthy and beautiful Queen of Sheba, who features in the holy books of Christians, Jews and Muslims. The town centre in the middle of this image, known today as Crater, is towered over by the extinct volcano within which lie the ancient cisterns.

One of many cisterns built in the mountains above the port of Aden to provide water to visiting ships.

THE ORIGINS OF COFFEE

As if *Arabia Felix* did not have enough going for it with frankincense, myrrh, gold and fine horses, this land also yielded another commodity that would become a luxury and later a necessity in Europe: coffee. The coffee plant was 'discovered' west of the Red Sea in Ethiopia, where the pleasant taste and energising effects of chewing its leaves were enjoyed by people who had first observed its effect on goats; but it was on the eastern shores that the plant was first cultivated and its berries or beans roasted to create a hot infusion, the drink of coffee. Seeds may have been brought there from Ethiopia, the first of many transplants of *Coffea arabica,* possibly in the sixth century, but it initially had no commercial significance and it took several centuries for coffee to become a drink, let alone a habit.

ADEN, Arabiæ foelicis emporium celeberrimi nominis, quo ex India, Æthiopia, et Perside negotiatores conueniunt: vrbs est magnifica, situ et structura bene munita, ædificiorum nitore atque frequentia celebris, muro et præcelsis septa montibus, in quorum summitatibus ardentes faces nauigantibus portum ostendunt. Peninsulæ formam quondam obtinuit, nunc autem hominum industria, vndique aquis ambitur.

Braun and Hogenberg's depiction in 1575 of the fortified port of Aden, at the time an island off the southern coast of Arabia. Water cisterns were built in the volcanic mountains.

It was on the Arabian peninsula that coffee acquired its Arabic name, *qahwa el-bon*, the wine of the bean, and its reputation as the Islamic world's alternative to hard liquor and thus the soubriquet 'Islamic wine'. The Arabic word for wine, *qahwa* or *kahwa*, is probably the origin of the English word coffee and other derivates, such as the Turkish *kahve,* though an alternative explanation is that it is named after the Kaffa region of Ethiopia.

The Red Sea port of Mocha (*el-Makkha*) became synonymous with fine coffee after developing a lively export trade feeding a growing appetite for this new beverage in Europe. Ships queued to load beans, only for them to be unloaded again further north at an Egyptian port on the opposite side of the Red Sea and the beans to be taken by camel and riverboat to the Mediterranean, as spices had been earlier, helping give new life to the

trading emporium of Alexandria. Later demand and profits were such as to justify shipping coffee beans direct to European and American markets by the long route round the Cape of Good Hope.

The Ottoman Turks were responsible for the spread of coffee into Europe after they captured Yemen in 1536 and developed their own addiction. Turkish coffee, drunk thick and sweet, remains a popular delicacy throughout the former Ottoman empire. As the empire expanded, so coffee reached new markets as far west as Vienna, where the empire's expansion was halted in 1683. Turkish soldiers are said to have left behind several bags of beans before retreating, which may have caused the citizens of Vienna to develop their own coffee-drinking culture. Some historians claim that coffee itself was an instrument of power – both because of the strength that any monopoly invests and because of the stimulating effect of the beans. For at least 150 years the port of Mocha was kept busy satisfying the tastes of European coffee connoisseurs.

The German coffee historian H. E. Jacob tells of an early example of brand marketing.[19] Arabia could not produce enough coffee to satisfy European demand, so Brazilian beans were shipped by windjammer around the Cape of Good Hope to Arabia, although the long, damp voyage destroyed its aroma. It was dried under the Arabian sun, rechristened 'Mocha' and shipped back round the Cape, in steamships this time, to satisfy European coffee drinkers. Calling coffee 'part of the history of the mind of man' Jacob

A scene of coffee roasting in Egypt, from Description de l'Égypte, *1809.*

argues that its discovery was 'as important as the invention of the telescope or of the microscope ... for coffee has unexpectedly intensified and modified the capacities and activities of the human brain'. While this view would have won the support of Napoleon, Beethoven, Voltaire and Pepys, all of whom frequented coffee-houses, it seems today somewhat exaggerated; it is easier to agree with another of Jacob's contentions, that the discovery of coffee extended the working day by helping to stimulate the mind.

While the Turks were spreading a taste for coffee, the Dutch and the French were expanding the sources of supply by transplanting the plant that produces the bean. Coffee's arrival in Amsterdam in the early seventeenth century is of particular significance since it led to its cultivation on Java in the East Indies. According to some accounts, a coffee tree was shipped from Aden to Amsterdam in 1616, though other versions suggest that cuttings were taken to Amsterdam and successfully cultivated under glass. As Arabia's monopoly ended, so began the decline of Mocha which lost importance as a trading port to Aden with its deeper harbour.

The trading partner that features most prominently in the story of Egypt is India, the source of many of the spices that Europeans coveted. At the close of the fifteenth century, neither Venetians nor Alexandrians could have been aware that their role in the trade with India was about to collapse as a result of the success of Portugal, a non-Mediterranean nation, in finding a direct route to the sources of spices.

GOA. GOA.

3/

GOA AND THE MALABAR COAST

A view looking south across the Mandovi River to Goa around 1700, by German cartographer Joseph Friedrich Leopold.

On 20 May 1498 the Portuguese nobleman turned mariner Vasco da Gama landed at Kappad beach, 15 kilometres north of Calicut on India's Malabar coast. It was nine and a half months since he set sail from Lisbon on the first direct sea voyage from Europe to India. From Malindi in east Africa, da Gama employed the services of a pilot for the final stretch across the Arabian Sea. He directed the Portuguese towards Calicut – now known as Kozhikode – on the Malabar coast in the pepper-growing region of southern India (pictured in a 1575 print by François de Belleforest and Sebastian Münster, overleaf).

On being asked why they had come, da Gama's mariners replied that they had come in search of 'Christians and spices'. The *zamorin* or king of Calicut was unimpressed by the presents the Portuguese brought from King Manuel of Portugal, having had his expectation for gold or silver set by Arab traders. He told da Gama: 'In my land, there is much cinnamon, and much cloves and ginger and pepper and many precious stones. What I want from your land is gold, silver, coral and scarlet cloth.' He was presented with cloaks, hats, striped cloth, branches of coral, brass vessels, a chest of sugar and a cask of honey. He refused the Portuguese permission to set up a *feitoria* or trading post, and after a stay of three months they set sail back to Lisbon with bags of spices, not as many as they had intended, promising to return with more substantial goods to trade. They started their return journey against the prevailing wind and took five times as long to reach the African coast as on the outbound crossing.

This was the first of many trading voyages from Lisbon. Da Gama himself returned twice, though his relationship with the *zamorin* hardly improved. For a time there was open war between the Portuguese and the people of the Malabar coast, which in turn led to strained relations between King Manuel I and da Gama, who was initially passed over for the new post of Portuguese viceroy of India. After Manuel died and his son succeeded him as King João III, da Gama was eventually appointed viceroy. He set sail in April 1524 to take up the post, only to die soon after reaching India. He had played an important part in giving Portugal control of the Indian Ocean, boosting its status in Europe.

Nearly fifty years after da Gama's arrival in what is now the state of Kerala, Sebastian Münster produced a map from Basel, Switzerland, which

The port of Calicut near where Vasco da Gama landed after the first 'round the Cape' voyage, pictured in 1575 by François de Belleforest and Sebastian Münster, showing that it was already a centre of shipbuilding.

demonstrates how raw and inaccurate was European understanding of India – or 'the Indies'. Based on the calculations and guesswork of the first-century mapping pioneer Claudius Ptolemy, the map fails to show the large subcontinental projection into the Indian Ocean. We see the River Indus rising in the mountainous north and flowing into the Indian Ocean, and further eastwards the mouths of the River Ganges, which appear to enter 'off stage' from the east.

Portugal's 'discovery' of a new continent, known for being the source of spices and the fantastic tales of Marco Polo, captured the imagination of Europeans. Indians had been used to foreign traders since at least the first century, when Hippalus had identified the south-west 'monsoon' winds which came to bear his name. Da Gama was the pioneer of a new class of visitor from the West who did not just want to trade, but also exhibited a sense of superiority towards the peoples they encountered; this was based on their Christian faith and their shipbuilding and navigational skills. 'We have arrived here via a long and tortuous journey,' they seemed to be saying, 'and you should regard us as your saviours.' Portugal's self-satisfaction found support from the most powerful authority in Europe when Pope Nicholas V,

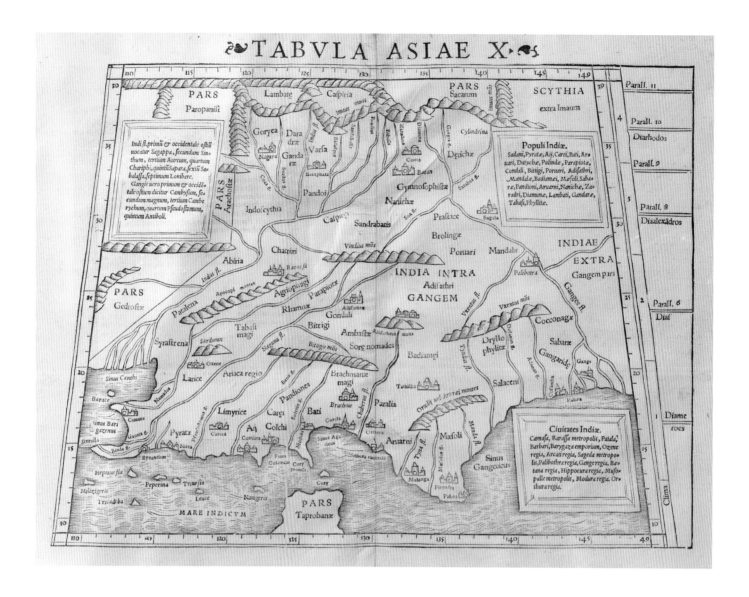

in the first of a series of *bulls* or edicts, authorised the Portuguese to take possession of any land that was not already ruled by Christians.

ARIKAMEDU AND MUZIRIS

India had been a magnet for traders from the West from early times, drawn there by its spices, pepper and cinnamon. Babylonians, Assyrians, Egyptians and later Arabs, Phoenicians and Romans all came to India looking for spices. When Romans took control of Egypt in 30 BC they sailed eastwards to trade with the Arabian peninsula, where grew the trees that gave the fragrances frankincense and myrrh, and to India for spices. Strabo wrote that 'when Gallus was prefect of Egypt [in 26–24 BC] ... I learned that as many as one hundred and twenty vessels were sailing from Myos Hormos [on Egypt's Red Sea coast] to India whereas formerly, under the Ptolemies, only a very few ventured to undertake the voyage and to carry on traffic in Indian merchandise'.[1]

Artefacts of Greek or Roman origin, including coins from the first century AD, have been found at several places in southern India; and as

Claudius Ptolemy's very limited understanding of India appears to be based on the Rivers Indus and Ganges, as shown in his Tabulae Asia, *reproduced in 1545.*

testimony to trade in the opposite direction, a statue of the Indian goddess Lakshmi was found in the ruins of Pompeii in AD 79. Two Indian locations stand out. On the east-facing Bay of Bengal coast just south of Pondicherry (now Puducherry) lay the ancient port of Arikamedu, a flourishing industrial centre which traded with the Roman empire through Egypt as early as 200 BC. Graeco-Roman *amphorae* or jars found there were used to transport wine, olive oil and fish sauce. It is not certain when spices became part of the return cargo, though sandalwood brought down the Cauvery River was traded from an early stage. It is likely that this east-facing port on India's Coromandel coast also conducted trade with China and the Malay peninsula, and may have been on the route that brought the Hindu religion and Sanskrit language from India to the islands of Indonesia. Arikamedu flourished until the sixth century, and was still trading shortly before Vasco da Gama arrived on the opposite coast; but it was no longer a port by the time Portuguese, Dutch, English, French and Danish voyagers in turn set up trading posts along this coast.

The second key location is the port of Muziris on the west-facing Malabar coast which the Romans reached much earlier, before the foundation of Arikamedu. The Malabar region, now the northern part of Kerala state, was rich in pepper, cardamom, cinnamon, ginger and turmeric as well as sandalwood and ivory and was the natural destination for ships carried eastwards from Arabia or the coast of Africa by the south-west monsoon winds. Muziris may have been in use as early as 1200 BC when visited by the Phoenicians, pioneer seafarers and traders. Muziris was also a destination for the Sumerians and Assyrians. More fancifully, Kerala sources have suggested that Muziris was the biblical city of Ophir and that ships of King Solomon sailed there in search of gold and precious stones, returning with wood used to build the temple at Jerusalem in around 930 BC.[2]

Pliny the Elder, the Roman naturalist and philosopher, wrote a *Natural History* around AD 77 in which he calls Muziris 'the first town of Merchandise in India'. Pliny had been Rome's naval commander, so knew something of the sea. When embarking from Ocelis on the Red Sea, Pliny wrote that 'if the wind called Hippalus happens to be blowing it is possible to arrive in forty days at … Muziris' and you can make the return journey within a year by setting sail for Egypt in December or early January, when the wind blows from the south-east. On reaching the entrance to the Red Sea, ships are blown northwards by the same wind, the Hippalus, which enabled the outward journey to India. Pliny says that Muziris is not the most desirable port for disembarkation on account of the pirates who maraud in the area; he mentions that its main attraction, pepper, is brought downriver by flat-bottomed boats from the hinterland. Probably timber for boatbuilding was brought to the coast the same way.[3] The port of Beypore on the Chaliyar River south of Calicut, renowned as a boatbuilding centre from the first century AD, was visited by Romans, Greeks, Chinese, Syrians and Arabs. In the same century the *Periplus of the Erythræan Sea* tells us that Muziris 'abounds in ships sent there with cargoes from Arabia and by the Greeks'.[4] Keralite historian V. Sankaran Nair says that Muziris is also mentioned in Tamil literature around this time. He quotes a source as describing Muchiri

– assumed to be Muziris – as 'where the beautiful large ships of the Yavans [Greeks], bringing gold, come splashing the white foam on the waters of the Periplus ... and return laden with pepper'. He makes a connection with the Red Sea port of Berenicê where, he says, objects of Indian origin were found.[5] (See the maps featuring Muziris and Berenicê in Chapter 2.)

Muziris was evidently close to the point where ships borne by the south-west winds reached the coast of India, and was situated near the mouth of a great river. Recent excavations suggest a location at the village of Pattanam, south of Cranganore (now Kodungallur), which today lies some distance from both the sea and the Periyar River. In 1341 a great sea flood inundated the Malabar coast, resulting in a significant change in the River Periyar's route to the sea and giving rise to Kerala's extensive 'backwaters' where fresh and sea water mix, important these days for fishing, transportation and tourism. This flood may have destroyed Muziris and caused the River Periyar to divert to where it now enters the Arabian Sea – part of the Indian Ocean – at Cochin (Kochi).

Marco Polo visited India in the 1290s while returning from China to Venice. Besides speaking of the abundance of pepper, ginger and cinnamon, he says that non-native spices such as cloves and spikenard, an aromatic oil used in medicine and perfumery, were traded there as well. Polo says that 'merchants come here [to Quilon, southern Malabar] from Manzi [Southern China] and Arabia and the Levant and ply a thriving trade for they bring various products from their own countries by sea and export others in return'. He tells of the dangers of vessels being captured and pilfered by corsairs or pirates off India's western coast.[6]

Another visitor from Venice was Niccolò de' Conti who arrived around 1440 on the Malabar coast, at Cambay to the north and Madras on the eastern-facing Coromandel coast, then venturing inland to the seat of the Vijayanagara empire in present-day Karnataka. He contributed to European understanding of the geography of Asia by informing the Venetian map-maker Fra Mauro, whose *mappa mundi* first appeared around 1450. An account written in Latin of de' Conti's travels would have facilitated da Gama's voyage, and a Portuguese language version was published after da Gama's return.

Among other early travellers from the West who reached India was the Moroccan, Ibn Battutah, who in 1342–3 visited Cambay, Malabar and Goa (known at the time as Sandabur), where he stayed several months before continuing his journey to China. Battutah described the harbour at Qaliqut (Calicut) as 'the largest in the world' and noted the presence there of thirteen large Chinese vessels, each with a thousand men, suggesting that Chinese mariners reached India well before da Gama. He described in detail how Chinese ships or *junks* were constructed.[7]

Signs of early Chinese contacts with the Malabar coast include the pivoted fishing nets known as *cheena vala* (Chinese nets) which, according to legend, were introduced by the Chinese sailor Zheng He (whom we shall meet in Chapter 5) and are still in use at Cochin; also Chinese silk or *cheena pattu* and cooking and

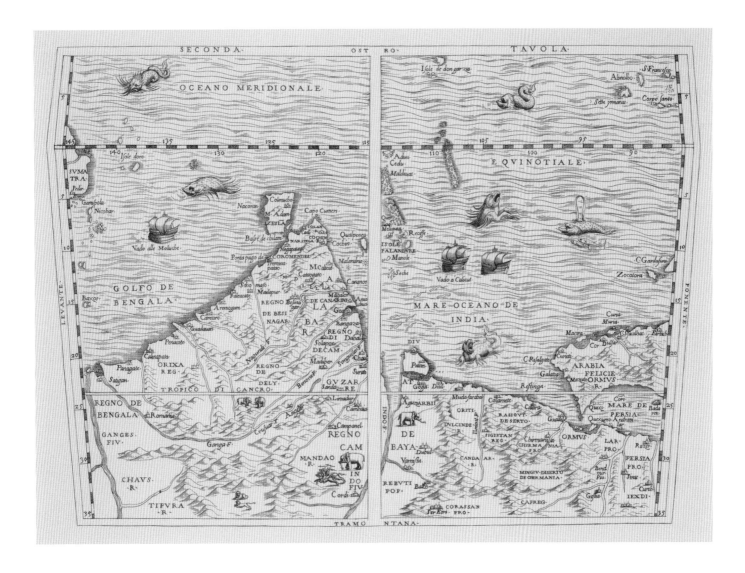

SECONDA. OSTRO. TAVOLA.

Giacomo Gastaldi's 'upside-
down' image of 1565 is one
of the earliest maps of India,
and shows the Indian Ocean
from the Persian Gulf to
Sumatra, featuring Ceylon and
the Maldives. The caravels
pictured suggest it is based on
Portuguese sources.

storage vessels such as the wok-style pan known as *cheena chhatti* and a clay
storage pot *cheena bharani*. Many words prefixed with *cheena-* have entered
Kerala's language of Malayalam.

A CENTRE OF RELIGIONS

The Malabar[8] coast of Kerala has wider significance as the point at which
three of India's non-indigenous religions first came ashore, borne by the
prevailing south-westerly winds. It is said that Christianity first arrived in
AD 52, brought by Jesus's disciple Thomas, who landed at Cranganore to
spread the gospel.

Also at Cranganore is India's earliest mosque, Islam having been
introduced there around AD 629, during the lifetime of the prophet
Mohammed. The so-called 'Malabar Jews' came ashore here in the twelfth
century. Traders from Arabia and the Jewish homeland, they are known
as the Black Jews to distinguish them from later migrations. After the
1341 flood, they moved south to Cochin where they were joined in the late
fifteenth century by a second influx of Jews, those expelled from Spain
and Portugal known as the White Jews. An ancient synagogue still stands

in Cochin's Fort area, though very few descendants of either community remain. Islam spread more rapidly than Christianity or Judaism, and trade between India and the Arabian birthplace of Islam was for several centuries dominated by Arabs and Mamluk Turks from Egypt and Muslims from Gujarat on India's north-western coast, renowned for producing the best wood for shipbuilding.

Da Gama's arrival put an end to Muslim domination of trade with the Red Sea and the Persian or Arabian Gulf, though it took some years and many sea battles for the Portuguese to establish themselves as the masters of Indian Ocean trade. Successive Portuguese voyages set up *feitorias*, trading bases or – in English terminology – factories, along the Kerala coast at Cochin (1500), Quilon (Kollam) further south (1502) and Cannanore (Kannur) to the north (1505).[9] Having established their trading positions, the Portuguese built forts to enforce their control over the Indian Ocean. They were the first Europeans to understand what became evident to later empire-builders: 'Whosoever commands the sea commands the trade; whosoever commands the trade of the world commands the riches of the world, and consequently the world itself.'[10]

PORTUGAL'S CONQUEST OF GOA
The conquest of Goa happened almost accidentally. Afonso de Albuquerque, the second Portuguese governor, or viceroy, of India, set out in February 1510 from Cochin with an armada of 23 ships and more than 2,000 men and an unknown number of locally enslaved people to secure the Persian Gulf island of Hormuz; but he was persuaded by a Malabar pirate named Timoji to divert to Goa. Timoji, who claimed to have been born in Goa, was determined to revenge its capture by the Muslim king of the inland state of Bijapur, Yusuf Adil Shah. He told the Portuguese that the Mamluks were building new ships in Goa with help from King Yusuf Adil Shah, who was also known as Hidalcão. Albuquerque was authorised by King Manuel to secure control only of Aden, Hormuz and Malacca – but not Goa.

Cranganore port on the Malabar coast, where several religions arrived in India. This 1708 image from a book by Wouter Schouten gives prominence to a church as well as the fort built by the Dutch after the port's capture from the Portuguese in 1662.

The Portuguese armada sailed into the Mandovi River estuary and captured a fort at Panjim – later known as Panaji – from Mamluk mercenaries. They found a largely Hindu community who, unhappy at their Muslim rulers, gave the Portuguese their support. It took several months and a second naval assault for Albuquerque's forces to secure full control of the city and hinterland after a counter-attack by Muslim forces loyal to Bijapur. St Catherine's Day, 10 November 1510, was the date when Goa became a domain of the Portuguese king, making St Catherine of Alexandria the city's patron saint, a curious link with Alexandria. Albuquerque doubtless felt he had furthered the crusading objective of the motherland in defeating a Muslim force, though the conquest was more blatantly commercial than religious. In a coincidence of timing, the Bijapur monarch Yusuf Adil Shah died ten days after losing control of Goa.

Goa became Portugal's principal trading port in India, though Calicut, renowned for the coarse 'calico' cloth produced there, remained under Portuguese control for many years. Portugal's capture of Goa is regarded as the start of the era of colonisation which would see European powers take control of large swathes of territory and their inhabitants on several continents. Afonso de Albuquerque, the founder of Portugal's Indian empire, was compared with Alexander the Great, whose territorial conquests reached only as far as the River Indus in present-day Pakistan.

Goa had advantages over the Malabar coast: not least that its harbour in the mouth of the Mandovi River was well suited for trading with the powerful inland Vijayanagar kingdom which held sway over southern India. Horses from Arabia, carpets from Persia, pearls from the Gulf, precious stones from Pegu (in Burma), cloth from Bengal and silk and porcelain from China were exchanged there for Malabar pepper and ginger, sesame and cardamom from Siam, cinnamon from Ceylon and cloves, nutmeg and mace from the Spice Islands. One of Albuquerque's first acts in Goa was to create a mint to facilitate trade that produced a gold coin called the *São Tomé,* after Jesus's disciple St Thomas. A later viceroy would establish Asia's first printing press.

Goa was also well suited for enforcing Portugal's self-claimed trading rights at other Indian ports and those around the Red Sea. Its seizure of Hormuz in 1515 gave Portugal control over the Persian Gulf. Goa's shipbuilding tradition was important for repairing Portuguese vessels and building new ships. By the late sixteenth century vessels five times the size of those in da Gama's fleet were being built at Goa using local teak. Larger ships could carry more arms so were better able to fend off attackers, as well as being able to carry larger cargoes to Portugal in the yearly trading convoys known as the *carreira da Índia.*

An early Portuguese visitor to Goa was the apothecary Tomé Pires. Travelling between Goa and China in 1512–15, Pires reported to King Manuel in a series of letters that were only published in the twentieth century.[11] Pires is associated more with Malacca, but nonetheless made perceptive observations about Goa: saying it was the most important part of India, civilised and plentiful in foodstuffs. Writing that the betel or areca nut popular for chewing was better in Goa than anywhere, he added: 'The men in these parts can sustain themselves on betel for three or four days without eating anything else.' It helps digestion, comforts the brain, strengthens the teeth and 'those who eat it have good breath'. Pires tells his monarch: 'Merchants will rejoice under our administration more than they ever did under the Moors [Muslims].' It was a good port, he continues, and its wood and craftsmen were 'especially suited to the business of raising armadas'. Albuquerque was doing just that: preparing an armada to consolidate his control of Hormuz, suppress the pirates of Malabar and enforce Portugal's dominion over the Indian Ocean.

Pires said that Goa, which was wealthy before the Portuguese took control, would become 'the greatest place in the world'. Goa *Dourada* or Goa the Golden, as it was known, became a destination for many young Portuguese men eager to make a living as traders or to build a new life tilling land for crops not found in Portugal. Some took refuge there after falling out with the authorities for one reason or another. This left a manpower shortage back home, since Portugal's population in the early sixteenth century only just exceeded one million so could scarcely spare the men needed to run its overseas territories on three continents. Those that settled in Goa engaged in business as masons, carpenters, bakers, innkeepers, barbers, tailors, cobblers, hat-makers and sail-makers, livelihoods that the Portuguese preferred to keep for themselves rather than employing local people.

Except in their fighting vessels, there is no evidence of Indians being enslaved, though local girls were often 'adopted' as temporary wives as there were hardly any Portuguese-born women in Goa. Albuquerque encouraged Portuguese men to marry local women, who were then required to convert to Christianity. Portugal's mission was to convert as many local people as possible. In Portugal, orphaned girls, so called 'orphans of the king', were encouraged to travel and seek husbands in the *conquistas,* or conquests, as the Portuguese called their overseas settlements.

Viceroys enjoyed near absolute powers, including the power to make war on any nation which threatened what they called the *Estado da Índia,* the Indian State. They were advised by a Council of State on which both civil and religious leaders sat, but were not bound to follow their guidance. Portuguese administrators serving in India were usually *fidalgos*, members of the nobility, and some born of lesser rank made the award of a title a condition for their service.

Twenty years after the Portuguese arrived in Goa, it was a cosmopolitan and bustling metropolis. It may have been an exaggeration to suggest it was 'more thickly populated' than London or Paris, as the French writer Rémy claimed, though possible that it 'housed more ambassadors than Lisbon itself',[12] most of whom are likely to have represented principalities within India. With a population in the late sixteenth century of 200,000, Goa was not much smaller than the Portuguese mother city of Lisbon. It was busier and more prosperous than anywhere else on India's west coast and probably anywhere in the interior. Its port received vessels from distant parts of the East and West according to the prevailing winds. An early-seventeenth-century traveller called Goa a noble city, while noting 'it does not produce anything, and is so barren that, some few Lambs and Goats excepted, it is not

GOA

MORM

CABO

BARDES

A map of Goa, an island at the time, drawn by Portuguese mariner and cartographer Pedro Barreto de Resende, from Livre de Estado da India Oriental, *1640–46.*

able to sustain anything'. What can be found is the product of industry not of nature 'and all other provisions are brought thither'.[13] Yet to early visitors it was one of the most magnificent cities on the face of the Earth, giving rise to the sentiment at the head of this chapter: that if you have seen Goa, you did not need to visit Lisbon.

THE CATHOLIC CHURCH

In Portugal King João III, known as 'the Pious', succeeded Manuel in 1521 and would reign for thirty-six years. He became concerned that trade and profit were overshadowing the crusading spirit in Goa which had become 'intoxicated by its own wealth'. In Europe, the Christian Reformation had begun with the German theologian Martin Luther emerging as a critic of the ways of the Catholic church, such as its practice of selling 'indulgences' for the remission of sins. Though not apparent at the time, divergence between Catholic and Protestant branches of Christianity would become a major factor in rivalry between the Portuguese, Dutch and English for control of territory in Asia.

The emergence of Protestantism in northern Europe prompted a reassertion of Catholic orthodoxy elsewhere, for example the founding in Paris in 1534 of the Society of Jesus, the Jesuits. The founders included two Spanish priests, Ignatius Loyola and Francis Xavier, both of whom would be declared saints of the Catholic church.[14] King João saw the society as an answer to his prayers for something to be done about the state of spiritual life in this distant territory, to re-enforce what he regarded as the primary purpose for settling India; so he appointed Francis Xavier as his spiritual ambassador to India with the papal rank of Apostolic Nuncio. Xavier arrived in Goa in May 1542 with authority to spread the gospel and serve the church in all its Eastern territories, with the unofficial title of 'Apostle of the Indies'. Rémy wrote that 'five months had not gone by since his arrival in Goa the dissolute, and the place was changed. The churches became too small to hold the faithful who flocked to them ... and there were scarcely enough priests in the city to hear all the penitents.'

The extent to which the Portuguese forced its religion on the people of India is less clear. There is evidence that attempts to do so caused an exodus of Goan Hindus, who did not want to become Christians. Xavier regarded proselytisation as part of his role and wrote what appeared to be an admonition to his monarch: 'God has given to the king of Portugal these far off lands not to enrich the royal treasury but to extend the kingdoms of Jesus Christ.' He advised the monarch to punish the territory's governors for their failings if he wanted himself to avoid punishment by God at his last judgement. The work Xavier started was carried on by resident archbishops with the designation Primate of the East and Patriarch of the East Indies, whose role was 'to Christianise' the share of the world Portugal had been allocated by the pope.

Xavier took the gospel to Ceylon, Borneo, the Spice Islands and Japan; he was on the point of becoming the first Catholic missionary to visit China when he died of a fever in 1552. His body was brought to Goa and preserved at Bom Jesus, the largest of many churches there. Four and a half centuries later his tomb draws a steady stream of pilgrims, though the glass and silver casket is only brought out on rare occasions. Xavier epitomises Portuguese rule in the East and had more lasting influence than did government representatives, as a jingle popular in seventeenth-century Goa related: 'Viceroys come and viceroys go, but the Jesuit Fathers are always with us.'[15]

An earlier saint, Jesus's disciple Thomas (known as Doubting Thomas for his refusal at first to believe in the resurrection of Christ), is reputed to have arrived on the Malabar coast in AD 52 and converted many inhabitants to Christianity, before attempting to do the same in the south-east region known now as Tamil Nadu. There he was less successful and was martyred on a hill outside the city of Madras (now Chennai) for challenging their traditional faith. His body is said to lie at San Tomé, Mylapore, the oldest Portuguese church in that city, shown as Maliapor in the 1603 map by Bertius.

A Goa-born priest of mixed Goan and Portuguese parentage by the name of José Custódio de Faria came to prominence in the mid-eighteenth century. Despite being implicated in a 1787 conspiracy to oust the Portuguese after the church refused to promote priests of local origin, de Faria earned the patronage of the Portuguese king who sent him to study in France where he became a pioneer of what he termed 'lucid sleep' – later known as hypnotherapy. In 1789 he took part in a protest movement that would grow to become the French Revolution and overthrow the country's monarchy.

After a period of imprisonment near Marseilles, he became professor of philosophy at the University of France in Nîmes. Abbé Faria, as he is better known, is commemorated in Goa's capital Panjim, with a statue of him hypnotising a woman; he was also supposedly the fictional priest of the same name in Alexander Dumas' novel *The Count of Monte Cristo*, where he is referred to as *un homme savant*, a wise man.[16]

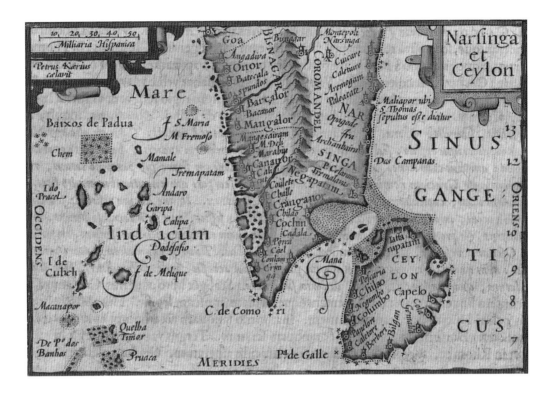

South India and Ceylon pictured in 1603 by Petrus Bertius, showing Calicut, where Vasco da Gama landed, Goa, Cranganore, Cochin and, on India's east coast, Maliapor (Mylapore) where St Thomas was allegedly martyred.

LUÍS VAZ DE CAMÕES AND GARCIA DA ORTA

Among those who made Goa their home in the early years of Portuguese rule were a poet and a doctor who became known in Portugal and the wider world as a result of books they started to write there. Both were from the Portuguese university city of Coimbra, and in Goa they became close friends. The poet was Luís Vaz de Camões, who became a national hero for his versified celebration of the role of Vasco da Gama and others in making Portugal great. The doctor and sometime professor of logic at Coimbra was Garcia da Orta, who in India pioneered the use of plants for their medicinal properties and would publish a celebrated book on the subject. Making play on da Orta's surname, which comes from the Latin *hortus* meaning 'garden', Camões penned a homage to his friend's research which includes the lines:

> Look, how in your lifetime
> A remarkable Garden produces many herbs
> In the Lusitanian fields,
> Herbs which those wise sorcerers
> Medea and Circe never found
> Because the laws of Magic outwitted them.[17]

Camões and da Orta were in self-exile in Goa for different reasons. Camões, it seems, admired a beautiful noblewoman in the service of the king. He wrote her a poem expressing his love, which got him into trouble at court and he was briefly imprisoned. Knowing he would never be allowed to marry someone above his station, he joined a ship which sailed from Lisbon in March 1553. This took him to Goa, Malacca and the Spice Islands among other places on a voyage that would lead him to write his famous epic of the Portuguese era of discovery, *Os Lusíadas*, featured in the next chapter.

Garcia da Orta was descended from a Spanish Jewish family which migrated to Portugal to escape the Spanish persecution of Jews. In 1497 – just as Vasco da Gama set sail for India – King Manuel followed Spain in ordering that all Portuguese Jews convert to Christianity. They were henceforth known as *Cristãos Novos*, New Christians, in line with Spanish practice, with the implication that they were not fully to be trusted. In 1531 a papal bull ordered that the Inquisition be established in Portugal as it had been in Spain, on the grounds that some New Christians were returning to the Judaic ritual they had abandoned. Garcia da Orta interpreted that as a threat to his position, so set sail for Goa to take up a post as personal physician to the viceroy. There he began work on the great pharmacopoeia which would make his reputation as one of the heroes of Portugal's age of exploration. His book, elaborately entitled *Colloquies on the Simples, Drugs and Materia Medica of India and some of the fruits found there*, was published in Goa in 1563, only the third book published there and the first on a non-ecclesiastical subject, following the introduction of printing in Goa seven years earlier. With it da Orta's name took its place beside that of Pliny and other great botanists who were to follow, such as Alfred Russel Wallace and Georg Eberhard Rumphius, who would carry out pioneering research in Java and the Spice Islands and whom we shall meet later. Da Orta himself reappears when we look at Bombay.

Garcia da Orta died in Goa a natural death, aged nearly eighty, but was not immune from the anti-Jewish mood of the times even in death. His sister, Catarina, was burned at the stake for 'practising Judaism' and da Orta was condemned for the same crime. In this most Catholic of cities da Orta's bones were exhumed and burned for this 'sin'. By this time, many Iberian Jews had fled, some finding refuge in Kerala where they were able to practise their religion freely.

JAN HUYGEN VAN LINSCHOTEN

Jan Huygen van Linschoten spent five years as secretary to the Portuguese archbishop of Goa in the 1580s, surprisingly so for the son of a Dutch Protestant family, and was responsible for one of the earliest maps of Goa. It appeared in his book *Itinerario*, published in Amsterdam in 1596, which gave detailed navigational instructions on how to reach Goa using appropriate winds, as well as intimate details of life there and elsewhere in the East. It was rare for a European map-maker to have first-hand knowledge of the place he was depicting.

Linschoten's south-facing view of Goa is an early depiction of a city as if from the sky, following those pioneered by Braun and Hogenberg. It shows

A map of the Portuguese settlement at Goa looking south, created by Dutchman Jan Huygen van Linschoten during his time as secretary to the archbishop, published in 1596.

the Mandovi River and the settlement now known as Vela (Old) Goa, the capital of Portuguese India and seat of government for all Portugal-ruled territories in Asia until 1843. The Arabian Sea is to the right. Ships made their way into the wide yet weather-protected Mandovi River to dock close to the Portuguese settlement. Elephants are depicted at work on the waterfront where ships unloaded and loaded; these were repaired at what became known as the arsenal. The customs house (*alfandega*) is at the left of the waterfront, close to the large market (*bazar grande*), and the timber yard lies beyond. Linschoten tells us that ships of up to 200 tonnes could load and unload at the town wharf, while larger vessels needed to dock on the northern bank of the river where the depth was greater.

Standing back from the waterfront is the viceroy's palace (*terierio do vizorey*), and beside it the Viceroy's Arch, built by Vasco da Gama's grandson Francisco da Gama, through which an incoming viceroy made his ceremonial entrance into the city. Beyond the archway is Rua Dereita or Straight Street, popularly known as *Leilaõ* from a Portuguese word meaning 'auction'. This was where traders assembled and transactions took place to fill the ships for their home-bound journeys, an early international marketplace. Linschoten likens the daily gathering of traders from many nations with 'the meeting upon the bourse in Antwerp', but says the variety of goods on offer is greater in Goa. Among its wares were 'all kinds of spices and dried drugges'.[18] Commenting on the wares on offer, Linschoten writes that Cochin on the Malabar coast produced enough pepper to fill two ships each year and says the cinnamon grown in Ceylon was far superior to that of India and commanded a much higher price. Portugal had already turned

its attention to Ceylon (later Sri Lanka), enlarging the area over which it claimed a virtual trading monopoly through the sixteenth century (see the earlier map by Bertius, page 71).

A view of Old Goa by German map-maker Joseph Friedrich Leopold (which opens this chapter) is literally more down-to-earth, showing the city from across the Mandovi River and including in the foreground activity on the river's northern bank where larger vessels docked. The Viceroy's Arch is near the centre of this picture, while the green hills beyond the city caused Linschoten to write of Goa as a green and fertile city which 'lyeth upon hills

The capture of Cochin by the Dutch from the Portuguese is pictured in 1682 by Johan Nieuhof, who worked for the Dutch East India Company.

and dales like Lisbon'. Neither view shows evidence of the many churches which would lead to the city being dubbed the 'Rome of the Orient'.

Linschoten tells of the life of Portuguese settlers. The town was 'well built with fair houses and streets, after the Portugal manner ... they commonly have Gardens and Orchards at the backe side of their houses full of all kinde of Indian fruits ... The town hath in it all sorts of Cloysters and Churches as Lisbone hath' and was only wanting for nuns 'for the men cannot get the women to travell so far as to let themselves be shut up and forsake Venus'. He says: 'The Portingales [men] in India are many of them married with the natural borne women of the country' and describes the children of such unions as being 'yellow' though the subsequent generation 'does seem to be naturall Indians, both in colour and fashion'. Linschoten felt strongly about the lack of privileges accorded to these so-called *Mestiços,* children of mixed marriages, by the Spanish monarch who also ruled Portugal at the time, and he introduces us to a new use for spices, telling us that cloves, ginger and pepper all gave rise to 'fiery desires'. A later traveller from Germany adds nutmeg to the list of supposed aphrodisiacs.[19]

One can detect a measure of criticism of the Portuguese administration in Linschoten's writing, but nowhere was he as bold as a later editor of *Itinerario* who says in an introduction to the book: 'Everyone learned that the colonial empire of the Portuguese was rotten, and that an energetic rival would have every chance of supplanting them.'[20] Linschoten says that viceroys and other servants of the king were poorly paid and these low salaries had encouraged graft or corruption. This became apparent as Portugal found difficulty paying for its vessels and sailors, let alone finding the funds to purchase spices. But some seventeenth-century viceroys managed to accrue considerable wealth during their tenure.

Goa was in decline by the mid-seventeenth century. One cause was Portugal's expensive war with Spain to regain its independence (achieved in 1640), which undermined investment in new ships and crews for the *carreira da Índia.* Another reason was growing competition from the Dutch East India Company, which was building better vessels with an enhanced ability to reach and return from India. Many Portuguese vessels were lost en route, as the difficulty of finding crews and goods to trade resulted in them sailing from Lisbon after March and becoming prone to adverse weather around the Cape. Portugal was fast losing its control over the Indian Ocean.

Monopolies survive only as long as they can be maintained. From 1603 onwards, Goa and other Portuguese-controlled territories in India came under attack from the Dutch, who blockaded the entrance to the Mandovi River from 1636, eventually capturing Cochin in 1663 after a sea battle with Portugal, depicted in the portrayal by Dutch map-maker Johan Nieuhof; other Malabar coastal ports soon followed.

Other rivals for a share of the Indian Ocean trade included the Marathas, a powerful warrior clan from India's western Deccan[21] plateau who rose to power in the 1670s and made several attempts to take control of Goa. The Portuguese held on and even expanded the area under their control. Another reason for Goa's decline was that Portugal was making bigger profits from its Brazilian *conquista* through the port of Pernambuco.

END OF EMPIRE

Portugal extended its territory around Goa in the eighteenth century, making it considerably larger than the island originally captured. During the Napoleonic Wars, Britain took over administration of Portuguese territories as they did the Dutch-ruled East Indies, handing both back to their respective colonial powers after Napoleon was defeated. Long after most of Portugal's other trading posts in Asia had fallen to the Dutch or British, and after the rest of India gained its independence in 1947, the Portuguese were driven from Goa and its smaller enclaves of Daman and Diu by Indian military action in 1961.

India took control of what remains its richest and most literate state. Goa's distinctive Portuguese Catholic heritage, together with its fine beaches, provide a holiday draw to both Indians and Europeans. Goa's cuisine is Portuguese-influenced: dishes such as pork vindaloo – which is not easily found elsewhere in India, at least not using pork – which originated in Portugal's Atlantic Ocean island of Madeira, though one of its main ingredients, chilli, was introduced by the Portuguese from Mexico. Goa's *feni* liqueur, made from the fruit of the cashew nut tree that the Portuguese brought from Brazil, is popular beyond the state.[22] If you want to buy India's most succulent mangoes, ask for them by name: Afonso, named after the second governor of Portuguese India.

The Viceroy's Arch at Goa as it appears today.

A Portuguese carrack depicted in a book of travels by Hieronymus Cöler the Elder of Nuremberg, 1533.

After standing for three and a half centuries, the Viceroy's Arch collapsed in 1948 and was restored by Portugal with the version that stands today. A statue of Vasco da Gama dominates the south side of the arch and an inscription and family crest within the portals recalls his role in the foundation of Goa. On the south side of the archway, facing the river, is the statue of a crowned woman, possibly St Catherine, Portuguese Goa's patron saint, with her foot on a local ruler which is said to symbolise the victory of Christianity over Islam. Surprisingly, this has survived Goa's return to Indian rule.

Several Portuguese forts in India survive, though little remains of the one at Cochin which gives the Fort area its name. North of Cochin is a hexagonal fort at Pallipuram dating from 1503, which is claimed as the oldest surviving European building in India. Fort Aguada at Goa remains largely intact, as do Portuguese forts in Daman and Diu. Portugal's first base in India, Calicut, was absorbed into the princely state of Malabar which, after India's independence from Britain, was incorporated with Cochin and Travancore into the state of Kerala.

par la vertu de la procuration q̃
il auoit espousa madame phͤe
de landastre ou nom et pour le
roy Jehan de portingal quy en ce
lauoit ordonne et institue Si les
espousa larcheuesque de braghee
Et furent sur vng lit courtoise
ment ainsi comme espeux et es
peuse doiuent estre, Ce fait a
lendemain la dame atout son ar
roy prest pour partir print congie
a monseigneur le duc de ladastre
son pere A madame sa mere A
ses seurs Et a tous ceulx a quy
Il apartenoit A grans ploure

Et tenreurs Elle monta sue vne
haguenee richement appareillie
Et bien amblant plusieurs da
moiselles auecques elle Sa seur
bastarde la femme du mareschal.
En sa compaigne furent ordonnez
daler messire Jehan de hollande
messire thomas de persy, messͤ
Jehan daubrecicourt Et cent
lances dangleterre eslus auecques
deux cens archiers Puis quant
ces seigneurs et dames furent a
dexniu mis Ils cheuaucherent
en bonne ordonnance vers la cite
de port en portingal.

Er fait mention comment le roy Jehan de portingal espousa phelippe de
landastre fille au duc Jehan de landastre sollempnelement en la cite
de port en portingal, Chapitre. xxxiiije.

4/

LISBON, QUEEN OF THE SEA

Vasco da Gama set sail from Lisbon, the only European capital that faces onto the Atlantic Ocean. In fact it lies 20 kilometres upstream on the Rio Tejo or Tagus, alongside the Mar da Palha, marked as Bay of Wares or Sea of Straw in the chart of 1756, which forms a large natural harbour. Portugal's challenge had been to find a direct route around the continent of Africa, bypassing the indirect way pioneered by Roman and Venetian mariners. Only when that key was found could Lisbon take advantage of its geography. First, it had to find out how to make use of the prevailing Atlantic winds.

As early as the fifth century, Herodotus wrote that the Mediterranean and 'what is called the Atlantic beyond the pillars of Hercules, and the Indian Ocean ... are in reality parts of a single sea'.[1] Claudius Ptolemy, a Roman subject of Egypt in the second century, reached a different conclusion: the Indian Ocean like the Mediterranean Sea is surrounded by land, which explains the preoccupation on the part of Venetians and other early traders to build a canal to connect the two supposedly landlocked seas. As greater awareness of the fabled Spice Islands dawned, European explorers and their sponsors became keen to find a direct route to the source of spices. In the late fifteenth century, Venetian merchants suspected that someone would break their European spice monopoly by finding a direct route. They thought it would be the Genoese, their main Mediterranean rivals.

In 1291 the Vivaldi brothers had set out in two ships from Genoa to the Straits of Gibraltar (then known as the Straits of Ceuta) 'in order that the galleys might sail through the ocean sea to India and return with useful merchandise'.[2] They carried two Franciscan friars, intimating that the voyage was not exclusively about trade, but no one ever returned. Evidence from later expeditions suggests that they called at the Canary Islands[3] and sailed beyond the Cape Verde peninsula, the westernmost point of mainland Africa, but did not reach the Guinea coast, famed for its gold.

Sebastian Münster created a map of Africa in 1540, using Claudius Ptolemy's calculations to give Africa a reasonably accurate shape, though not quite like the Africa we know today. The continent, variously called Libya or Ethiopia, was considered to be a rich source of gold and the dominion of the mythical figure of Prester John.

In the 1480s another Genoese adventurer came to Portugal in search of sponsorship for a sea voyage to 'the Indies' by sailing west. He married a Portuguese noblewoman and lobbied King João II, who was looking for a direct route to the source of spices that had served Venice well. The explorer failed to convince the king that sailing west would be the quickest way to the fabled Spice Islands, so he left Portugal and sought sponsorship instead from the ruler of neighbouring Castile, Queen Isabella, whose marriage to King Ferdinand II of Aragon united the two kingdoms which would become Spain. Here the Genoese gentleman, whose name was Christopher Columbus,[4] was more persuasive. The fledgling Spanish dynasty was interested in any opportunity to beat its Portuguese neighbours to the spices of the East.

Columbus' 1492 voyage under Spanish sponsorship was the first to reach the Indies, the West Indies that is, thus 'discovering' the Americas for Europe. He did not find the spices that Venice was trading, though did bring back capsicum and allspice, insisting all along that he had reached the Spice Islands. There is no doubt of the significance of Columbus' discovery for Europe, Spain in particular, but it left open the challenge of finding a direct route to the oriental Spice Islands that had made Venice and Alexandria rich.

King João II was making his own plans to outflank both Venice and Genoa in bringing pepper, ginger and cinnamon to Europe. 'What was so special about Venice and Goa,' he reasoned, 'except that they had good shipyards?' It is said that the Venetian *doge* Francesco Foscari, who held office from 1423 to 1457, provided the Portuguese monarch with a copy of Marco Polo's *Travels*, which may have fuelled his ambition.

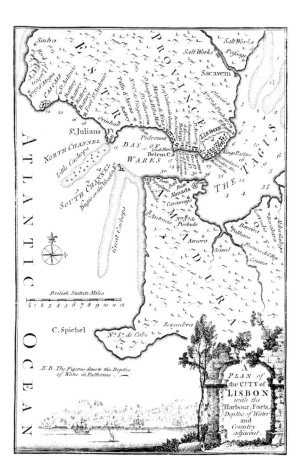

A chart of Lisbon harbour on the River Tagus by Robert Baldwin published in the London Magazine *around 1756. The river mouth appears to be heavily fortified.*

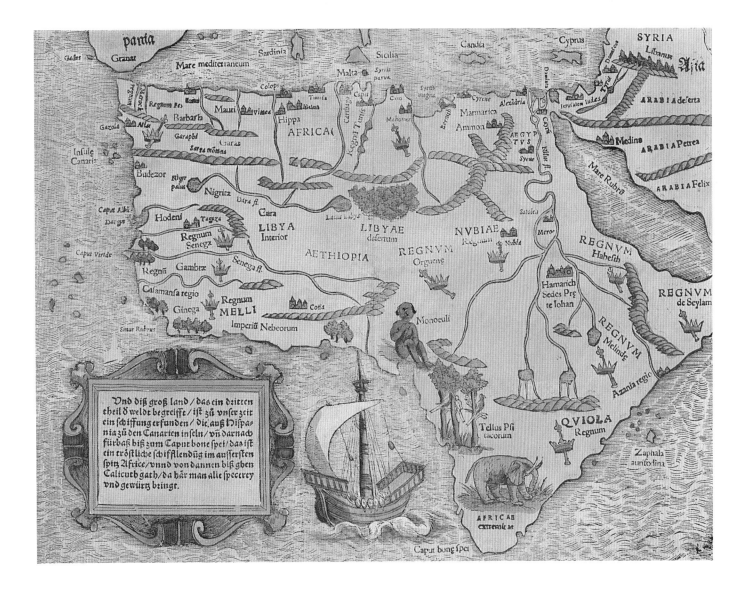

Sebastian Münster's 1540 map
of Africa based on Ptolemaic
calculations.

THE FOUNDATION OF LISBON

Lisbon was founded around the seventh century BC by one of the earliest race of seafarers, the Phoenicians, on an expedition from their homelands in the eastern Mediterranean. In the second century BC the city was settled and fortified by the Romans, who built roads and initiated the Portuguese language. The Portuguese name *Lisboa* is derived from Rome's name for the city, *Olissipo*. After the western Roman empire collapsed in the early fifth century AD, the city on the River Tagus fell under the sway of different groups of Barbarians – meaning foreigners – including the Vandals and the Visigoths, before the arrival in AD 711 of Moors – Berbers and Arabs from north Africa – who transformed Lisbon into an Islamic city, which it would remain for more than four hundred years. Its population under the Moors did not exceed 20,000.

In 1147 an army led by Afonso Henriques, a Christian of Franco-Spanish descent from the northern town of Guimarães, besieged the city for nearly four months before recapturing it, restoring the religion introduced by the Romans. This event, known as the *reconquista* or reconquest, marks the foundation of the Portuguese dynasty, Afonso becoming its first monarch. Catholicism was the defining ideology of the kingdom, which was more loyal to the pope in Rome than was Venice. The recapture of Lisbon by Christians is regarded as a highpoint of the Second Crusade, though it was another century before Muslims were driven from the south of the country.

By the end of the twelfth century Lisbon was a city of churches rather than mosques. It replaced Coimbra as capital of the Catholic kingdom in 1256. In due course the city expanded to cover the seven hills on which it now stands. It took longer to develop the world-beating shipbuilding skills and seamanship which enabled Portugal to outclass Venetians and Genoese – though not the Spanish – in maritime exploration. Lisbon enjoys a close relationship with both the river, the greater part of which flows through Spain, and the sea to which the river gives access.

As part of its assertion of independence from Spanish kingdoms, Portugal signed an alliance with England, the Treaty of Windsor, in 1386. It was marked, as such events often were, with an alliance of another sort between royal houses, when King João I married Philippa of Lancaster, daughter of England's John of Gaunt and sister to King Henry IV (see the beautiful portrayal opposite the chapter opening). Treaty and marriage created an Anglo-Portuguese alliance providing strength against that between France and Portugal's neighbours and rivals, the Castilians. Anglo-Portuguese relations faced strains nearly three centuries later after another royal marriage between the two nations, which we shall recall in the later chapter about Bombay.

HENRY THE NAVIGATOR

King João set the target to usurp Venice's position as the most powerful trading nation in Europe; his third surviving child, Henrique, born in 1394, is regarded as the instrument of that ambition. Henrique grew to be one of the most prominent members of what was dubbed *Ínclita Geração,* the Illustrious Generation. Better known as Prince Henry the Navigator, he is regarded as the father of Portugal's era of exploration, though he did not live to see the first voyage around the Cape which changed the map of the world and the fortunes of Portugal. Henry's reputation has taken a knock in recent years with the refutation of the myth that he founded a school for navigators, and the realisation that the farthest he ever travelled by sea was to Ceuta, on the north African coast opposite Gibraltar.[5]

In 1415, at the age of 21, Henry took part with his father and brothers in the capture of Ceuta, from where Barbary pirates were making raids on Portuguese ships. Prior to Portugal's conquest of Ceuta, it had been Genoese sailors based at the Andalusian ports of Seville and Cadiz who managed Ceuta's onward trade with Europe.

But Henry's move was part defensive operation and part religiously-motivated crusade against Islam.[6] There were also commercial motives, since Ceuta was an entrepôt for wheat at the northern end of the trans-Saharan trade route, which also delivered to the Mediterranean gold and enslaved people. Portugal was the first European nation to engage in African slave trading, setting a pernicious precedent.

Prince Henry assumed responsibility for protecting and provisioning Ceuta through the *Casa de Ceuta*, or Ceuta agency, in Lisbon. Being cut off from its wheat-producing hinterland, Ceuta was a constant drain on the royal finances. The difficulty of supplying foodstuffs may have encouraged Portuguese vessels into the Atlantic Ocean, where they found and colonised the island of Madeira around 1419 and the Azores some twenty years later. Madeira was a source of sugar, while the more distant Azores became a wheat basket.

By the 1440s his countrymen had sailed past the most westerly point of Africa to reach the Guinea coast, with Henry directing the voyages from Lisbon. Guinea, between the Tropic of Capricorn and the Equator, was a rich source of trading goods: gold, ivory, black pepper and enslaved people, feeding a ready market for either purchase or onward shipping in Europe. Portugal claimed exclusive trading rights over areas it reached first, setting up *feitorias* or factories, equivalent to the Venetian *fondaci*. It pioneered the principle of monopoly trading, meaning that ships, whether Portuguese or of any other nation, could only trade in areas under Portuguese control with the permission of the king, which was granted on a profit-sharing basis.

The Guinea coast engraved by Dirck Cornelissen Swardt for an atlas produced in Amsterdam by Johannes Cloppenburg in 1632, by which time the Dutch had built several forts along the coast.

Henry may not have been quite the navigator once believed, but he is credited with designing the caravel, a sailing vessel with a more aerodynamically shaped sail than those used in the Mediterranean. It was adapted from a fishing vessel to cope with the complicated geography of the port of Ceuta, which sometimes required a vessel to sail against the wind to enter the harbour. The Venetian sailor Cadamosto, writing in the mid-fifteenth century, described caravels as 'the best ships that travel the seas under sail ... the ideal craft for exploring the unknown and difficult waters of the West African coast'.[7] Columbus is said to have gained his sailing skills on Portuguese caravels. The caravels' triangular sails made them more versatile than the traditional and less manoeuvrable square-rigged vessels, with an ability to sail at 30° off-wind. Portugal's caravels displayed the square cross of the Order of Christ on their sails and eyes were painted on each side of the prow, which Africans believed gave them the ability to find their destinations in uncharted waters. Like the galleys of Venice, caravels carried oars for manoeuvring into and out of ports and river mouths.

The development of the caravel is the main reason the Portuguese won the race to be first around the southern tip of Africa. With favourable winds, caravels were capable of impressive speeds of 6 knots. Sailing northwards, they could tack to the north-west, towards the Azores, to overcome the effect of the trade winds blowing from the north-east. This enabled them to make the round trip to Guinea in a matter of months. Papal decrees forbade the Portuguese from teaching 'infidels' about navigation and shipbuilding, an early example of a restrictive practice.

The arms of Portugal are depicted on the sail of this vessel on an earthenware bowl originating in the Islamic kingdom of southern Spain.

ROUND THE CAPE

Navigation was fairly primitive, based on the stars and hugging the coast where possible. Latitude had yet to be devised, though a primitive version of the astrolabe, a device for determining position by measuring the altitude of stars, was used on Portuguese ships by the mid-1450s. Henry's 'own unshakeable self-confidence that it was his destiny to succeed as a sponsor of oceanic exploration communicated itself to mariners and sea-going knights and squires alike, even before caravels started to trade profitably in Guinea'.[8]

Trade with Guinea was sufficiently profitable to keep Portuguese mariners and their royal sponsors content, though the only spice found in west Africa, a type of cardamom known as *melegueta*, did not have the same appeal to European tastes. It would be some years after Prince Henry's death in 1460 before efforts were renewed to reach the southern cape and find a route to India. Portuguese vessels crossed the Equator in 1471, after which Henry's great-nephew, Prince João, was tasked by his father, King Afonso V, with ascertaining the southern limit of the continent. The king also commissioned Fra Mauro in Venice to produce a *mappa mundi* or map of the world. (The version provided to Lisbon has not survived.) Portuguese mariners erected stone pillars or *padrões* with a cross on top as they reached further south, to what we now know as Congo and Angola, claiming the newly discovered lands as Portuguese territory. After the

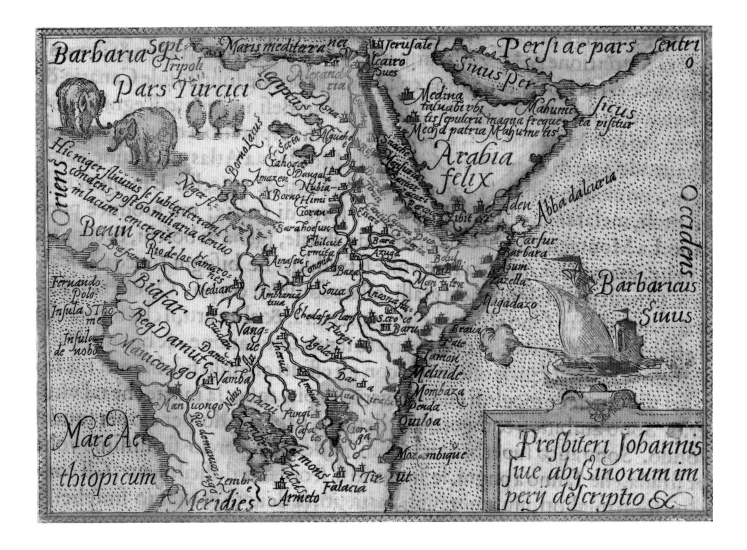

The map shows the following labels (as they appear):

Barbaria Sept · *Tripoli* · *Maris mediterranea* · *Jerusale* · *Persiae pars* · *centri* · *Icairo* · *Sues* · *Siuus Per* · *Pars Turcici* · *Ægiptus* · *Alexandria* · *Asua* · *Medina talnabi vbi tis sepulcru magna freque ta visitur* · *Mahumeticus* · *Arabia felix* · *Mecha patria Mahumetis* · *Aden* · *Abbadalcuria* · *Hic niger fluuius se subter terram condens post 60 miliaria denuo in lacum emergit* · *Niger fl.* · *Borno lacus* · *Sesta* · *Algueb* · *Tahoga* · *Amazen* · *Daugala* · *Nubia* · *Boeno Himi* · *Goran* · *Carfur* · *Barbara* · *Asum* · *Gazella* · *Benin* · *Biafar* · *Rio de los Camarones* · *Sarahoesum* · *Ergimita* · *Chilcut* · *Comoni* · *Bara* · *Azuga* · *Beul* · *Beda* · *Man itten* · *Ferriando Polo* · *Insula S Thome* · *Biafar* · *Reg Damut* · *Mediar* · *Annasen* · *Ambianca tua* · *Soua* · *Baza* · *Ancon fu* · *Braua* · *Pate* · *Magadazo* · *Barbaricus Siuus* · *Insule de nobo* · *Manicongo* · *Vang ue* · *Chedaf Tam* · *S.ce ce* · *Baru* · *Lamon* · *Melinde* · *Damut* · *Cucuan* · *Vamba* · *Agolath* · *Thoua* · *Dan a* · *Mombaza* · *Penda* · *Man uongo* · *Rio de manuo* · *Taqui* · *Zembi* · *Aua* · *Quiloa* · *Mare Ae thiopicum* · *Zembr* · *mons* · *fungi* · *Casa tes* · *Gor ga* · *Mozambique* · *Tit ut* · *Falacia* · *Armeto* · *Meridies* · *Occidens* · *Oriens* · *O*

Cartouche: *Presbiteri Johannis siue abysinorum imperij descriptio &c*

The mythical figure of Prester John, a Christian said to rule a kingdom in east Africa, is the subject of this 1593 map by Antwerp-based Abraham Ortelius which exaggerates the length of the River Nile.

prince became King João II in 1481, he accelerated what was known as 'the India project', sponsoring an expedition by Bartolomeu Dias which was to make the breakthrough.

A subsidiary – or possibly principal – objective was to discover the domain of the mythical Christian king known as Prester John, who was believed to rule over a land of fabulous wealth. This 1593 map by Abraham Ortelius, titled 'The Kingdom of Prester John', depicts the Atlantic Ocean as the Ethiopian Sea. Ethiopia was a label used to describe the African continent. With a similar degree of vagueness, the terms 'India' and 'the Indies' encompassed the region that began in east Africa and reached as far as the Spice Islands.

With a flotilla of three ships, Dias rounded the southern cape during a heavy storm in February 1488, landing at the mouth of the Bushman's River, east of Port Elizabeth, where he erected a *padrão*. He sighted what we know as 'the Cape' only on his return journey, naming it *Cabo das Tormentas* or the Cape of Storms. King João subsequently renamed it *Cabo da Boa Esperança,* the Cape of Good Hope.[9]

It was nine years before another attempt was made to reach India, by which time King Manuel I was on the throne. In the intervening period the Genoese Columbus had reached the Americas, claiming to have discovered India. Whether through shortage of funds or a feeling of having been defeated by the neighbouring Castilians, the Portuguese took their time to push eastwards. They may have been deterred by the bad weather encountered by Dias, or else the king was preoccupied by his principal crusading aim to capture Jerusalem.

VASCO DA GAMA

King Manuel 'the Fortunate' was on the throne throughout Portugal's era of discovery, from 1495 until his death in 1521, so was both main sponsor and chief beneficiary of Vasco da Gama's 'discovery' of India. Da Gama, a minor nobleman rather than a mariner, was aged just 28 when appointed to lead the flotilla of four vessels carrying 170 men which set sail from Lisbon on 8 July 1497 'to make discoveries and go in search of spices'. The vessels were a caravel and two *nau* or carracks, a version of the caravel with four masts to give greater stability on stormy oceans and with greater carrying capacity. The fourth vessel, described as a supply ship, was not up to the voyage and was scuttled in southern Africa. The flotilla followed the route pioneered by Guinea coast traders, before making a considerable deviation westwards towards the coast of Brazil; it then made use of the South Atlantic westerlies to tack back towards southern Africa.

The sailors crossed open sea with no land in sight before reaching the African mainland, replenishing their food and water at Helena's Bay, which faces westwards, and Mossel Bay, which faces south-east. The sailors had a violent encounter when local people responded to their attempts to obtain water by throwing spears, one of which wounded da Gama in the thigh.

Da Gama and his mariners then entered the unknown waters of the Indian Ocean, sailing up the eastern coast of Africa, giving the name *Natal*

The arrival in 1498 of Vasco da Gama on the coast near Calicut, pictured on Portuguese azulejos *tiles, displayed in the library at Panjim, Goa.*

to the area they passed on Christmas Day 1497. In March they called at Mozambique Island, but fell out with the sultan over the insufficiency of the gifts they offered him. This was their first encounter with Muslim traders. It is clear from the chronicles of the journey that they were seeking 'friendly' Christian territories with which to trade and were hostile to Muslims, or Moors as they were inclined to call them after the inhabitants of Morocco.

They stopped at the major port of Mombasa, but again were forced on their way after allegedly looting Arab merchant vessels in an act of piracy. However, they were well received at Malindi, whose ruler was in competition with the sultan of Mombasa and Kilwa for control of the well-established trade with India. There da Gama hired a pilot to guide them across the Indian Ocean, and they embarked across open sea on 24 April 1498. The pilot was well practised at using the monsoon winds to reach the pepper region at Calicut on India's south-western Malabar coast. The crossing took 23 days, completing a total journey of nine and a half months since leaving Lisbon. They told one of the first people they met, 'We came to seek Christians and spices', and apparently misidentified Hindu temples as churches. Da Gama's arrival at Kappad beach near Calicut is depicted in *azulejos*, Portugal's distinctive blue and white tiles, in the public library at Goa's capital Panjim. Palaces and public buildings in Portugal and its overseas territories were decorated with *azulejos* from the sixteenth century onwards as a way of showing off the country's new wealth.

MAPPING THE ROUTE TO INDIA
The map of the Atlantic or Ethiopian Ocean on page 88 gives an idea of the impressive 10,000 kilometre route from Lisbon to the Cape of Good Hope. It shows the easternmost tip of Brazil, towards which ships headed on the outbound journey to pick up the westerly winds to send them round the Cape. This map, produced a century after da Gama's voyage, claims to show 'all harbours, islands, reefs, raised sea-beds and shallows' and the 'true width of the Ethiopian Ocean from east to west'. It was produced by the Dutchman Jan Huygen van Linschoten in his book of navigational instructions, *Itinerario*, and comes close to representing the true shape of Africa when compared with the equivalent map published by Sebastian Münster fifty years earlier (page 81).

Linschoten also produced a map of the Indian Ocean (page 88); while it under-represents the size of the Indian subcontinent, it shows how relatively close is the distance from east Africa to India. Neither Dias nor da Gama had access to Linschoten's or Münster's maps, but based their navigation on the spoken tales of previous mariners. A map that da Gama and his fellow sailors may have seen is that which accompanied the *Nuremberg Chronicles*, one of the earliest printed books which constitutes a summary of the biblical story, classical mythology and history. A map from the *Chronicles*, published the year before da Gama sailed (see page 90), is unlikely to have been of much use since it shows the Indian Ocean to be enclosed, whereas da Gama's voyage proved conclusively that it was not. Produced in 1496 by the German cartographer Hartmann Schedel in

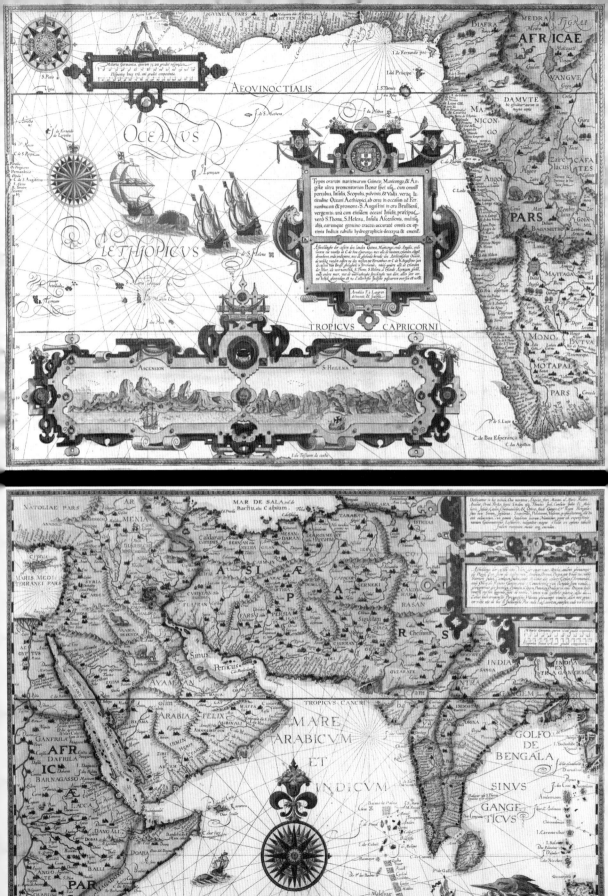

Nuremberg, it ties in with a biblical view of the world; in the corners are depicted the three sons of Noah, who are said to have divided the world between them after the great flood, foreshadowing how popes would later share much of the world between Spain and Portugal. According to the text, Shem and his descendants took Asia, Ham took Africa and Japeth was assigned Europe.

The accompanying text reveals a slender grasp of India where are found 'people with the heads of dogs, who bark when they speak' and others 'who have but one eye, which is in the forehead above the nose'. The map makes a division between India 'this side of the Ganges' and 'beyond the Ganges'. From da Gama onwards, any new information about this mythical land was regarded as commercially sensitive. King Manuel banned the distribution of maps to thwart any attempt to supplant the Portuguese, an early attempt to copyright geographical information. Linschoten's maps would in due course enable the Dutch Republic to gain an upper hand over Portugal in trade with the East.

DA GAMA'S RETURN

Da Gama's return journey took rather longer. Leaving Calicut on 29 August 1498 after a stay of three and a half months, he ignored advice that the prevailing winds were not suited for the return journey. He drifted northwards and anchored for some weeks at the island of Anjediva off Goa before sailing westwards to Malindi, a journey of more than four months. Half the crew died on the voyage and others were sick with scurvy from a shortage of fresh food. At Malindi they scuttled another ship and limped back to Portugal with two vessels, reaching Lisbon in July or early August 1499. Da Gama himself arrived a month later, having stopped in the Azores to attend to his brother Paulo, who had fallen ill on the voyage, and then to bury him.

In Lisbon da Gama was greeted as a hero. Notwithstanding the loss of a hundred or more men, two ships and the hostile reception his men had encountered at their destination, they did at least bring pepper. He had discovered the direct route by sea to India, something no one else had achieved. Alexander the Great at a similarly young age had reached India with a land army after conquering much of west Asia, but da Gama had travelled further into the Indian landmass, bypassing Muslim Egypt, Arabia and Persia, fulfilling Europe's crusader purpose by upstaging Muslim rulers.

Da Gama's success enhanced King Manuel's standing with the pope and throughout Europe. It was a commercial success too, since Lisbon now rivalled Venice as principal spice market of the continent. Venice received advanced news of the Portuguese success via Alexandria; but according to diarist Girolamo Priuli, they found it hard to accept. A Florentine merchant rubbed salt on the wound by suggesting the Venetians should give up trading 'and become fishermen'.[10] The king boasted to his neighbours in Castile that Portuguese mariners 'did reach and discover India [and] found great cities and great edifices and rivers and great settlements, in which is conducted all the trade in spices and [precious] stones that passes in ships ... throughout the world'. He told them that the seafarers had brought back cinnamon, cloves, ginger, nutmeg and pepper, making the point that Columbus brought no such spices.[11]

The follow-up was faster than after Dias' breakthrough, with a second armada of thirteen ships and more than a thousand men leaving Lisbon barely six months after da Gama's homecoming. King Manuel appointed Pedro Álvares Cabral to lead it and Bartolomeu Dias captained one of the vessels, but da Gama himself was not on board. This flotilla plied so far west in its search for the South Atlantic westerly winds that it inadvertently 'discovered' Brazil, allowing Portugal to steal a lead on Spanish exploration of the Americas by claiming a slice of the southern continent.

Arriving in India, this flotilla was better equipped with trading goods, but made little headway with the *Zamorin* of Calicut; however, it did succeed in setting up a local factory or trading base at Cochin (now Kochi), close to the rich pepper-growing region. This entrepôt also provided cinnamon from Ceylon as well as cloves, nutmeg and mace from the Spice Islands. From 1500 onwards Portugal claimed a monopoly over the trade in 'Indian spices', which it was hardly in a position to enforce even if it was the only nation there with armed ships. But it did succeed in denying trade in spices to Muslims, Arabs in particular, after taking control of the island of Hormuz at the mouth of the Persian (or Arabian) Gulf in 1507; it would have been more successful had it captured Aden, which commands the entrance to the Red Sea. It did take control of the east African port of Sofala in Mozambique, building a fort there in 1505.

A food writer who has examined medieval cookery books says that European tastes were changing at this time, with turmeric and cardamom going out of favour and cinnamon becoming more popular, alongside pepper, ginger, cloves, nutmeg and mace.[12] Such changes would explain why the Portuguese turned their attention at an early stage to Ceylon, which

The best guide the Portuguese would have had for the route to India was this 1496 map produced for the biblical Nuremberg Chronicles by cartographer Hartmann Schedel.

grew the best cinnamon, superior to the cassia or 'false cinnamon' which
grew in India. It is likely that the market was adjusting to what the ships
brought back: initially *Piper nigrum* or black pepper, the peppercorn of
southern India.

An oddity is that the spice we most associate with India today, the
chilli, also known as 'hot' or 'red' pepper, is part of the capsicum family
that originates from Mexico and is unrelated to *Piper nigrum*. It was
introduced by the Portuguese to Europe and India as well as to east Africa,
where it is known by its Swahili name of *peri-peri*. The Portuguese are also
credited with bringing to Europe from South America the turkey, known
in Portuguese as *peru* after its country of origin.[13] Later Portuguese traders
would bring from China the sweet orange known in the Turkish and Arabic
languages as *portugalis*. (The English word 'orange' also came from the East;
it was adapted from the Sanskrit *nāranga* via Persian and Arabic.)

Da Gama made two further voyages to India and was appointed to the
senior post of viceroy – the sixth holder of that office – by King Manuel I's
successor, João III, nicknamed 'the grocer king' for his sponsorship of trade.
Da Gama's somewhat haughty manner in dealing with local rulers may have

been the reason why King Manuel had favoured Francisco da Almeida as the first Portuguese governor or viceroy of India; he was followed by Afonso de Albuquerque, the chief strategist for the expansion of Portugal's control of the Indian Ocean and territories.

Da Gama was to die in Cochin three months after taking up the viceroy post; he was buried there at St Francis' church, which still holds a memorial to him. His body was later returned to the motherland and, some 400 years after his epic voyage, laid to rest in the Jerónimos Monastery at Belém.[14] Da Gama's six sons all followed their father into seafaring and exploration; five were associated with the next Asian entrepôt that Portugal conquered, becoming in turn 'Captain of Malacca'.

Meanwhile Portugal's Asian empire, or *Estado da Índia*, expanded. After the settlement of Cochin in 1500 and Goa in 1510, Portugal took control of Malacca (1511), Timor (1512), Ceylon (1517) and the Spice Islands (1529), strengthening its hold over the spices on which its trading profits depended; these were followed by Bombay (1534) and Macao (1557). As a consequence Lisbon became one of Europe's busiest and wealthiest cities. As the sixteenth century progressed, the *carreira da Índia* convoys from India became more regular; along a single street in Lisbon you could purchase 'Chinese porcelain, Indian filigree, bolts of silk and other fine cloth, incense, myrrh, precious gems and pearls, pepper, ginger, cloves, cinnamon, nutmeg, saffron, chillies, ivory, sandalwood, ebony, camphor, amber, Persian carpets and handsomely bound books'.[15] Meanwhile enslaved people who arrived from the Guinea coast were marched in chains to the prison of the Casa dos Escravos before their physical evaluation and auction in the public square known as Pelourinho Velho.

PORTUGAL'S TRIUMPH

Vasco da Gama's success gave rise to an extraordinary outpouring of nationalism in a relatively young country. By the early 1500s most of Europe's pepper supplies arrived at Lisbon in convoys of Portuguese vessels. The city embarked on a *Século de Ouro* or Golden Age. Venice, engaged in a costly war with the Ottomans, was in no position to compete. In a final humiliation for the city that had started the 'spice race', vessels from Venice came to Lisbon to meet its customers' spice needs.[16] Damião de Góis, who chronicled the reign of King Manuel, awarded Lisbon the epithet Queen of the Sea on the grounds that it had vanquished the Castilian port of Seville.[17]

Nowhere was the sense of triumphalism more apparent than in *Os Lusíadas*, an epic poem written in 1572 by Luíz Vaz de Camões, which tells how the Christian Portuguese had defeated distant peoples of all faiths. Invoking mythology, Camões compared the fame that da Gama brought to Portugal with that which Homer brought to Greece and Virgil to Italy. The poem, which runs to 226 pages in English, is a lyrical history of how tiny Portugal earned its place as one of Europe's leading nations, a geography of Portugal's conquests and a virtual deification of Vasco da Gama.

> Goa, you will see, seized, from the Muslims
> And come in the fullness of time to be
> Queen of the Orient, raised up
> By the triumphs of her conquerors.
> From that proud, noble eminence,
> They will rule with an iron fist
> Idol-worshipping Hindus, and everyone
> Throughout that land with thoughts of rebellion.

Camões had no doubt that Portugal had taken over leadership of the world from Venice, and lists some of the material benefits that the heroes brought back, underlining the fact that sailors in the service of the Spanish crown had not succeeded in their aim of discovering the sources of spices.

> There was mace from the Banda Islands;
> Then nutmeg and black cloves, pride
> Of the new-found Moluccas, and cinnamon,
> The wealth, the fame, the beauty of Ceylon.[18]

Camões celebrates brave pioneers who 'Risking all, In frail timbers on treacherous seas, By routes never charted, and only Emboldened by opposing winds' had brought such prestige to a grateful nation. With such support from Camões, Portugal – especially its capital Lisbon, whose shipbuilders made the vessels in which the mariners sailed – acquired a new confidence. In due course the country paid its own tribute to Camões by placing his remains at the Jerónimos Monastery at Belém close to those of da Gama.

As far as can be known, the Portuguese were the first to round the Cape of Good Hope. Strabo and Pliny both refer to Eudoxus of Cyzicus, who may have sailed around the Cape in the second century BC in the service of

Ptolemy VIII, but there is no clear evidence that he did. Herodotus, writing in around 446 BC, refers to a claim that an Egyptian king, Neco, 'after calling off the construction of the canal between the Nile and the Arabian Gulf, sent out a fleet manned by a Phoenician crew with orders to sail round and return to Egypt and the Mediterranean by way of the pillars of Hercules', before adding, 'I do not myself believe [this account] though others may'.[19] Herodotus is also unlikely to have been convinced by a twentieth-century claim by a British former submarine commander that the fifteenth-century Chinese mariner, Zheng He, of whom we shall hear more later, sailed around the Cape half a century before Dias, discovered America seventy years before Columbus, and circumnavigated the world nearly a century before Magellan.[20]

PORTUGUESE–SPANISH RIVALRY

As crusaders, Portugal's seafaring motive was initially to fight and defeat Muslims, though trade was a secondary objective. After the capture of Ceuta, the search for the source of gold on the Guinea coast took precedence. Then the desire to seek out Prester John, the mythical ruler of a Christian realm 'in the Indies' and a potential ally against Muslims, became their driving force. By the time of da Gama's voyage, the search for spices had become pre-eminent. As if to re-emphasise both the crusading and commercial motives, the mint in Lisbon in 1457 struck gold coins called *cruzado* for the purpose of trading in newly-found lands. This was Portugal's equivalent to the Venetian *ducat*.

As long as the fight against Muslims was dominant, Portugal could count on the support of the pope, ideologically or spiritually the most powerful ruler in Europe. Support was expressed in a series of papal *bulls*[21] or edicts. In 1452 the pope authorised the Portuguese monarch to attack Muslims and other non-Christian peoples and take possession of their lands. Three years later a further *bull* recognised Portugal's settlement of the Atlantic islands of Madeira and the Azores, its arrival on the Guinea coast and its intention to circumnavigate Africa, by granting it a monopoly of navigation, trade and fishing in all present and future such regions 'as far as the Indies'. As 'the Indies' embraced a wide and then unknown area eastwards from the coast of Africa, this gave the Portuguese an exceptionally wide 'licence', affirmed in a third *bull* under a new pope in 1456.[22]

In 1494, between Spain's success in reaching the Americas and Portugal's arrival in India, leaders of the two countries met at Tordesillas in north-west Spain to share out newly discovered land. Under a deal proposed by Ferdinand and Isabella of Spain, Pope Alexander VI awarded half the world to each country in a further papal *bull*. The line it drew in the Atlantic Ocean was not exact, since neither longitude nor the means to determine it were understood until the eighteenth century. Indeed, the notional line was subsequently revised to 'give' Portugal Brazil. The significance of the Treaty of Tordesillas was the role that popes took in sharing out land between two of Europe's leading Catholic kingdoms. The *bull* provided that neither country could claim territory already ruled by a Christian monarch.

Thus the final decade of the fifteenth century inaugurated an era of trade, colonisation and discourse between continents. This was shortly before Niccolò Machiavelli wrote his treatise on statecraft published as *The Prince* (1513), a century before William Shakespeare wrote his play about international trade, *The Merchant of Venice*, and two centuries before Daniel Defoe wrote his fantasy on sea travel, *Robinson Crusoe*, the first English novel.

The Scottish father of the study of economics, Adam Smith, would write in *The Wealth of Nations* (1798) that 'the discovery of America and that of a passage to the East Indies by the Cape of Good Hope are the two greatest and most important events recorded in the history of mankind',[23] though he went on to express reservations about colonisation as a system of trade and to describe monopoly power as 'growth retarding'. Smith says the Eastern discoveries were of greater significance, though they lacked the sources of gold and silver of the Western discoveries. Since European colonisers traded these wealthy commodities in the East for spices and other goods, the two discoveries neatly complemented one another.

MAPPING LISBON

The bird's-eye plan of Lisbon by Braun and Hogenberg in 1598 would have been among the most sought-after of their maps. It appeared a century after da Gama's triumphant return, by which time Lisbon was one of Europe's

Braun and Hogenberg's north-facing 'aerial view' of Lisbon on the River Tagus, produced in Cologne in 1598.

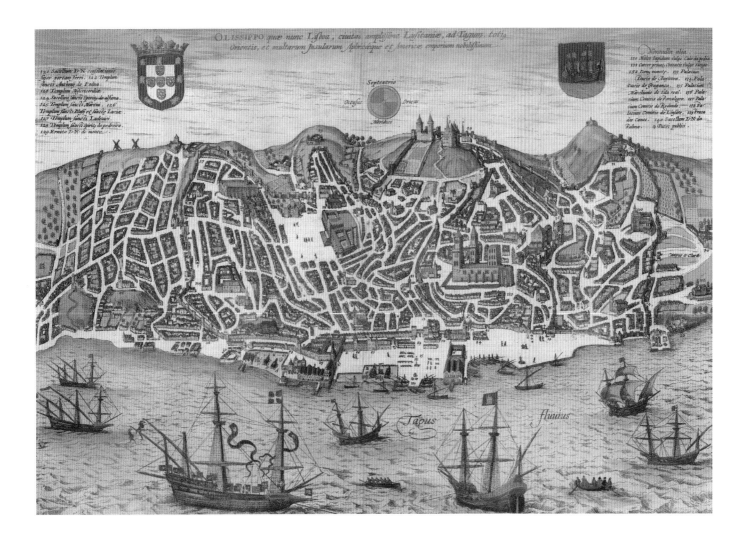

most prosperous cities, dominating East–West trade, and with around 350,000 inhabitants, a quarter of the country's population. Indeed, one of the country's problems in fulfilling its new role as spice merchant to Europe was a shortage of vessels and men to crew them. The view looks north, the River Tagus flowing into the Atlantic Ocean some way to the left. It is headed 'Olissippo, which is now Lisbon, the largest city of Portugal, on the Tagus, and a well known place of trade for the whole East and of many islands of Africa and America'. It is shown occupying seven hills on the northern bank of the River Tagus and protected by a wall which weaves across the hills, giving access to the city through a number of gateways. Caravels are being built on the river bank.

At the waterfront in the centre is the *Terreiro do Paço* or Terrace of the Palace, named for the *Paço da Ribeira* or Palace of the River Bank across the square on the left. Also on the square (now known as *Praça do Comércio*) is a small shipbuilding yard and stone wharf. Wharves for coal and timber are at the right of the picture. To the left and back from the river is a distinctive long building described as 'the place where ships ropes are made'. There is a second shipyard, and between the two a row of buildings is identified as *Casa da Índia* or New India House; Old India House is next to the Palace of the River Bank, from where the king could oversee the India trade. Behind the *Terreiro do Paço* is 'the wide new road of the merchants' lined by warehouses.

Ships sailing for the Indies departed from Belém[24] downstream (to the left), where the river is wider. Fleets were given a ceremonial send-off and blessing; and the fortunate ones were welcomed back laden with spices and other oriental produce two or more years later. Investors who financed the voyages and families of sailors would have no news during that time, nor advanced notice of a ship's return until it was spotted beating its way up the Portuguese coastline towards the mouth of the Tagus.

German map-maker and publisher Matthäus Seutter produced this image of Lisbon after the earthquake of 1755.

THE EARTHQUAKE OF 1755

Portugal had its dark days also. The year that da Gama first sailed to India, it followed Spain in forcing Jews to become 'New Christians'. Many refused and sailed to India to escape persecution. Christians old and new fell victim to the Inquisition after 1536. Then the country itself fell under the control of Spain in 1580 when King Sebastião died without an heir. The Portuguese throne passed to King Philip of Spain,[25] a grandson of King Manuel I, and the country was a province of Spain for what came to be known as the Sixty Years Captivity. Portugal becoming sovereign again in 1640, when it negotiated its independence from Spain under João IV 'the Restorer'.

Lisbon's most disastrous day was 1 November 1755, All Saints Day, when the city was hit by Europe's largest ever earthquake. It was a Sunday and many citizens were at mass when the quake struck. It lasted no more than six minutes but wrought immense havoc, with fissures as wide as 15 feet (5 metres) opening on the city streets. Stone churches collapsed, killing worshippers, and church candles started fires which raged for several days and were not extinguished by the massive tsunamis which followed the quake. The image by German map-maker Matthäus Seutter shows the city with fires ablaze.

By the time the disaster subsided, nearly a quarter of the city's population of 200,000 were dead and much of the city was destroyed. Gone was the *Paço da Ribiera* or Palace of the River Bank, containing famous paintings including works by Titian and Rubens, the customs house and the *Casa da Índia*. The king and his family survived and his prime minister, the Marquis of Pombal, launched a project to rebuild the city with the grand squares and wide avenues that characterise it today, especially the downtown area known as *Baixa*. The architectural style of rebuilt Lisbon is known as *Pombaline*, contrasting with the *Manueline*

style of the era of Manuel I. The city's Moorish quarter, *Alfama*, largely survived the earthquake. An engraved view of Lisbon from as late as 1782 still depicts the city as it was before the earthquake, showing that it takes as long for traditional views to adjust to new realities as it does maps.

The earthquake led to philosophising by writers such as Immanuel Kant in Germany and Voltaire in France on the nature of a religion that could not save its followers, a key moment in the period of intellectual ferment in Europe known as the Age of Enlightenment. Catholics attempted to explain it as God's wrath on the sins of the Portuguese, while Protestants blamed the Portuguese for being Catholic. Voltaire argued against the presence of an all-powerful god, saying there could not be a benevolent loving deity who intervened in human affairs to reward the virtuous and punish the sinful. The great Lisbon earthquake changed the appearance of the city significantly and is credited with development of the science of seismology and the construction of buildings able to withstand earthquakes. Lisbon would never recover its previous grandeur, as by this time another northern European city, Amsterdam, was fast gaining supremacy in the spice trade. But meanwhile let us turn to another highly significant Eastern port.

(above) An imaginary view of Praça do Comércio, *as it might have been reconstructed after the 1755 earthquake, published in 1757.*

(opposite top) This waterfront scene at Lisbon by Thomas Sparrow appeared in George Millar's Universal System of Geography in 1782, but depicts the city as it was before the earthquake 27 years earlier.

(opposite bottom) Lisbon in 1889 by an unknown artist, looking towards the harbour and sea beyond. A square edged by columned porticos in the Pombaline style can be seen on the left.

La tierra
R. de S. Graco
R. de Tormo
Baia hermosa

Cabo frio
Rio brauo
C. Hermoso

Mar Ver-
mejo

Pontes de buena
na speranza
Ancon de S. Andres
S. Augustin.
Laguna del rastro.
R. de S. Francesco.
Laguna de
caldera

Noua Hispania.

Messico.

MARIS

SIVE M

Florida

Cali-
formia

Mossos
Islas de los
Cedros
Islas de
los diamantes

P. de Pedro y S. Paulo.

Cuba

Y. de S.
Thomas
La anublada

P. di. na i
vidad
Colima
Curilimbo
Guatulco
Cocomisco
Stapa
Pasado

La tambre
Islico olim.

S

Iamaica

Rocca partida

Cagaius
C. de los
Farillones
Repeque
Rimallo
Remedios
Lempa
Badia de Gt.
S. Pt.
Nicaragua
Medeco

P. de mca
gualco

IVCATAN

R. de per
dicion

Blanco

Nombre de Dios

Cartagena

ACIFF-

QVOD VVLGO

Y. de Cocos

Monigo
Coiba

Caian

23° 24° 25° 26° 27° 28°

Y. de Galopagos

29°

Malpelle
P. de Gue
rura

30°

C. de forta
Rio de S. Ioan
Mangrales
Rio de S. Tiago
P. de S. Matheo

Quito.

ombre de Iesus
sola Atreguada
Las Marias
S. Catalina.
S. Anna

Circulus Aequinoctialis.

Isola de la
plata
S. Clara.
Isola de
lobos

Badia de caraque
Charapanton
de puna
R. de S. Iago
R. de tambes
R. de S. Miguel
Paira
C. de laguia
P. de Salinas

Peru.

NO MI-NANT,

Sa-

Isolas de lobos

Limocin
Civdad de los reiz
Pachacania
Garico
Laguna

Los Tuberones

Isolas de
cuervos.

Laanasca
Machate
R. de Montagn

ricorni.

S.

Isleo de
arecife

R. Decumana
R. de arocigro
Tamborale
R. de buena madre

MAR

C. de Fortuna

DEL

Cunhamu
co

Arbol
C. Blanco.
Las A.
Badia

Prima ego velivolis ambivi cursibus Orbem,
Magellane novo te duce ducta freto.
Ambivi, meritoq; vocor VICTORIA: *sunt mî*
Vela, alæ; precium, gloria; pugna, mare.

C. dela isla

C. d
los

ZVR.

AVSTRALIS,

GELLANICA NON=

DETECTA.

Cum privilegijs Imp. & Reg. Maies tatum,
nec non Cancellariæ Brabantiæ, ad decennium.

Fret

5/ MALACCA AND THE MALAY WORLD

Malacca was an early settlement on the Malay peninsula and birthplace of the Malay nation, first known to travellers by its harbour. One map of 1598 marks the entire peninsula as Malacca, probably because Europeans had not penetrated the thick jungle. Yet the harbour attracted migrants from Sumatra, where Malay was the dominant language. A slightly later map, of 1652, still shows the Malay peninsula connected to Sumatra (both on page 102). In the first century AD Pliny was referring to the Malay peninsula when he wrote in his *Natural History* of an island called Chryse which 'consists of gold and silver'.[1] This may have inspired Claudius Ptolemy to characterise the peninsula as *Chersonesus Aurea* or the Golden Peninsula in his *Geographia*. The term Golden Chersonesus was used in Indian, Roman and Greek accounts, giving the peninsula mythical status as a source of gold. Marco Polo was probably referring to Malacca when he wrote of 'a large and splendid city ... Malayur, which plies a flourishing trade especially in spices, of which there is great abundance'.[2]

The west coast fishing village that would become Malacca was founded at the start of the fifteenth century by a Muslim prince or sultan called

Parameswara; he came from the legendary Srivijaya empire based across the narrow straits in Sumatra on the Musi River, near the modern Indonesian town of Palembang. Srivijaya had been weakened by a series of raids from the Chola kingdom of southern India, and would be eclipsed by the more powerful Java-based Hindu Majapahit empire, of which it had become a vassal state. An ancestor of Parameswara whose name is lost to history recognised that an empire needed access to the open seas to survive; he felt that the eastern shore of the Malacca Straits was better suited. He crossed the straits in 1389 and took control of an island at the southern end of the peninsula then known as Temasek. When Majapahit influence spread further, Parameswara fled up the coast to establish a new kingdom at the mouth of the Malacca River.

Nature gave Malacca the navigational advantage of being at the point where two separate seasonal winds meet. Ships sailing from India on the south-west monsoon between April and September would arrive at Malacca after three to six weeks, returning to India from October when the wind direction changed. Vessels arriving from China sailed south on the north-east monsoon between October and March before entering the Malacca Straits for the final stretch northwards. This made Malacca an ideal location, receiving traders from West and East and commanding the important straits between Sumatra and the mainland. The river mouth provided a sheltered harbour.

The village had fewer than a thousand inhabitants when Parameswara created a trading centre there, developing a navy to protect traders from the scourge of piracy in the straits. He introduced regulations administered by *shahbandars* or harbourmasters to ensure orderly trading. Under Parameswara, Malacca had four *shahbandars* representing traders from China, Java, Gujarat and Bengal. One of his successors introduced an early form of 'laws of the sea' which were enforced by a *laksamana,* or admiral, giving Malacca status as a maritime power.[3]

(left) Even in 1598 the European view of south-east Asia was extremely vague, as demonstrated in this map by Abraham Ortelius and Jodocus Hondius where the entire Malay peninsula is identified as Malacca.

(right) This later map by Jan Jansson of the Indian Ocean in 1652 suggests that the island of Sumatra (Aurea Chersonesus) was attached to the Malay peninsula (Aurea Continens).

The traditional story of how the village acquired its name is that it came to Parameswara while sitting under a *Pokok Melaka*, a fruit tree. The name of the tree derived from the Sanskrit word *amlaka* meaning 'sour tasting', an accurate description of the fruit whose only use was in folk medicine. An alternative version has it that traders named the port *malakat*, an Arabic word meaning a gathering of merchants. Whether the name was first applied to the river or the port is unclear.

Malacca was the successor state to once powerful Srivijaya, whose rulers claimed descent from Alexander the Great.[4] Parameswara, also known as Iskandar Shah, was its first sultan, the first of any Malay state and one of many migrants from Sumatra who settled on the Malay peninsula. The Malay language used Jawi, a script based on Arabic. Islam, brought to Malacca by Arab traders, became the state religion during the reign of Parameswara's son, Sultan Megat Iskandar Shah, 1414–24. According to one historian of the city 'Malacca was the crucible where Malay-ness got defined: speaking the Malay language, observing Malay *adat* (custom) and worshipping God according to Islam'.[5]

By the late fifteenth century, Malacca controlled the entire peninsula and much of Sumatra, giving Parameswara's successors mastery of the straits. Early maps, such as that by Petrus Bertius and Benjamin Wright, first published in single colour in 1598, depicted the entire peninsula as Malac. The name Malaya derived from an earlier Melayu kingdom on Sumatra.

Historians suggest that the emergence of Malacca coincided with a breaking away from Indian influences, manifested in both Hinduism and Buddhism, which characterised both the Majapahit and Siamese empires. The sultanate traded in Indian cloth, Chinese porcelain, silk, camphor and

This 1612 version of a map by Petrus Bertius and Benjamin Wright charts the island of Sumatra, the Malay peninsula and the Malacca Straits which separate them much more accurately; it also makes one of the earliest references to Singapore (Sincapura), apparently situated on the mainland.

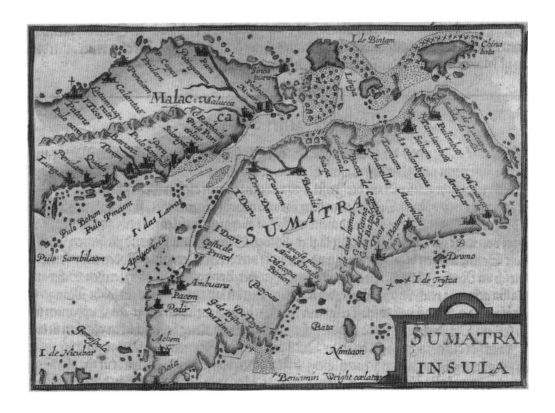

iron as well as sandalwood, fish and forest products from the archipelago. The Bugis, seafaring people from the island of Celebes (now Sulawesi), brought to Malacca the spices that so appealed to Europeans, while gold was brought from Sumatra and tin from Phuket (now in Thailand) and Tavoy (Burma). Later, tin was discovered within territory controlled by Malacca and became a trading currency.

By moving out of Majapahit control, Parameswara fell under the sway of the more powerful ruler of the kingdom of Siam (modern Thailand) based at Ayutthaya, north of present-day Bangkok. The port was constantly under threat of invasion by the king of Siam, to whom Parameswara paid an annual tribute in gold. It took an armada led by a Muslim admiral from China to break the hold on this fledgling state by the Buddhist king of Siam to the north and the Hindu Majapahit rulers of Java to the south. The Chinese admiral was the eunuch Zheng He, also written as Zheng Ho or Cheng Ho. His arrival in Malacca with a fleet of 200 so-called 'treasure ships' marked an important juncture in the development of Malacca as a port and in establishing a Chinese presence there.[6]

ZHENG HE AND CHINA'S TREASURE FLEET

In fifteenth-century China, castration was common practice for orphaned boys or those taken into servitude by victorious generals. Zheng He was born into a Muslim family of Uzbek descent who served the Mongols in Yunnan province. He was aged ten when Chinese forces ousted Mongols from Yunnan, the last province they held, establishing China's Ming dynasty. The third Ming ruler, the Yongle emperor who came to power in 1403 soon after the Malaccan sultanate was founded, was intent on opening China to the world, so built a massive fleet of vessels to sail into 'the southern seas' and create alliances and exchange goods with other nations, in other words to trade. Evidence from the remains of the docks in Nanjing where the fleet was built suggests that the treasure ships were far larger than anything built in Europe at the time. This was nearly a century before Columbus or da Gama set out to navigate the oceans.[7]

The first of seven great armadas of around 200 vessels including 62 treasure ships set sail in 1405 and visited Champa (Vietnam), Java and Sumatra (Indonesia) and Calicut (India). All the subsequent voyages visited Malacca, known to the Chinese as *Wu Shu* or Five Islands. In 1409 one of the voyages called at Ayutthaya, and Zheng He is said to have warned the Siamese against attacking Malacca where the Chinese had built a *guangchang*, a stockade or storage base, to provision their ships. Malacca lies roughly halfway between Nanjing and the east African coast, the fleet's furthest reach.

On the third voyage, Admiral Zheng He presented Parameswara with an inscribed stone recognising Malacca as a kingdom, granting him a seal of office and appointing him king with silk robes and a ceremonial

A model of one of Zheng He's treasure ships at the Tamkang University Maritime Museum in Taiwan.

Zheng He, regarded as the
Chinese founder of Malacca.
Illustration from a fictionalised
account of the sea voyages of
Zheng He, printed c.1600.

golden umbrella which has remained a symbol of Malaysia's kingship. That ceremony in 1411 is regarded as the foundation of Malacca as an independent state and the birth of Malaya, a Muslim nation recognised as independent by a Chinese admiral brought up a Muslim. To China the ceremony marked the transfer of Malacca's allegiance from the king of Siam and sultan of Majapahit to the emperor of China.

Zheng He may have mastered some Malay words. The first Chinese–Malay dictionaries date from this time, well before Malacca had any direct contact with Europeans. Zheng He would have practised using the language when Parameswara and a large retinue sailed with him for a first visit to China by a Malay sultan, during which he paid his respects to the emperor. These contacts with China made a deep impression on the Malay city, where Zheng He is venerated for the role he played in the birth of the nation. He helped Malacca establish control over the straits by capturing a notorious pirate leader operating from Sumatra. Zheng He's travels are represented by Chinese *junks* on Fra Mauro's *mappa mundi* produced in Venice in 1459 (page 18).

Early diplomatic relations between China and Malacca were marked by the exchange of gifts and triggered a steady migration to Malacca by southern Chinese. For example, they brought tea to Malacca two centuries before the drink reached Europe. At periods in Malacca's history citizens of Chinese origin outnumbered Malays, known as *bumiputera* or 'sons of the soil'. According to a leading historian, in making Malacca his regional capital Zheng He 'greatly enhanced Malacca's position as the most important trading centre in south-east Asia',[8] enabling the port to reach the height of its power a century before the Portuguese arrived.

Two more Malaccan sultans made 'tribute missions' to China, and one married a Chinese princess in a grand ceremony at Malacca in 1459. As in Europe at that time, cross-cultural marriages had more to do with diplomacy and the forging of trading alliances than of love or individual choice. Sultan Mansur Shah and Princess Hang Li Poh are considered to be the progenitors of Malacca's *Baba Nyonya* heritage, which blends Chinese and Malay traditions of dress and cuisine. Chinese born in Malacca are known as *Peranakan* or 'Straits Chinese'. Their homes often display silk tapestries and mother-of-pearl inlay furniture brought from China alongside traditional Malay cooking utensils. *Peranakan* eat off Chinese porcelain, and use their hands according to Malay tradition rather than chopsticks. The royal marriage started a tradition of migration from China to Malacca and other destinations in south-east Asia – in

Chinese terminology, *Nanyang* or the South Seas. The large entourage the emperor's daughter brought with her settled on *Bukit Cina*, China Hill, now incidentally the site of the largest Chinese cemetery outside China.

This opening to the world by an otherwise introspective empire lasted only until 1433 when Emperor Yongle's successor brought down the shutters once more, prohibiting China from trading with other states. Thirty years was long enough for China to have built the largest naval force the world had seen until then, numbering 250 vessels and nearly 30,000 men, and for it to sail as far as Africa and the Red Sea in seven epic voyages.

THE COMING OF EUROPEANS

Europeans viewed Malacca as the gateway to the array of islands from Sumatra eastwards which included the Spice Islands. Afonso de Albuquerque was so fired by his success in taking control of Goa that he now turned his attention to Malacca. This port, along with Aden and Hormuz, was on the target list issued by King Manuel in 1509 for controlling the Indian Ocean, unlike Goa which Albuquerque captured on his own initiative. Lisbon knew of Malacca's reputation as a source of spices, and Albuquerque would have encountered vessels in Goa that had come from Malacca bearing spices and goods of Chinese origin.

Albuquerque's crusader motive was uppermost when he spoke of 'the great service which we shall perform to Our Lord in casting the Moors [Muslims] out of this country and quenching the fire of this sect of Muhammad so that it may never burst out again'. Yet identifying Malacca as 'the headquarters of all the spices and drugs' which the Moors carry every year in forty or fifty ships bound for Mecca, he added: 'If we take this trade of Malacca away out of their hands, Cairo and Mecca will be entirely ruined and to Venice will no spices be conveyed except what her merchants go and buy in Portugal.'[9]

Albuquerque sent a reconnaissance mission under Diogo Lopes de Sequeira, which arrived in Malacca in September 1509. In a minor skirmish with the sultan's forces, Portuguese sailors were killed and others taken hostage. De Sequeira reported to Albuquerque that as many as two thousand trading vessels from all over the East were anchored in Malacca harbour. He depicted the reigning sultan, Mahmud Shah, as weak, vulnerable and unable to stand up to superior Portuguese firepower. Albuquerque himself set sail from Goa in 1511 with 14,000 men in nineteen vessels, ostensibly to rescue the Portuguese hostages, though he made additional demands on the sultan: including that Portugal build a fortress – presumably on the instructions of his king.

When negotiations with the sultan failed to achieve his purposes, Albuquerque fired canons onto the port, causing the sultan to flee. Malacca fell easily into Portuguese hands and would remain so for 130 years. An 'aerial' view by Pedro Barreto de Resende shows the bridge on which Albuquerque focused his attack. Capture of the port was followed by a brutal massacre of Muslims, while Buddhists and Hindus were spared. Hindus had facilitated the Portuguese in taking control of the port from Muslims, so Albuquerque appointed their leader, Nina Chatu, as an additional

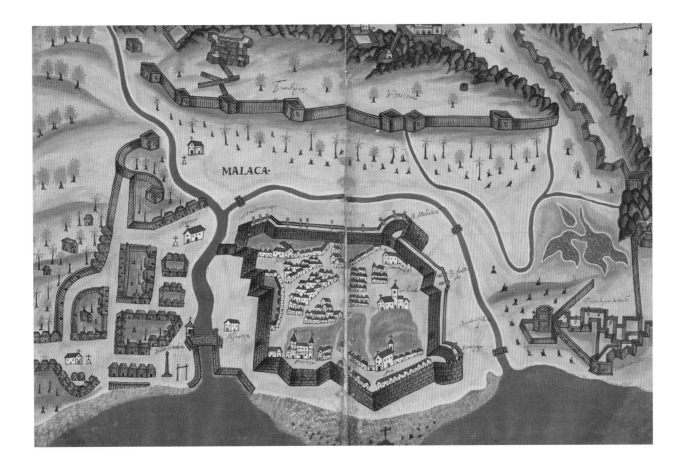

MALACA·

An 'aerial view' of the
Portuguese settlement at
Malacca from the Livro de
Estado da India Oriental
1640–46 by Pedro Barreto de
Resende.

shahbandar to represent traders of South Indian origin. Two years after
the port's capture, the Portuguese destroyed a fleet of 300 ships in the
Malacca Straits sent from Demak, a Muslim sultanate on the north coast
of Java which was growing in strength as that of Majapahit was declining,
confirming Portugal's control of the port and the straits it commanded.

The Portuguese built a fortress known as *A Famosa,* the famous, on the
hill where the sultan's *istana* or palace had stood, above the point where
the Malacca River enters the sea. They fortified the town from attack from
land or sea and built dwelling places for Portuguese settlers within. Atop
the hill they built a church, the first in south-east Asia, a headquarters for
the Jesuits and symbol of Portugal's missionary purpose.

Portugal created a *feitoria* to trade in the products that had made Malacca
and its Arab traders wealthy, though Goa remained its main trading base in
Asia. The Portuguese apothecary Tomé Pires gave testimony that 'whoever
is lord of Malacca has his hand on the throat of Venice' adding 'it is a city
that was made for merchandise [of which] men cannot estimate the worth
... on account of its greatness and profit'.[10] According to another writer, the
capture of Malacca 'gave the Portuguese the complete command of the spice
trade, and eventually of the Chinese and Japanese trade. It struck the final
blow at the Muhammadan commercial routes to Europe.'[11]

The Portuguese slotted themselves in as 'a new competitor in the old-
existing pattern of political and commercial rivalry and power'[12] alongside
the many sultans who ruled territory on the peninsula and across the

archipelago. None would risk confrontation, because of superior Portuguese firepower. Collectively the sultanates – especially Muslim ones like Aceh and Demak – limited Portugal's further expansion in the region. However, Malacca had the advantage of controlling the straits so it is no wonder that European nations would later compete to occupy the port. Albuquerque meanwhile returned to his beloved Goa in January 1512, arriving just in time to prevent it being recaptured by Muslim forces.

REACHING THE SPICE ISLANDS

The capture of Malacca was an opportunity for the Portuguese to extend their reach through diplomacy. They set about cultivating links with the many trading communities, sending envoys to establish trading relations with Ayutthaya in Siam, Pegu in what would become Burma, to Cochin China and Tonkin in what would become French-ruled Indo-China and later Vietnam, and to nearby Sumatra. Tomé Pires, who was secretly reporting to King Manuel, was sent on the first Portuguese mission to China, though it was not a success. The Chinese had got on well with the Malacca sultans so were displeased at the arrival of Europeans; they chose instead to ship their porcelain and silk through other ports.

Malacca's most important diplomatic mission was to the Spice Islands. Albuquerque sent three ships there under his most trusted captains, António de Abreu and Francisco Serrão. They sailed along the coast of Java

A view of the Dutch settlement of Malacca in 1726, with A Famosa *fort on the right with its hilltop church, and the Dutch Village on the left, by Dutch priest and naturalist François Valentijn.*

to Flores and Timor before turning north and arriving at the Banda Islands, the source of nutmeg and mace. Serrão was the first European to 'discover' this archipelago of eight islands in the middle of the Banda Sea, dominated by an active volcano. They then travelled northwards to Ambon, the central island of the Moluccas. Attempting to return to Malacca, Serrão's ship became separated from the others and, after being shipwrecked, he reached Ternate, another volcanic island, which with Tidore, Motir, Makian and Bacan were the native home of the spice clove. The islands lie off the coast of the much larger island of Gilolo (later Halmahera). Ternate was the only Spice Island named on Sebastian Münster's 1540 map (page 16). It must have felt like reaching the end of the rainbow to find the source of Venice's and Alexandria's riches, a further triumph for Portugal's mariners and king.

There is a wildly inaccurate map by the Flemish mathematician and theologian Petrus Bertius (page 110) on which you can trace their route from Timor on the left (south) to Banda and then Ambon (Amboina) before Serrão alone crossed the Equator to reach Ternate (Terenate). There Serrão befriended the sultan, who was at war with the sultan of neighbouring Tidore. Serrão would never return to Malacca; he died in Ternate in 1521, after allegedly being poisoned by the sultan of Tidore, just as a friend from his days in Malacca was attempting to reach Ternate from the opposite direction.

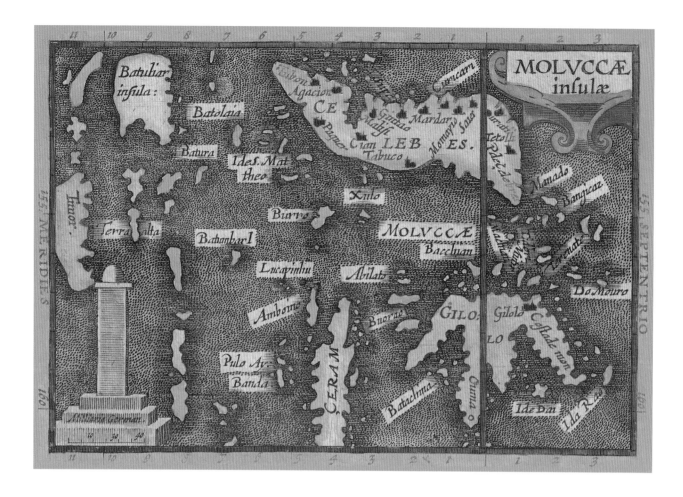

ROUND THE WORLD

That friend was a Portuguese nobleman by the name of Fernão de Magalhães, better known as Ferdinand Magellan. In Malacca Magellan hatched an ambitious plan to find a more direct route to the Spice Islands by following the lead of Christopher Columbus in sailing westwards from Europe. On his return from Malacca to Lisbon, Magellan presented his plan to King Manuel I, the monarch who had backed da Gama, but he declined to finance this expedition. Magellan instead took his proposal to the Spanish monarch Charles I.[13] Flushed with the success of three voyages by Columbus, Charles agreed to back him, so in 1519 Magellan set sail from Seville under the Spanish flag to find a route to the Spice Islands by sailing west.

In five ships with 237 sailors, Magellan crossed the Atlantic Ocean before facing the challenge of finding a way around the southern tip of the Americas. This he managed via the passage that now bears his name, the Magellan Straits, skirting an area he named *Tierra del Fuego* or 'land of fires' because he saw fires burning there. Portuguese sailors had found the routes round two great continents, Africa and South America, though the latter was achieved in the name of Spain.

Magellan sailed on across the ocean he named *Mar Pacífico* or Pacific Ocean, because he said it was more peaceful than the Atlantic Ocean he had left behind. After several weeks sailing he reached an archipelago lying between China and the Spice Islands. An encounter with 'native kings' on

This west-facing 1618 map of south-east Asia by Petrus Bertius marks the Clove Islands of Ternate, Tidore, Machian and Bacchan (part of the Moluccas) but does not show how to reach them.

Mactan Island off the coast of Cebu resulted in Magellan being killed. His fellow mariners persevered to reach the fabled Spice Islands, arriving in November 1521 at the island of Tidore, neighbour to Ternate. They befriended the island's ruler, Sultan Manzor, who willingly pledged allegiance to the king of Spain, offering to rename his island 'Castile' in his honour.

Sultan Manzor said that his island, part of the Moluccas group for which Magellan had been searching, was one of only five where the clove tree grew. He told them it grew in the mountains: 'The tree is tall and as thick across as a man. Its branches in the centre spread out widely, but at the top they grow into a kind of peak ... The cloves come at the tip of branches, ten or twenty together ... When the cloves sprout they are white; when ripe, red; and when dried, black.' Europeans had never previously seen cloves growing. They were also given descriptions of nutmeg and mace, which the sultan said grew on the adjacent island of Gilolo; of ginger, which grew on all the islands; and cinnamon, which he said grew on an island to the south called Ende, better known as Flores.[14] Among presents that the sultan sent to his newly recognised monarch were two dead birds of paradise, known locally as *bolon divata* or 'bird of god', renowned for its colourful plumage.

The mariners filled their vessels with cloves, but had to abandon one when it sprang a leak. They sailed their remaining vessel, the *Victoria*, south of Java and Sumatra to avoid any unwanted encounter with the Portuguese in the Malacca Straits. As the chronicler recorded it, 'we left [the island of Sumatra] on the right hand to the north for fear of the king of Portugal'. After crossing the Indian Ocean, they rounded the Cape of Good Hope and arrived back in Seville in September 1522. Only eighteen of the thirty-seven sailors who had set sail nearly three years earlier returned home.

Besides discovering the source of key spices, Magellan's crew made another discovery. They kept a close tally of the days, so were surprised during a replenishment stop at the Cape Verde Islands to find it was a Thursday rather than Wednesday as they believed. It then dawned on them that by constantly sailing westwards around the globe they had gained a day. This notion gave birth to the International Date Line, an imaginary north–south line which bisects the Pacific Ocean in a way that the line created by the Treaty of Tordesillas never did.

This Spanish-funded first circumnavigation of the world highlighted the intense maritime rivalry between Spain and Portugal; it revived the ongoing argument over territorial rights fuelled but not resolved by the pope-backed Treaty of Tordesillas of 1494 which had shared the world between the two Catholic powers, based on an imaginary line of longitude drawn in the Atlantic Ocean. There was an assumption that the notional line extended to the other side of the globe across the Pacific Ocean, determining whether Spain or Portugal could claim the Spice Islands. The two powers were not able to measure precisely where the *linea de demaracación* lay. It depended on the islands' distance eastwards from Malacca, which no one could easily determine. Before long Europe's Protestant powers would challenge their rights anyway, so Portugal and Spain agreed by the Treaty of Zaragosa of 1529 that Portugal, by virtue of its primary occupation, would retain control of the Spice Islands or Moluccas; Spain would take exclusive rights over the islands to the north, to be named the Philippines for Philip II of Spain. Meanwhile in Malacca, Portugal was coming under pressure from one of those Protestant powers.

THE PORTUGUESE-DUTCH WAR

Portugal now commanded a substantial part of Europe's trade with 'the Indies'. The main losers were Arab traders, 'the moors of Cairo, of Mecca and of Jeddah', as Albuquerque described them. 'Moors' of north Africa dominated the southern Iberian peninsula until 1492, and Albuquerque believed he was furthering the campaign against the spread of Islam that his Spanish neighbours were pursuing nearer home. Portugal's control of Malacca gave it the power to determine who sailed through the Malacca Straits, which was why Magellan's fellow mariners avoided that route on their return to Europe. Malacca presides over the narrowest part of the 930 km-long waterway; so, with Portugal in control, Arab merchants turned their attentions to the lesser ports of Bengal, Burma and Sumatra.

Spices transported around the Cape in Portuguese vessels could be found on sale at the Rialto in Venice; but before long Portugal's capital Lisbon took over as the main market place for such delicacies in Europe. This small European nation with a population of no more one and a quarter million citizens at the end of the sixteenth century had over-reached itself, since it lacked both the shipping and the manpower to defend its long supply lines. This may not have mattered while its main enemies were pirates. But other forces were at large in Europe, where the main seafaring nations were engaged in war against each other, initially over domains in Europe and subsequently for more distant territory.

These wars kicked off with the Spanish Armada of 1588, when a combined Spanish and Portuguese fleet under Philip II tried to invade England, whose navy was supported by Dutch forces in resisting the Iberian onslaught. Naval historian George Ballard wrote that 'no short war ever ... produced an effect on the subsequent history of so great a portion of the surface of the globe as the defeat of the Spanish Armada'. He went on to argue that had 'the wall of Spanish maritime ascendancy' not been demolished by the northern Europeans, 'New York would never have been either Dutch of British – and might never have come into existence at all'.[15]

The Dutch were already fighting to overthrow their Spanish Hapsburg rulers in the Eighty Years War (1566–1648), and the Portuguese were seeking to recover their independence from Spain with whom they shared a monarch from 1580. Then there were the colonial struggles of which the most prolonged was an attempt by the northern United Provinces – later the Netherlands – to gain ascendancy over the Portuguese. These began with an attack by the Dutch on Portuguese shipping off west Africa in 1598, and lasted until 1663 by when the Dutch had taken control from Portugal of Ceylon, the Malabar coast and Malacca and established a base at the Cape of Good Hope, whose earlier conquest had given Portugal command of the oceans. The Portuguese–Dutch War was as much about sugar and slaves as spices; and while the Dutch were victorious in Asia, they just matched the Portuguese control of the west African slave trade, and were losers in

This 1603 image by Theodore de Bry shows a confrontation in the mouth of the Johore River (Rio Batastubar) off Singapore (on the left) between the Dutch and Portuguese. The Dutch captured the Portuguese galleon Santa Catarina *whose cargo is said to have raised 3.5 million guilders when sold in Amsterdam.*

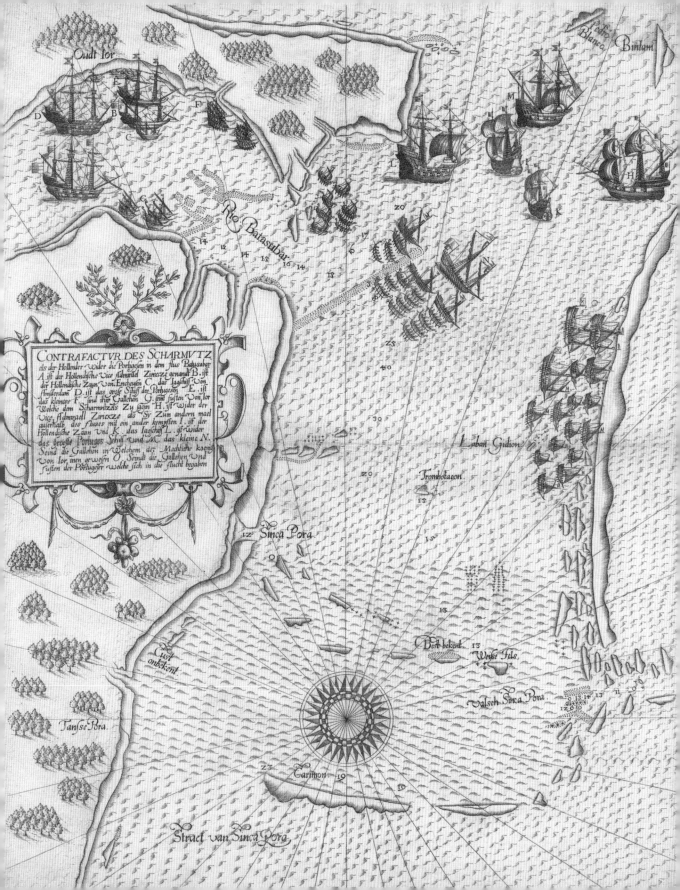

Oudt Ior

Rio. Batasabar

Pedro Blanco

Bintam

CONTRAFACTVR DES SCHARMVTZ
els der Hollender wider die Porhuosen in dem flus Bajusabar
A. ist der Hollendische Vice Admiral Zirixzee genandt B. ist
der Hollendische Zaan von Enchusen C. das Iagtschiff von
Amsterdam D. ist das grose Schiff der Porhuosen E. ist
das kleinere F. sind ihre Gallehen G. sent sustten von Ior
Welche dem Scharmutzel zu sagen H. ist wider der
Vice Admirael Zirixzee als Sy zum andern mael
auserhalb des fluses mit ein ander kempsten I. ist der
Hollendische Zaan Und K. das Iagtschiff L. ist wider
das groeste Porluges Schiff und K. das kleine N.
Seind die Gallehen in welchem des Mechtiehr koenig
von Ior, inen gewesen O. Seindt die Gallehen und
sustten der Porhugeser welche sich in die flucht begaben

Laban Gidion

Tronhotavon

Sinca Pora

Cust onbekent

Gut bekent

Weisse Fels

Valsch Sinca Pora

Tansse Pora.

Strael van Sinca Pora.

Carimon

the battle to control the Brazilian sugar trade.[16] Victory by the Netherlands in Asia, says historian C. R. Boxer, was down to three factors: 'superior economic resources, superior manpower, superior sea-power'.

The Asian confrontation is sometimes dubbed 'the Spice War', since it was about access to pepper in Malabar, cinnamon in Ceylon and cloves, nutmeg and mace in the Spice Islands of the Malay archipelago. As well as a struggle between Europe's northern Protestant nations and its southern Catholics, it was a contest about royal enterprise, as practised by the Spanish and Portuguese, versus the private enterprise model introduced by the Dutch and English at the turn of the seventeenth century, which consisted of private 'chartered' companies authorised by the state to bear arms and engage in war where necessary. Under this model trade was funded by private investors hoping to turn a profit from spices. At this stage neither companies or nations were thinking in terms of building an empire. Yet this was a time, writes Admiral Ballard, when European private companies wielded more power than 'the Mogul Emperors on the Peacock Throne [in India], or the Sons of Heaven in the Great Hall of Audience of Pekin, or the Kings of Persia in the Courts of Ispahan'.[17]

The clash between the two systems of trade was paramount when three ships of the newly-formed Dutch East India trading company, *Vereenigde Oost-Indische Compagnie* (VOC), seized the 1,500-ton Portuguese carrack *Santa Catarina* close to the southern entrance to the Malacca Straits in 1603. The vessel, returning from Macau on the coast of China, had a cargo of Chinese silk and porcelain and the perfume ingredient musk. The value of this one ship was so great that it allegedly enhanced the capital worth of the VOC by 50 per cent. An early map by Theodore de Bry of the sea off Singapore depicts an encounter in the war (page 113).

Malacca had first enacted laws of the sea under Sultan Muhammad Shah, and this seizure off the Malay peninsula triggered a wider legal debate about who owned the high seas. Portugal's claim to *mare clausum* – the right of a nation to control or close a given sea – was pitched against the contrary notion of *mare liberum*, under which the seas were open to all. This latter principle, advanced in a document by the Dutch lawyer Hugo Grotius in 1609, was espoused by the Dutch, though they were less committed to the principle when it was a matter of excluding other countries' ships to protect their own claimed trading monopoly. Seizure of the *Santa Catarina* marked the end of Portugal's monopoly control of the eastern seas. It also marked the ascent of Europe's Protestant powers, the Dutch Republic and England, over the Catholic powers of Portugal and Spain, who had started the competition for both souls and spices.[18]

A sea battle off Malacca in 1615 ended Portugal's naval domination of the straits and foretold the collapse of its outpost at Malacca a quarter-century later. The Dutch blockaded the port from 1634 to prevent vessels entering or leaving, which encouraged arriving vessels to divert to Batavia (Jakarta) in Java, which they controlled from 1619. These tactics led to the decline of Malacca and the blossoming of Batavia as the region's main entrepôt. The Dutch also challenged Spanish control of the Philippines, though with less success than in their battles with the Portuguese. Things

Looking north from A Famosa
hilltop towards the mouth
of the Malacca River, with
Kampung Belanda, *the Dutch
Village, beyond; by an unknown
artist around 1870.*

did not always go in favour of the Dutch, as is shown by their unsuccessful
attempts to capture Goa, Macau, the sandalwood-producing island of Timor
to the south of the Spice Islands, and the east African victualling station of
Mozambique, all of which remained in Portuguese hands until the second
half of the twentieth century.[19]

Midway through this drawn-out Catholic–Protestant war, Portugal
recovered its independence from Spain when the Duke of Braganza became
King João IV, nicknamed 'the Restorer' (1640), and the United Provinces
were granted their independence by the Treaty of Münster (1648), which
ended the Eighty Years War, though for all intents the Dutch Republic (as
the country restyled itself) had been self-ruled from 1580. Portugal's losses
in Asia caused it to seek a military alliance with the English against the
Dutch in 1661, as we shall see when we consider the story of Bombay.

By the time the Portuguese–Dutch War ended in 1663, Portugal had lost
control of Ceylon (1638), Malacca (1641), the Malabar coast (1663), and of
Hormuz to a combined Persian–English force (1622). Through Malabar the
Dutch gained control of the trade in pepper; Ceylon gave it access to the best
cinnamon; while its successful ousting of the Spanish and Portuguese from
key Spice Islands enabled it to monopolise the trade in cloves, nutmeg and
mace. By establishing a base at Cape Town in 1652, the Dutch took control
of the direct sea route to India and the Indies. Malacca's fall to the Dutch
ended 130 years of Portuguese domination there; and control of Java and
other parts of the archipelago enabled the Dutch to exercise monopoly over
the lucrative trade in spices reaching European markets. It also 'sealed the
fates of [powerful sultanates] Mataram and Aceh as commercial powers'.[20]

Under the Dutch an area to the north of the bridge across the Malacca River – which played a role in Albuquerque's capture of the port – came to be known as *Kampung Belanda* or Dutch Village. During the Dutch era, tin became an important export through Malacca. It was especially plentiful in Perak, a sultanate north of Malacca. (*Perak* means silver in Malay: apparently when tin was discovered there it glistened like silver.) However, Malacca was never again the major entrepôt it had been under the Portuguese, because the Dutch had invested heavily in Batavia on the north-west coast of Java, which was closer to the Spice Islands and more plentiful in food. Malacca was self-sufficient only in fish and fruit; rice and other goods were brought from Batavia.

Other reasons for Malacca's decline were the silting of the river mouth as larger trading vessels needed greater displacement when laden, as well as rivalry from ports controlled by Malay sultans closer to the tin-producing region. Dutch dealings with local rulers revolved around tin. The sultans of Kedah and Johore exerted their authority, as did the Bugis traders from Celebes. Malacca's main importance for the Dutch was that it enabled them to control who sailed through the straits. The VOC held Malacca for nearly two hundred years, longer than the rule by Portugal.

A DUTCH-BRITISH SWAP OF TERRITORY

The takeover of Malacca by the British in the late 1700s was dictated by events in Europe, where Napoleon was extending his ambit and eyeing up both the Dutch Republic and its overseas territories. Britain, through its East India Company, developed a port at Prince of Wales Island (later Penang) further up the coast, which became a British settlement in 1786 by agreement with the sultan of Kedah to whom annual rent was paid. The sultan's successor extended the settlement (and the bounty) to include part of the mainland bordering the tin-producing state of Perak. Britain's first settlement east of India became a fourth presidency of British-ruled India alongside Bombay, Madras and Calcutta. It joined Malacca and Singapore in the new colony of the Straits Settlements in 1826.

Besides trading tin, Prince of Wales Island served the East India Company's lively trade with China, a notable part of which consisted of tea. It was also well positioned for Britain to challenge Dutch domination of the trade in spices from the archipelago. By the time the fourth Anglo-Dutch War ended in 1784, Britain and the Dutch Republic were close to becoming allies, feeling their commercial interests – or those of their respective East India companies – were threatened by Napoleon-ruled France. When France invaded the Dutch Republic in 1795, the Dutch *stadhouder* William V of Orange fled into exile in Britain, which then extended the 'custody and protection' of King George III over Malacca on behalf of the Dutch prince, since both nations feared it would otherwise fall into French hands – or those of 'a native prince'. The governor-general of India, Lord Minto, then extended Britain's reach further by sanctioning the temporary occupation of Java, a much larger and more significant Dutch-controlled territory.

Malacca's subsequent transfer to the British (in 1825) was a matter of consolidating spheres of influence and trade of the respective European powers. The port had prospered because of the winds which met there and the shelter that its river mouth afforded sailing vessels, but it fell into decline from the 1830s as a result of the different needs of steamships. Britain inherited a province that could not grow enough rice to feed its inhabitants – and did not have Java as a rice-bowl, though Chinese farmers developed tapioca as an alternative. Britain invested in tin production on the peninsula, and then introduced rubber as a source of wealth. In the early twentieth century mineral oil was discovered off the east coast and in Borneo, and vegetable palm oil became a major export crop in the 1960s. Migrants from India added to Malacca's diversity in response to British planters' need for manpower to work the estates.

The Dutch persuaded Malacca to use the Latin alphabet to write the Malay language (*Melayu*), though the Arabic-based Jawi script remained in use for Islamic rituals. *Melayu* is a variant of *bahasa Indonesia* – *bahasa* being a word of Sanskrit origin meaning language. Through their trading contacts, both Indonesia and Malay adopted words from Pali and Sanskrit, which were Indian classical languages, and from Arabic, while the Malay words for church (*gereja*), flag (*bendera*) and pineapple (*nanas*) all derive

This map of east Asia by Jan Huygen van Linschoten, in its 1607 version, has east at the top. It was instrumental in showing the Dutch how to reach the Spice Islands (top right) without sailing through the Malacca Straits.

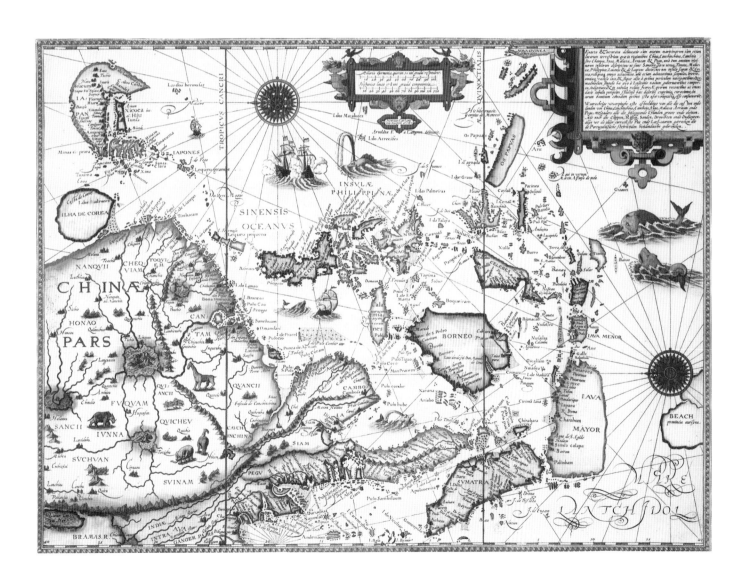

from Portuguese. Malay words have entered the languages of Portugal, the Netherlands and Britain. For example, *kampung*, meaning village, has entered all three: in English it is the origin of compound, an area adjacent to a house or factory. The expression to run amok, meaning to behave in a wild and uncontrollable manner, comes from Malay where *meng-amuk* has the same meaning. Tea may have come into English from the Hokkien dialect *tê* via the Malay *teh*. The Portuguese adopted *chá*, also used colloquially in English, from the same word in Mandarin. Paddy, meaning rice in the husk (while growing), comes from the Malay word *padi*. Ketchup, popularised in America under various spellings to mean tomato sauce, comes from the Cantonese *keh jup* via Malay, where *kecap* means any variety of fermented savoury sauce.

JAN HUYGEN VAN LINSCHOTEN

Before leaving Malacca we should credit the man who, quite literally, put south-east Asia on the map, at least in Europe. We recalled Jan Huygen van Linschoten, a Dutchman who served the Portuguese archbishop of Goa, for his map of Goa and descriptions of Portuguese life there. Linschoten never visited Malacca or any south-east Asian port, yet when he returned to his homeland and published *Itinerario* in 1596 it included a full description of Malacca gained second-hand from colleagues in Goa who had ventured further east.

His book included the most comprehensive map so far of the Malay world, peninsula and islands. It was remarkable for its relative accuracy of a region that few Europeans had visited. Those who followed Linschoten's map and instructions learned that they did not need to sail through the Portuguese-controlled Malacca Straits to reach Java and the Spice Islands. A more direct – and unmonitored – route lay through the Sunda Straits that separate Java from Sumatra, after which they could plot a course to Banda, Ambon or Ternate with little chance of crossing the path of marauding Europeans or the notorious Malacca Straits pirates. As well as being descriptive of Portuguese rule, *Itinerario* gave the impression that Lisbon's administration was inefficient, fundamentally corrupt and would easily succumb to the power of a mightier navy such as that of the Dutch Republic.

As if the Dutch sea-power advantage over the Portuguese were not sufficient, Linschoten had given his country a major navigational aid. First to realise it were the van Houtman brothers, Cornelius and Frederik, who sailed through the Sunda Straits in 1595 with an early version of *Itinerario*.[21] Linschoten's map proved its worth a few years later when the Dutch Republic created the VOC, or United East India Company. The VOC's determination to find its own route to the Spice Islands was fuelled by Philip II denying entry by Dutch vessels to Spanish and Portuguese ports.

Parameswara's dynasty came to an end in 1528 during the reign of the seventh sultan, who went on to found the Johore-Riau sultanate that adjoins Malacca to the south. Malacca is regarded as the fount of ethnic Malay culture, as well as of the racial diversity that makes up multicultural Malaysia. Alongside the Malacca River, on what is believed to be the site of Zheng He's stockade, stands a museum celebrating the man and his voyages. The river, the

A watercolour of Malacca from the sea by Jan Keldermans, 1764.

city and the state that surrounds it are now written 'Melaka' to conform with modern Malay orthography. The Malay Federation was renamed Malaysia in 1963 with the incorporation of two states in northern Borneo.

Evidence of Portugal's 130-year rule survives in a community of Portuguese who intermarried with other races, some still bearing Portuguese names and speaking a version of the Portuguese language dating from the sixteenth century. The Dutch left their building style in the *stadthuys* or town hall and street names such as *Heeren Straat* or Gentlemen's Street – mirroring Heerengracht Canal in Amsterdam – in *Kampung Belanda* or Dutch Village and *Jonker* Street, from *yonkheer* meaning young gentleman. The British left behind their language and system of government when Malaya – later Malaysia – gained its independence in 1957.

Melaka has given the world the Melaka cane, a walking stick made from jungle-grown rattan, and *gula Melaka*, sugar produced from coconut and other palm trees often served as a dessert. Most of all it has given its name to the adjacent waterway through which passes a quarter of world trade. Melaka has long been upstaged as a trading centre by the port which guards the southern entrance to the straits, once known as Temasek and now as Singapore, the subject of a later chapter.

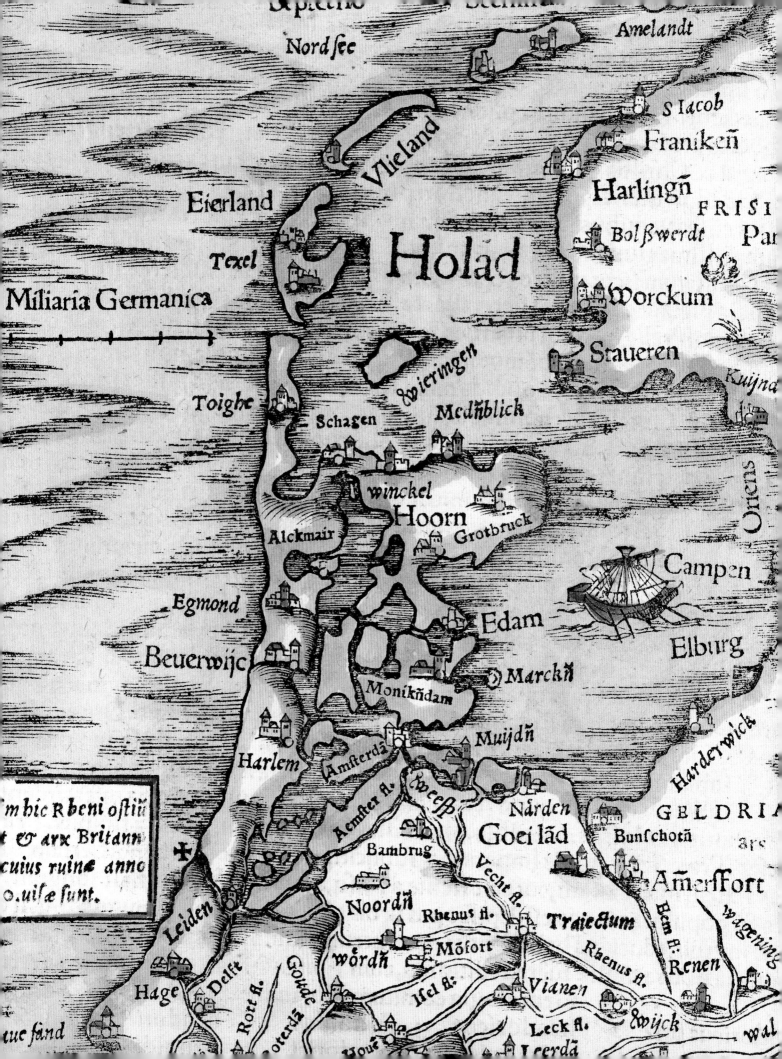

Nordsee

Amelandt

Vlieland

S Iacob

Franikē

Holād

Harlingñ

FRISI

Bolßwerde

Par

Eierland

Texel

Worckum

Miliaria Germanica

Staueren

Kuijnā

Wieringen

Oriens

Toighe

Schagen

Medñblick

winckel

Hoorn

Grotbruck

Campen

Alckmair

Egmond

Edam

Elburg

Beuerwijc

Marckñ

Monikñdam

Muijdñ

Harderwijck

Harlem

Amsterdā

Nārden

GELDRIA

Aemster fl.

Koreß

Goei lād

Bunschotñ

ars

Bambrug

Āmersfort

Leiden

Vecht fl.

Noordñ

Rhenus fl.

Traiectum

Bem fl.

Wagening

Hage

Delft

Rhenus fl.

Renen

Goude

Mōfort

Vianen

sterdā

Isel fl.

Leck fl.

Zwijck

tue sand

Youe

Leerdā

wal

m hic Rheni ostiū
et arx Britann
cuius ruinæ anno
o. uisæ sunt.

> *'I looked with respect upon the city which is the warehouse of the world ... We met the governor going about on foot without lackeys in the midst of the general populace. One does not see there anyone who has to pay court ... They know only work and modesty.'*

VOLTAIRE, 1722

6/ AMSTERDAM AND THE BIRTH OF THE NETHERLANDS

Amsterdam sits at the south-western end of the Zuiderzee. Ships reached the open sea after passing the island of Texel, shown in this pre-independence, 1559 map by Sebastian Münster, who did so much to update the first-century cartography of Claudius Ptolemy.

By the time the distinguished French thinker Voltaire visited Amsterdam, it was unrivalled as the busiest, richest and most important trading port in the world. Apart from the work ethic and modesty of its citizens, Voltaire was impressed by the large number of ships in the harbour. The puzzle is how this port, lying 100 kilometres inland from the North Sea, fashioned from land reclaimed from marshes, attained global status within little more than a century.

Amsterdam was created by damming the River Amstel near its confluence with the River IJ[1] in the late thirteenth century, an early attempt to control the flow of water into the large seawater bay, the Zuiderzee or Southern Sea. The land now known as the Netherlands or 'low countries' was created by draining marshland to enable human settlement and farming. It became a land of dykes, artificial embankments holding back water, and polders, the low-lying land between the dykes. The country's independence was achieved by its inhabitants gaining control over the mouths of three great rivers: the Scheldt, the Maas and the Rhine. Dutch novelist Cees Nooteboom sets the scene:

The land is marshy and vulnerable under a high, ever-changing sky; the only mountains are the dunes in the west, the Dutch mountains. They have a sea in front of them and a sea behind them: the North Sea, Zuiderzee. A river writes its way through the land of Amestelle. The counts of Holland and the bishops of Utrecht quarrel over this wet, uncertain peat bog in a remote corner of the realm of Nether Lorraine. Stelle: safe place, protected place. Ame: water. The land gives its name to the drifting river ... Where it ends in the Zuiderzee, the water is called IJ, and there the river invents a city, a city on the water. Now the game can begin.[2]

THE FOUNDATION OF AMSTERDAM AND THE NETHERLANDS

Amsterdam received its city[3] charter in around 1306, when it had fewer than 25,000 inhabitants, and was incorporated into the province of Holland soon afterwards. Holland in the sixteenth century was controlled by the Habsburg dynasty which ruled large swathes of Catholic Europe: much of Germany, Hungary, Croatia, Bohemia, Austria, Spain and the United Provinces, together constituting the Holy Roman Empire. When Emperor Charles V abdicated in 1556, this empire was divided between his brother Ferdinand and his son Philip, the latter becoming king of Spain and the United Provinces, the area covering present-day Netherlands, Belgium and Luxembourg. He would later inherit Portugal through his mother. Philip[4] was born into an age of empire-building, with both Spain and Portugal intent on extending their domains on all continents. His Spanish great-grandparents, Ferdinand and Isabella, sponsored Christopher Columbus' westward voyages in search of the Indies; his Portuguese grandfather, Manuel I, sponsored Vasco da Gama's epic voyage; while his father sent Ferdinand Magellan on his round-the-world venture. Philip would himself be honoured in the naming of the Philippines.

Philip was born in Spain, and his accession triggered an anti-Spanish, anti-Catholic rebellion in the United Provinces. No less conscientious than his Flanders-born father in trying to hold Spain's empire together, Philip's many preoccupations included checking the spread of Muslim Ottoman power in the Mediterranean and attempting in 1588 to invade England. He found time to marry in succession four wives, adding the royal families of England, France and Austria to the family's Spanish and Portuguese heritage. To put down the revolt, he appointed a bloodthirsty Spanish nobleman, the Duke of Alba, who constituted a Council of Troubles as an instrument for implementing the Inquisition against anyone showing disloyalty to the Spanish monarchy or the Roman Catholic church. It came to be known as the Council of Blood for the numbers of death sentences passed against Dutch citizens who deviated from Catholic orthodoxy.

Leading the rebels' fight for independence was Willem of Orange, a nobleman from Nassau in Germany and prince of Orange in southern France, whom Philip's father had nurtured as a future leader of the United Provinces. Philip, confident in his Catholicism and loyalty, appointed him to the post of *stadhouder* – a position roughly equivalent to governor – of the provinces of Holland, Zeeland and Utrecht. But Willem the Silent, as he was later known, converted to Calvinism, making him a natural leader of the rebels and the

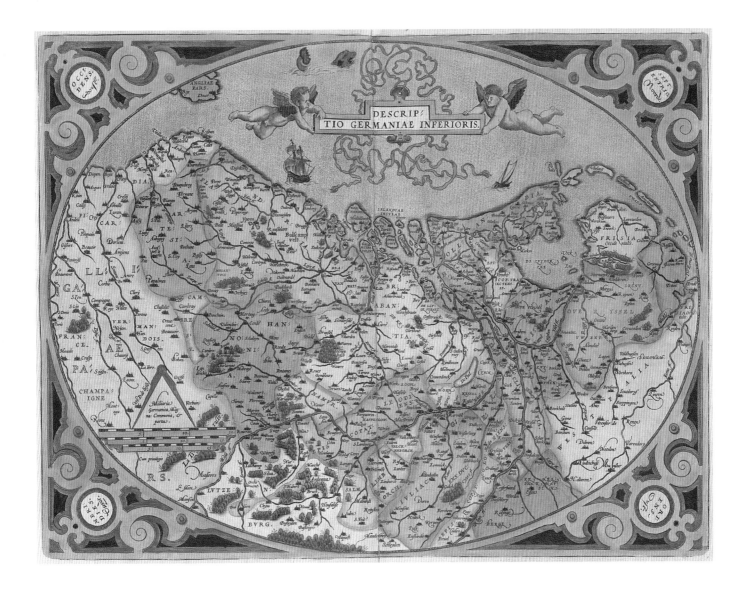

The United Provinces, or Lower Germany, mapped by Abraham Ortelius in 1598, with west at the top. Zeeland, Holland and provinces bordering the Zuiderzee constituted the Dutch Republic of the Netherlands from 1579.

growing Protestant movement. He founded the independent Dutch Republic from the seven northern provinces (out of seventeen): Holland, Zeeland, Frieseland, Groningen, Overijssel, Gelderland and Utrecht.[5]

On 26 May 1578 the council of the staunchly Catholic city of Amsterdam was displaced by Calvinists, an event known as the *Alteratie* or 'Alteration' which is marked as the city's independence day. Other towns followed suit, effectively ending Spanish/Roman Catholic rule in the northern provinces. Dutch independence was affirmed by the Treaty of Münster in 1648, part of the Peace of Westphalia which ended thirty years of fighting within the Holy Roman Empire.

The 1598 map by Dutchman Abraham Ortelius shows to the north (right) of the River Maas the seven provinces which would form the Dutch Republic, later to be known as the Netherlands. To the south (left) are the ten provinces which would become Belgium and Luxembourg. Like other maps of the time it refers to the area embraced by the United Provinces as *Germaniae Inferioris* or 'Lower Germany'.

WHY AMSTERDAM?

To reach Amsterdam, sailing vessels had first to enter and sail through the Zuiderzee, as can be followed in the map that faces the chapter opening. Outgoing vessels reached the open sea when they passed the island of Texel. Amsterdam was an inland port, as was its main northern European rival, Antwerp, which lies 70 kilometres upstream on the River Scheldt.

A Spanish decree of 1494 required Jews to convert and become 'New Christians'. Many chose instead to migrate, and Antwerp was a popular choice because of its growth as northern Europe's main trading port: through which were imported wheat from the Baltic, salt from France and spices from Asia, in return for textiles and metal goods. Portugal followed Spain's lead with its own ban on Judaism fuelling further migration northwards, to Antwerp's advantage. Spain, anxious to prevent Antwerp and its province of Flanders from joining the Dutch rebellion, tightened its control over the city in 1585. The River Scheldt flowed through islands that fell within Zeeland, one of the rebellious northern provinces. Protestant rebels took control of the estuary and closed the river to shipping, strangling Antwerp. Ships were forced to unload their wares at Middleburg, a Zeeland port on the river mouth, or sail north to Amsterdam.

This destroyed Antwerp as a shipping centre and triggered a further migration or 'brain drain' of Calvinist and Jewish merchants who preferred the freer atmosphere of the north. Calvinists were easily assimilated in Amsterdam, while Jews were first tolerated then welcomed and finally allowed to worship openly, contributing to the city's reputation as a place where religion was less important than commerce and trade. A century later, the tightening of controls on religious worship in France brought another wave of Protestant migrants, the Huguenots, to the Dutch Republic.

Amsterdam was largely populated by these refugees from Iberia and Catholic cities in the southern United Provinces. Jews constituted as many as half of the city's inhabitants and made a major contribution to the city's rise through their business acumen. Amsterdam merchants benefited financially from the *asientos de negros*, a contract with Spain to ship enslaved people from Africa to Spanish-controlled territories in Latin America, though they would lose that contract to the English in 1713. The Dutch, like the Venetians, Spanish and Portuguese before them, and English afterwards, relied on slave labour to work the plantations in the territories they controlled, whether shipped from Africa or locally enslaved.

In 1594 Dutch ships were ordered out of Spanish and Portuguese ports and trade embargoes were imposed, part of Spain's effort to hold onto the United Provinces, which had the inadvertent effect of provoking the Dutch to found their own trading empire. Finding a way to the Spice Islands would be a start. They already had a lively maritime tradition in their herring fleets, which supplied much of Europe using the so-called 'herring buss' (*haring buis*), an early 'factory ship' where fish were gutted and preserved on board, enabling the vessel to stay at sea far longer. It was a three-master which needed only a small crew and provided plenty of cargo space. Adding guns to fight off privateers, a hazard of sixteenth-century shipping, enabled the vessels to sail further; so the ocean-facing provinces of Holland and Zeeland came to dominate shipping between the Baltic ports and France, Spain, Portugal and even the Mediterranean Sea as far as the Levant.

Dutch shipbuilding was given a boost by the invention of the wind-powered sawmill. Cornelis Corneliszoon, from the village of Uitgeest north of Amsterdam, in 1593 developed a crankshaft which converted the windmill's circular movement into the back and forth motion of a saw, making the building of ships both quicker and cheaper. This invention started Europe's industrial revolution centuries before the invention of steam, internal combustion or electrical power and played a major role in the republic's rise to greatness. At one time there were as many as two hundred wind-driven sawmills in the Zaanstad area of Holland, providing wood to sixty shipyards.[6] Shipbuilding was as dependent on the wind as was sailing. For ventures further afield, the most commonly used vessel was the *fluyt*, or flute. Designed by shipwrights in the Zuiderzee port of Hoorn, the *fluyt* proved so efficient and popular that it was copied by other countries.

While fighting for their independence, the Dutch had also developed considerable competitive advantage in the fields of water management, fishing and shipbuilding. By the time peace was agreed with Spain, their principal city of Amsterdam had overtaken Antwerp and Lisbon as Europe's main trading port, handling as much as half of Europe' ocean-going fleet.

THE DUTCH EAST INDIA COMPANY

A revolution in funding maritime trade came with the creation in 1602 of the *Vereenigde Oost-Indische Compagnie* (VOC), the [Dutch] United East India Company. The state granted it a renewable twenty-one-year monopoly on all trade east of the Cape of Good Hope, building on the 1494 Treaty of Tordesillas under which the pope had apportioned the world for trading purposes between the Spanish and Portuguese.

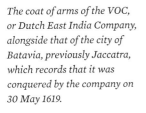

The coat of arms of the VOC, or Dutch East India Company, alongside that of the city of Batavia, previously Jaccatra, which records that it was conquered by the company on 30 May 1619.

As well as trading, the charter authorised the VOC to manage territory, maintain an army and wage war, even against its supposed 'motherland' of Spain. It acted like an arm of the state, yet was a publicly-owned company whose shares could be bought and sold, initially on the bridge at the mouth of the Amsterdam street known as Damrak. It was the world's first publicly-traded company. Through its 'initial public offering' (to use modern parlance), the VOC raised 6.5 million guilders,[7] enough to finance several voyages to the East, making Amsterdam not just a trading centre but a business centre too.

The VOC attracted funds from investors large and small across Holland and Zeeland. Initially dividends were paid in kind – sacks of pepper, nutmeg or ginger, for example. Spices brought from the East were much in demand as ingredients for *hutsepot*, a national dish of meat stew, and in beer, the drink of choice at every meal – notwithstanding a Calvinist argument that imported exotic flavours of supposedly pagan origins should be avoided. After tobacco was introduced from the American colony of Virginia, nutmeg and mace would be mixed with the leaf to give extra flavour.

The formation of the VOC – and of the English East India Company two years earlier – marked the birth of 'capitalism': investment in enterprises through share ownership. The company oversaw the process and managed the considerable risks, knowing it would profit by several multiples of the initial outlay when a ship returned from the East full of much sought-after spices. Profit depended on the company's 'monopoly' rights which prevented other enterprises, at least Dutch enterprises, from competing; and there was no limit to how much the company could charge for the spices it sold on the quayside at Amsterdam.

The buying and selling of shares in trading companies like the VOC led to the formation of the first 'stock exchange'. When traders started to buy cargoes that had not yet arrived, a trade in 'futures' began, leading to the establishment of a futures market. In 1609 the first 'bank', the *Wisselbank*, was formed. Amsterdam was also becoming a centre of publishing and printing. The first paper mill was built in 1616, and soon afterwards one of the world's first newspapers, a weekly called *Courante* (Current), was published in Amsterdam.

The fad for taking profit from investment took a curious turn when a bulb introduced from Turkey gave rise to a money-making craze. From 1634 punters fell over themselves to buy different varieties of tulip for high prices in the expectation they could be propagated to make bulbs of ever more vibrant colours. It was an early example of a speculative 'bubble'. Then, as suddenly as it had started, the market collapsed in early 1637 leaving people out of pocket and the Dutch somewhat wiser in the economic science of valuing assets and investments.

A model of the VOC ship Prins Willem *which from 1651 onwards sailed five times from Middleburg to Batavia before sinking with the loss of all on board on its final homebound voyage in 1662.*

The VOC gave employment to a great many Dutchmen and others in the territories it controlled and made use of locally enslaved people in Java. (Other Dutch trading companies engaged in the iniquitous slave trade, transporting – it has been calculated – as many as 50,000 Africans up until the trade was banned in 1829 – to territory they controlled in South America and the Caribbean.) The company's powers included running local industries, draining swamps, constructing canals, exploiting forests, operating mines, managing mills, building ships, administering justice with penalties (which could include imprisonment or execution), issuing currency, signing and ratifying treaties and creating cities – notably those of Batavia and Cape Town. Amsterdam's prosperity derived from the territory managed – 'exploited' might be a more apt word – by the VOC.

The VOC had six 'chambers' representing the ports of Amsterdam, Hoorn, Enkhuizen, Rotterdam and Delft in Holland and Middelburg in Zeeland. It brought their merchants together in an alliance of common purpose, presided over by a board of directors with each chamber represented. Its ruling body was the *Heeren XVII,* the Seventeen Gentlemen, eight of whom were elected by the port of Amsterdam, giving the city the dominant voice, though just short of an overall majority. They met regularly in a meeting room within *Oost-Indisch Huis* (East India House), which

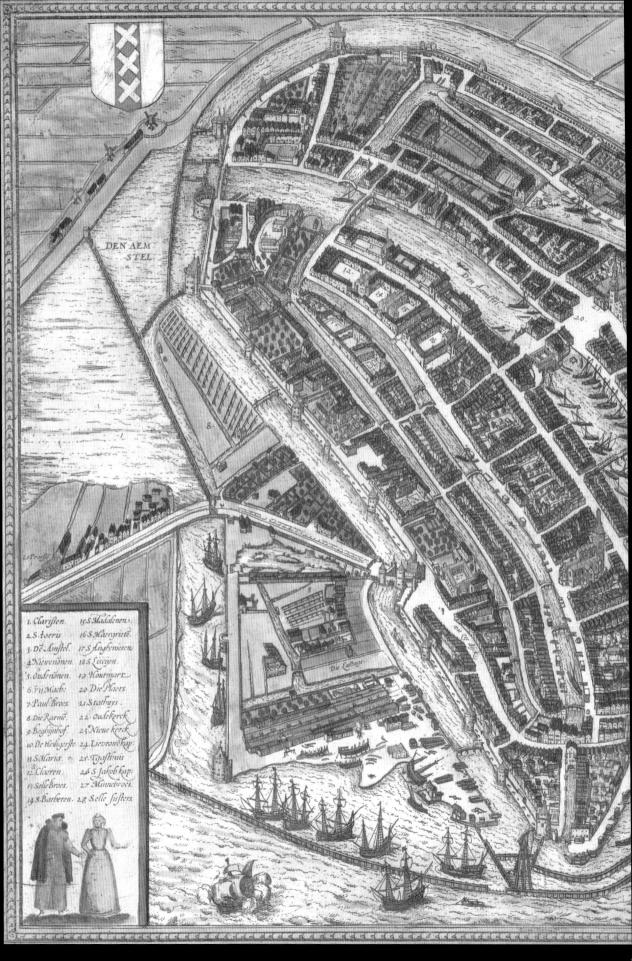

DEN AEM
STEL

Den Aemstel

Le Proost

Die Lastage

1. Clarissen.   15 S. Madalenen.
2 S. Ioeris.   16 S. Maergriet.
3 De Amstel.   17 S. Anghenierēe
4 Niewenōnen.   18 S. Luscijen.
5 Oudenōnen.   19 Houtmart.
6 Vij Mach: 20 Die Plaers.
7 Paul Broes.   21 Stathuys.
8 Die Raeme.   22 Oudekerck.
9 Beghijnhof.   23 Nieue kerck.
10 De Heiligprste. 24 Lievrowēkap:
11 S. Maria.   25 Tgosthuis.
12 Claeren.   26 S. Jakob kap:
13 Selle Broes.   27 Minnebroes.
14 S. Barberen.   28 Selle susters.

AMSTELREDAMVM, nobile Inferioris Germaniæ oppidum, ad
recipiendos, ex omnib. mundi partibus, mercatores, recenter natum, genus
hominum incolit mercimonijs deditum quæ quidem, tum blanda populi comi-
tate, ac sedula diligentiâ, indus Friæ; tum portus comoditate permagna, usq; adeo
incrementa sumpserunt, vt vix vllum mercaturæ genus excogitari possit, quod hîc
non exerceatur. Hinc fit, vt opum lucrique cupiditas, ex remotißimis etiam
terris, negotiatores, in hanc ciuitate inuitet, qui varia hinc bona, & maximè,
rem frumentariâ, in Brabantiam, cæteraq; longè dißita, totius vniuersi loca,
transferentes; ingentes ex eiuscemodi comnertio opes consequuntur.

the VOC shared with an arsenal and a slaughterhouse. It is now part of the University of Amsterdam, and on the wall of the meeting room still hang maps of the company's trading centres.

CITY OF MAP-MAKERS

A bird's-eye view of Amsterdam by Braun and Hogenberg in 1577[8] shows that it was already a busy and prosperous city, based on its trade with the Baltic and Mediterranean before voyages to the East Indies began. Amsterdam then had a population of around 30,000. At its centre is the *stadhuis* or town hall and the *Nieue Kerk* or New Church close to the point where the Amstel was first dammed.

The main shipbuilding ports were Zaanstad, just north of Amsterdam, and Hoorn and Enkhuizen on the Zuiderzee, though we see in the foreground that Amsterdam was equipped to build and repair ships as well. Indeed, the commentary tells us that 'there are very good and experienced shipbuilders here'. The 'New Bridge' (*Nieuwe Brug*), where the central channel of the River Amstel enters the Zuiderzee, was the main trading point, while harbour fees were collected at a nearby toll-house. The commentary says that 'Amsterdam is a well known city in Lower Germany that was arisen in recent times to accommodate merchants ... It is almost impossible to think of a commercial activity that is not practised here. Profit seeking businessmen are drawn to this city from the most far-away lands.' On the image's reverse, a poem by Nicholas Cannius records that Amsterdam had eclipsed Lisbon even before finding its own way to the Spice Islands.

At the bottom of the image is a small tower with a blue roof known as the *Schreierstoren*. This was the traditional point of departure for

(previous spread) Braun and Hogenberg's famous representation of Amsterdam in 1577 after the building of the city's canals. Ocean-going vessels offloaded cargo in the harbour onto smaller vessels to carry it through the canals.

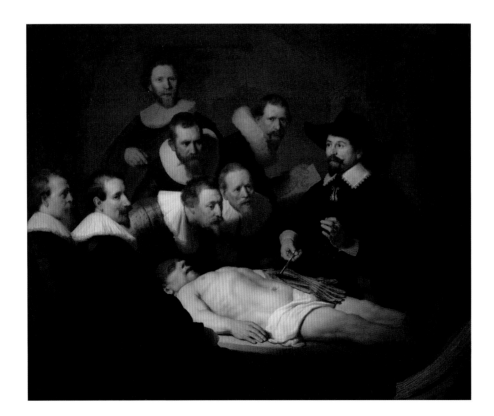

'The Anatomy Lesson of Dr Tulp' by Rembrandt van Rijn, 1632.

Portrait of Jan Huygen van
Linschoten from his book
Itinerario, 1596, with images
of Goa, Mozambique Island
and St Helena.

sailors embarking on long voyages, hence its nickname 'the Weepers'. One sailor who departed from there in 1609 was an Englishman, Henry Hudson. Tasked by the VOC to find a new route to the East, he instead 'discovered' the island of Manhattan – a disappointment to the company, though of major significance for the place of the Dutch Republic in the world.

Straddling the canal on which the *Schreierstoren* stands is a multi-turreted building, the *waag* or weighing house, which also served as an anatomical lecture theatre. Here Rembrandt painted his famous picture 'The Anatomy Lesson of Dr Tulp'. Dr Tulp, originally called Claes Pieterszoons, was a professor of medicine who changed his name to Nicolaes Tulp in celebration of the flower bulb introduced from Turkey. Rembrandt recognised in one picture two of the factors for which the city became renowned: the study of anatomy and the tulip.

By the late sixteenth century, Amsterdam had the ships but not the maps; then two gentlemen appeared who gained access to Portugal's sea charts. The first was Petrus Plancius, a Calvinist priest turned businessman originally from Flanders. Raising finance for an early trading mission to the East, he went to Portugal and bought navigational charts from a Portuguese merchant which enabled him to produce his own chart of the East Indies.

The second individual was Jan Huygen van Linschoten, whom we encountered as secretary to the Portuguese archbishop of Goa in earlier chapters. Born in Haarlem and brought up in the port of Enkhuizen, Linschoten returned from Goa in 1594. Plancius and Linschoten linked up with an Amsterdam bookseller, Cornelis Clæsz, who would publish their maps of the East Indies including the all-important Spice Islands. Clæsz also commissioned engraver Arnoldus van Langren to make detailed maps of the two oceans (shown in Chapter 4) through which ships passed when sailing from Europe to Asia.

Linschoten literally put the East Indies on the map in *Itinerario*, an account of his time in the East, published in Amsterdam in Dutch in 1596. It was a veritable encyclopaedia, detailing the value as trading items of pepper, cinnamon, nutmeg, ginger, cardamom and opium, among other products. Its text and maps were quickly translated into English and German and then French and Latin. Linschoten wrote that Malacca was 'as richly laden with costly marchandaises and spices as ships laden in India', saying 'it hath great trafficke and dealings with all shippes which sayle to and from China, the Molucos, Banda, the Islands of Java, Sumatra and all the islands bordering thereabouts'.[9]

He recommended Cananor in Malabar (now Kannur, Kerala) for its pepper, as well as being a good source of long masts for ships 'such as better cannot be found in all Norway'; he also advised that the cinnamon on the

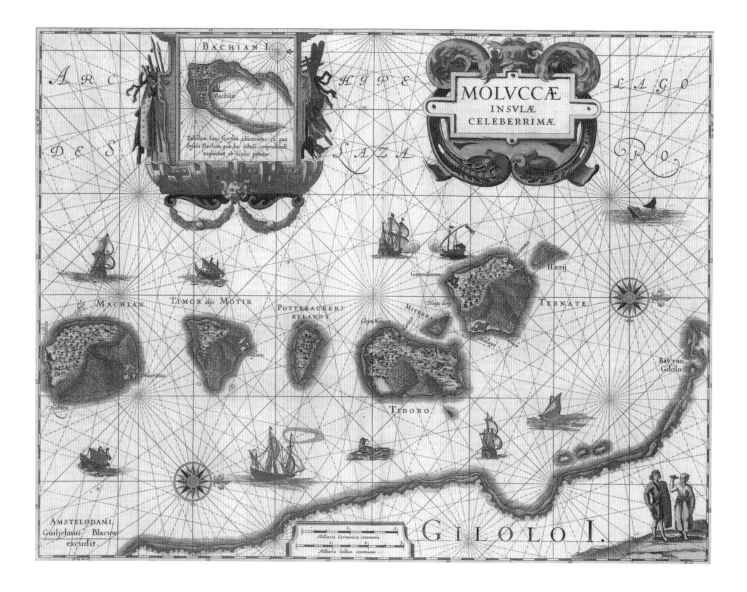

Malabar coast of India is not as good as that of Ceylon. He emphasised the importance of entrepôts like Hormuz in the Persian Gulf and the Atlantic Ocean islands of St Helena and Ascension used by Portuguese sailors as victualling stations. The book identified places where Portugal had built forts to defend its trading interests – in a way that would nowadays be considered a major security leak and Linschoten be taken as an industrial spy. It showed up the weaknesses in Portugal's trading network, implying that its dominance of the sea routes of the East was open to challenge. The young Dutch nation was set to benefit from this advice.

When Dutch 'bottoms' were banned from Iberian ports in 1594, Amsterdam traders started to challenge the Portuguese by venturing round the Cape of Good Hope in search of spices. The first venture to Asia in 1595 was by the de Houtman brothers, Cornelius and Frederik, who carried with them an early draft of Linschoten's book. The voyage was a disaster, returning with only a third of the 249 mariners who left Amsterdam and very little pepper; but it had successfully pioneered a route to Java through the Sunda Straits, shown on Linschoten's important map of south-east Asia,

Willem Blaeu produced this west-facing graphical view in 1650 of the Clove Islands of the northern Moluccas. Bachian, which lies just south of the Equator, is presented as an inset.

following his advice to avoid the Portuguese-controlled Malacca Straits. When *Itinerario* went on sale at the publisher's bookshop on Amsterdam's Damrak, the number of voyages to the East increased rapidly: fifty vessels sailed in eight fleets between 1598 and 1602.

This was a great age for map-making and Amsterdam and Antwerp were at its heart, the VOC its main sponsor. Petrus Plancius became the VOC's first official cartographer tasked with showing mariners the way to reach the source of spices, and advising Henry Hudson on his attempt to find a north-west passage to Asia. François Valentijn followed Plancius into the VOC's employment as pastor, cartographer and historian. He lived for a time in the Spice Islands, producing drawings and maps which were published in his own book.[10] Maps and images by Valentijn and by Amsterdam-based Peter Schenk and Pieter van der Aa are represented in this collection. In Flanders, Gerardus Mercator pioneered a new way of mapping – Mercator's Projection, made using a globe – which allowed accurate distances to be measured between ports while distorting the size or area of territory further from the Equator. Mercator popularised the globe as a means of displaying cartographic and navigational information.[11]

Abraham Ortelius of Antwerp collected his maps into an atlas while serving as court geographer to Philip II of Spain. Jodocus Hondius migrated from Flanders to Amsterdam and with his son (of the same name) and son-in-law Jan Jansson further enhanced the city's map-making reputation. Willem Blaeu, a student of the renowned Danish astronomer Tycho Brahé, and his son Joan produced another aerial view of Amsterdam in 1649, showing how the city had expanded in the seventy years since the Braun and Hogenberg version appeared. Willem Blaeu was among the first to produce a map of the Clove Islands of the Moluccas. Father and son would in turn hold the position of hydrographer to the VOC, with responsibility for charting harbours and waterways used by the company.

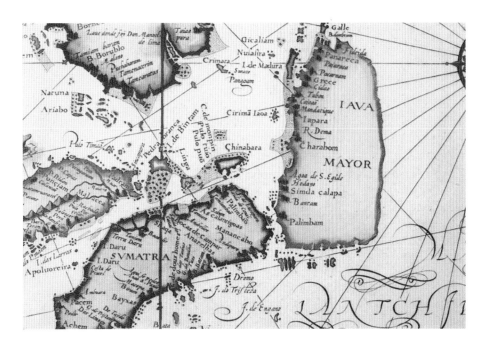

Linschoten's 1596 map of east Asia showed Dutch mariners how to avoid the Portuguese-patrolled Malacca Straits by sailing through the Sunda Straits between Sumatra and Java.

AMSTERDAM'S ERA OF PROSPERITY

By 1602 when the VOC was founded, Amsterdam had everything it needed to break the Portuguese stranglehold on bringing spices to Europe: the ships, the maps, the funding arrangements and a ready market. The year is often marked as the start of what was later to become known as the Dutch 'Golden Age', of which Holland's largest city, the country's capital, was the chief beneficiary. According to the 1617 edition of the Braun and Hogenberg view: 'Amsterdam wants for nothing, except that it has too much wealth. The city is like a store house from which not only neighbouring but far distant countries are supplied.'[12]

Amsterdam grew in stature and eminence, as shown in the 1752 view of the River Amstel along the Damrak. Characteristic of the age were Amsterdam's canal houses, distinguished dwellings which fronted on to the newly-built semi-circular canals, creating what has been dubbed 'the Venice of the North'. Houses which doubled as warehouses were identified by the pulley mechanism used as a hoist to lift goods from the barges which transported goods from the *fluyts* in the harbour. Amsterdam connected with the rest of the country through a pioneering venture in public transport: passenger-carrying barges plying the Vliet Canal between Amsterdam, Haarlem, Leiden, The Hague, Delft and Rotterdam. The Dutch seemed to believe they had conquered the world. National poet Joost van den Vondel wrote in a 1639 poem: 'We Amsterdammers journey, Where Ganges casts its waters down into the sea: Wherever profit leads us, to every sea and shore, For love of gain the wide world's harbours we explore.'[13]

The age was also characterised by a philosophical debate about the relationship between the individual and the state and the part played by religion. While war with Spain continued in the south, debate raged in Holland: whether the House of Orange should be rewarded for its service to the independence movement by being granted the status and rights of monarchy, or whether the state's republican structure be retained. It was part of a wider debate across Europe as the role of hereditary rulers was challenged by a system in which the people had a greater say in how they were governed. A leading Amsterdam advocate of the republican model was the influential Jewish philosopher Baruch Spinoza. His view was both unambiguous and influential: 'Now, seeing that we have the rare happiness of living in a republic, where everyone's judgement is free and unshackled, where each may worship God as his conscience dictates, and where freedom is esteemed before all things dear and precious ... without such freedom, piety cannot flourish nor the public peace be secure.'[14]

Spinoza was against both monarchical rule and 'the divine right of kings' as well as the concept of a state religion to the exclusion of other religions. He believed that rulers should be selected on merit, not by virtue of their birthright; and that faith should be a personal choice, not one imposed by the state. He had himself been barred from his synagogue for expressing such unorthodox views, helping the country and its chief city to stand out as free-thinking, which attracted philosophers from countries that were less free.

That ability gained Holland a reputation as a centre of enlightenment. Philosophers from countries that were less free began to seek refuge in the

Dutch Republic, men like Descartes from France and John Locke and Thomas Hobbes from Scotland who encountered difficulty publishing their work at home. In 1638, Galileo Galilei, a victim of the Inquisition in Rome, published his *Discourses and Mathematical Demonstrations* in Leiden, the university city where books on all subjects, no matter how controversial, were published. Leiden and Amsterdam set the bar high for what today we would call 'academic freedom'. It was at this time that the fundamentals of international law were laid down by the Dutch jurist Hugo Grotius in his treatise *De Jure Belli ac Pacis*, On the Law of War and Peace (1625). The historian of Western philosophy, Bertrand Russell, wrote in the twentieth century: 'It is impossible to exaggerate the importance of Holland in the seventeenth century, as the one country where there was freedom of speculation.'[15]

The pro- and anti-monarchy debate brought the republic into conflict with its neighbours, England, France and parts of Germany, though trading rivalry was a factor too; England was experimenting with its own version of republicanism in the so-called Interregnum (1649–1660) after

King Charles I was executed. France's invasion of the Dutch Republic in 1672 brought its 'year of disaster' or *Rampajaar*. The country's ruler, Johan de Witt, was assassinated, leading to the reinstatement at national level of the post of *stadhouder*.

Willem the Silent's grandson, also called Willem, was appointed to lead the defence against French forces. He would go on to become king – but not of the Netherlands, rather of Britain which in 1689 was in need of a Protestant monarch.[16] More than a century later, after a further period of occupation by the French during the Napoleonic Wars, the country again declared its freedom (1815) but this time as a monarchy. Amsterdam's famous town hall, or *stadhuis,* became a royal palace.

SCIENCE AND ART

The wealth flowing in from the republic's trading empire gave rise to a flowering of science and the arts. The mantle of astronomical research laid down by Copernicus and Galileo, and passed to the German Protestant physicist Johannes Kepler (who first used the word 'orbit' to describe the elliptical movement of the planets around the Sun), then fell upon the Dutchman Christiaan Huygens. He developed the reflective telescope and perfected the microscope, advancing the study of anatomy in which the Dutch were leaders. Both instruments benefited from Dutch expertise at grinding lenses – a skill adapted later for polishing diamonds. The microscope was invented in Delft by Antonie van Leeuwenhoek, who used his invention to discover human spermatozoa, thus unlocking the truth of human reproduction. The philosopher Baruch Spinoza had a practical side in that he earned a living by grinding lenses, collaborating scientifically with Christiaan Huygens. Huygens has been called Europe's greatest scientist of the age because of the range of his research: from his discovery of Saturn's first ring and its largest moon, through optics and the wave theory of light, centrifugal force, thermometers and accurate time-keeping, all of which advanced significantly during the seventeenth century.

The country which harnessed wind power to drain the marshland and build ships and then developed lenses for telescopes and microscopes also played an important role in the development of spectacles and wristwatches. Christiaan Huygens – whose father referred to him as 'a little Archimedes' – was central to these inventions. He also tried his hand at determining longitude at sea by adapting the pendulum clock first developed by Galileo. Other Dutch inventions using lenses included the magic lantern, forerunner of the slide projector, and the *camera obscura* used to capture scenes on a wall, a forerunner of the camera. In Huygens' *Cosmotheoros*, published in 1698 after his death, he speculated on the possibility of life on other planets. He spent time in Paris, where he was admitted to the *Académie des Sciences,* and made several visits to London, becoming a fellow of the Royal Society. The German physicist Albert Einstein would later credit Huygens with 'coming close' to the theory of relativity. Scientific advancement, publishing and cartography all thrived in Amsterdam.

The age also benefited Amsterdam's artists, who were commissioned by families made rich through trade to create paintings to adorn their affluent homes. A good example is Pieter Isaacsz's 1606 painting on the lid of a harpsichord, which shows the city as a maiden with one hand on a globe surrounded by Olympian gods looking out over ships against a background of world map – a perfect allegory for Amsterdam's rising position in the world. From this period, we particularly think of Johannes Vermeer of Delft (who depicted maps in several of his paintings) and the portraitist Frans Hals of Haarlem.

Rembrandt Harmenszoon van Rijn, described by the art critic Kenneth Clark as 'one of the great prophets of civilisation', the son of a Catholic mother and Protestant father, migrated from his birthplace in southern Holland to Amsterdam to produce most of his work. He is best remembered for his portraits, allegorical biblical and mythological scenes, and for Amsterdam pictures like 'The Night Watch' (*De Nachtwacht*) and 'The Anatomy Lesson of Dr Tulp'; another example is *De Brillenverkoper*, 'The Spectacle Seller', which demonstrates the city's role in the development of spectacles – but he painted no views of the city itself. Rembrandt's talent was first recognised by Constantijn Huygens, father of the scientist and secretary to the *stadhouder*. Though he never travelled abroad, Rembrandt's style was influenced by Italian painters like Michelangelo and Caravaggio and by the Flemish painter Peter Paul Rubens, with whom he is often compared. Rembrandt's drawings of Mughal rulers of India, including Shah Jejan who built the Taj Mahal and the emperors Akbar and Jehangir, indicate how he was influenced by Amsterdam's Asian connections. Rembrandt is so closely identified with the Golden Age that it was said that Amsterdam's fortunes went into decline when the artist died in 1669.

The city's fortunes did indeed dip towards the end of the seventeenth century, but that was hardly a consequence of Rembrandt's demise. Rather it was the result of the VOC facing stiffer competition in its Asian trade, notably from the British. While Dutch rivalry with Portugal led to war on the oceans, its fight with England to maintain the republic's self-claimed monopoly on the trade in spices took place largely in the North Sea and Thames estuary, where the two Protestant nations fought three wars between 1652 and 1674. The republic lost many vessels, but also inflicted severe damage on England's mercantile fleet during a daring raid on the latter's naval base at Chatham on the River Medway in June 1667. The Dutch objective

'Amsterdam as the Centre of World Trade' by Pieter Isaacsz, 1606, painted on the lid of a harpsichord.

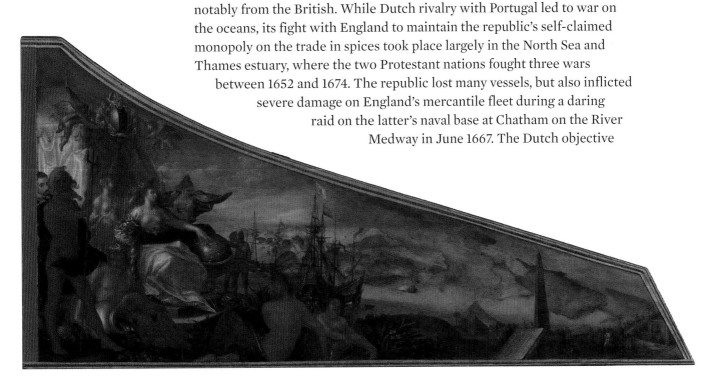

was to enforce its claimed spice monopoly and, as we see later, that purpose would take a curious twist.

Recognition of Amsterdam's prominence as a great city of trade, science and art was boosted by its many visitors. Peter the Great of Russia arrived in 1697 to study the arts of shipbuilding and cartography and later applied some of the city's planning ideas to St Petersburg, which was similarly reclaimed from marshes. Dubbed 'the Amsterdam of the East' because of its pattern of canals, St Petersburg became Russia's capital, its main port and the base of the new Russian navy. Arriving from France, Voltaire was impressed by the bustle of trade in the harbour, typified in the busy scene portrayed by Claes Jansz Visscher in 1611. His fellow countryman and philosopher Charles de Montesquieu was similarly entranced: 'The streets of Amsterdam are beautiful, clean, wide. There are broad canals lined with trees ... [and] boats pass directly in front of the houses. I like Amsterdam more than Venice because, in Amsterdam, one has water without being deprived of land ... It's one of the most beautiful cities in the world.' The French philosopher René Descartes, who spent much of his working life in Amsterdam, asked: 'Where else on earth could you find, as easily as you do here, all the conveniences of life and all the curiosities you could hope to see? In what other country could you find such complete freedom ... or find fewer poisonings or acts of treason of slander?' The English diplomat Onslow Burrish, commissioned to report on the policy and commerce of the United Provinces, was similarly ecstatic, describing Amsterdam as 'the glory of Holland and the wonder of the world'.[17]

Amsterdam seen from the River IJ, with merchandise being traded on the shore, portrayed by Claes Jansz Visscher, 1611.

Dutch mariners excelled not only in trade, but also in exploration. They were the first Europeans to make contact with both China and Japan. Anthony van Diemen, as governor-general of the Dutch-ruled East Indies, sent out the sailors who 'discovered' Australia, New Zealand, Tonga, Fiji and Tasmania, the last being named first Van Diemen's Land before the Dutchman Abel Tasman set foot there and changed its name. New Zealand was named for the Dutch province of Zeeland, its spelling being Anglicised later. In a different direction, the Barents Sea (part of the Arctic Ocean) was named after Dutchman Willem Barentsz, who tried to find a route to the East via the Arctic; and Cape Horn, the southern tip of South America, was named after the Dutch port of Hoorn. When we look at New York – previously New Amsterdam – we shall see Dutch names are also plentiful there.

Nineteenth-century engineering connected Amsterdam to the North Sea by the North Sea Canal, after which the development of larger seagoing vessels led to Rotterdam in southern Holland, at the mouth of the Rhine, taking over as the Netherlands' – and one of the world's – busiest ports. Twentieth-century engineering converted the Zuiderzee into a freshwater lake, renamed IJsselmeer, and transformed one of the country's largest polders into Amsterdam's Schiphol airport.

All of which leads us to the 'jewel' in the Dutch imperial crown that contributed so much to Amsterdam's wealth: Batavia – or Jakarta – on the island of Java.

> *'What the Cape of Good Hope is between Europe and every part of the East Indies, Batavia is between the principal countries of the East Indies. Almost all the ships, too, that sail between Europe and China touch at Batavia.'*
>
> ADAM SMITH, *THE WEALTH OF NATIONS*, 1776

7/ BATAVIA AND THE SPICE ISLANDS

Batavia was the name the Dutch gave to the ancient port once known as Sunda Kelapa, then as Jayakarta or Jaccatra, and nowadays as Jakarta. Situated on the north coast of Java, close to the straits which separate it from Sumatra, Sunda Kelapa was a trading centre from as early as 150 BC, providing a sheltered anchorage for sailing vessels coming from China, India and Arabia. It may have been the port through which Buddhism and Hinduism arrived in Java from India – and later Islam from Arabia. The bulk of its trade, however, was with the many islands of the Malay archipelago – known to Europeans as the East Indies – of which Java formed a central hub. In particular the seafaring Bugis people from Sulawesi – known to the Dutch as Celebes – in their distinctive sailing ships brought spices, sago and other foodstuffs from the remote and sparsely populated eastern islands, shipping back rice and pepper from Java and Sumatra, the westernmost islands of the archipelago.

The East Indies were ruled in early times by local chieftains or sultans who were often at war with each other, especially on Java, but also conducted trade between the islands. Sunda Kelapa was the sea outlet on

the River Ciliwung of the Hindu Sunda kingdom whose capital was inland at Pajajaran, known to the Dutch as Buitenzorg and nowadays as Bogor. *Kelapa* – sometimes written as *Calapa* – means coconut in the Malay and Indonesian languages, suggesting that coconut palms grew around the port.

The Venetian traveller Marco Polo mentions Java, though it is doubtful whether he visited the island. His fellow Venetian Niccolò de' Conti, who visited in the early fifteenth century, was most impressed by a bird he encountered there – probably a bird of paradise brought from its native New Guinea. Conti's journeys and those of Marco Polo helped with the compilation of early maps, including that drawn in Venice by Fra Mauro. Details of the Spice Islands were recorded in *The Suma Oriental*, a chronicle written in Malacca in 1512–15 by the Portuguese apothecary Tomé Pires in the form of secret letters to the Portuguese king.

Pires tells of the two main ways to reach the Spice Islands or Moluccas, the thousand or so islands at the eastern end of the Malay archipelago which included the natural homelands of the clove and nutmeg trees. He told travellers to head east along the northern coast of Java, sail past Lombok to the sandalwood island of Timor and then turn north towards the Banda Islands; alternatively, he wrote, they could skirt the southern edge of the large islands of Borneo and Sulawesi to reach Ambon, which was roughly midway between the Nutmeg Islands and the Clove Islands. Pires quotes Malay merchants as saying: 'God made Timor for sandalwood and Banda for mace and the [northern] Moluccas for cloves … merchandise [that] is not known anywhere else in the world except these places.'[1]

Portuguese vessels sent from Malacca under António de Abreu's command called at Sunda Kelapa in 1511 on their way to find the Spice Islands, and may have set up a *feitoria* or trading base there. Soon afterwards

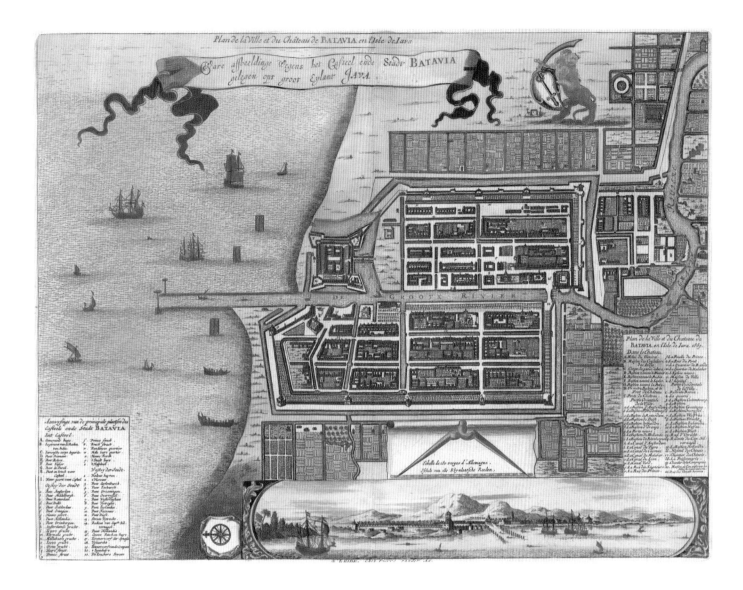

An 'aerial view' facing east by Pieter van der Aa of the castle and fortified town built at Batavia (Jakarta) on the Ciliwung River as the VOC's main trading base in the East, pictured in 1732.

the port was the subject of a takeover by the ruler of the Islamic sultanate of Demak in Central Java. He may have been responding to a call for help by the sultan of Bantam, a Muslim enclave opposite Sumatra in predominantly Hindu western Java, who feared his port was being upstaged by Sunda Kelapa. The Demak sultan fought a battle with the Sunda king[2] for control of the port. Once victorious, he declared a Muslim state and renamed the port *Jayakarta* meaning 'great victory', later shortened to *Jaccatra*. The day of the victory, 22 June 1527, is regarded as the foundation of the city now known as Jakarta, though for more than three centuries it would bear the name Batavia. Sunda Kelapa, or *Jaccatra*, was placed under the sultan of Bantam, a tributary state of Demak.

ARRIVAL OF EUROPEANS

There was little European contact with Java through most of the sixteenth century, and when contact resumed it was initially with Bantam thanks to Jan Huygen van Linschoten. Linschoten advised traders to approach the Indies through the Sunda Straits between Sumatra and Java to avoid the

Portuguese, who from their base at Malacca controlled shipping passing east of Sumatra through the Malacca Straits. Traversing the Sunda Straits meant passing close to the volcanic island of Krakatoa; its famous eruption in 1883, among the most powerful ever recorded, caused heavy loss of life on Java and Sumatra and could be heard as far away as Australia.

When sailing this way, Bantam was the first port on Java where vessels could dock. The Dutch and soon afterwards the British followed Linschoten's advice to land at Bantam. There they filled their ships with pepper from Sumatra and cloves and nutmeg brought from the Spice Islands. From Java, Linschoten told them, you can set sail for the clove islands of the Moluccas, such as Ternate, and the nutmeg-rich Banda Islands. His map of south-east Asia (in Chapter 5) showed Simda Calapa, probably based on a mishearing, and Bantam – also known as Banten – as the main ports in north-western Java. Farther along the coast, the map showed the River Dema, home of the Demak dynasty.

At the time the English and Dutch were united in their determination to oust the Portuguese from their dominant position – the Anglo-Dutch wars would come later. The Dutch VOC trading company tasked a seafarer by the name of Jan Pieterszoon Coen to find a place to make their chief port in the Indies, perhaps feeling there was too much competition at Bantam. It had to be accessible to the larger vessels the Europeans were now using, so needed harbours with good depth. Any settlement or trading base needed to be negotiated with whoever held sway over that area.

Coen chose *Jaccatra*, a day's sailing east of Bantam, planting the Dutch flag there. Subsequently, while Coen was on an expedition to the Banda Islands supervising purchase of the fruits of the nutmeg tree, the English company were invited by the *Jaccatra* ruler to oust the Dutch. The English Admiral Dale agreed, opening fire on Dutch ships in the port and helping the townsfolk to capture the Dutch compound. Coen raced back to retake *Jaccatra*, and sought his revenge by attacking English vessels in the harbour, causing them to scatter.

The incident made Coen realise that *Jaccatra* was the ideal place for the Dutch to build their headquarters, being better protected than Bantam and benefiting from a supply of fresh water from the Ciliwung River. He built a factory and castle to enforce the company's monopoly and keep the English out. The episode also showed that the VOC was in control and could not be pushed around by the English. Coen named the new settlement Batavia after the first settlers of Holland, the *Batavi*, who according to the Roman historian Tacitus settled on an island in the mouth of the River Rhine also known as Batavia. Henceforth the former Sunda Kelapa, now Batavia, would be the VOC's main trading entrepôt in the Indies, the capital of its expanding eastern empire.

The aerial view of Batavia in 1732 (page 143), imagined by Amsterdam cartographer Pieter van der Aa,[3] gives a vivid impression of the castle and fortified town that Coen built. The point where the Ciliwung River, described here as De Groote Rivier, enters the sea was the site of the ancient port visited by Portuguese sailors from Malacca. The view shows how the Dutch diverted the river into canals to provide a moat around the city,

(top) *A Batavia street scene along the central canal in 1805, by an unknown artist.*

(bottom) *Officials of the Dutch VOC going about their business within the fortified town of Batavia, looking north towards the Java Sea, by Franz Xaver Habermann c.1780.*

clearly modelled on Amsterdam. One of those canals features in a Batavia street scene in 1805 by an unknown artist, while a more formal picture gives an idea of the European lifestyle enjoyed by Dutch employees of the VOC living within the castle.

Jan Pieterszoon Coen is regarded as the founder of the Dutch East Indies. Having built the castle at Batavia, he set about extending Dutch control across the archipelago. He was a believer in the axiom that 'might is right' and tended not to wait for the *Heeren XVII* in Amsterdam to respond to his requests for approval, which could take many months to arrive. Instead he told them: 'We cannot carry on trade without war, nor war without trade.'[4] This philosophy was demonstrated by the brutal way in which he murdered his way to take control of the nutmeg-producing islands of the Moluccas.

A more generally claimed justification for the Dutch Republic's colonisation of the East Indies is that it was short of land at home: this was the motivation to cultivate territory overseas, the East Indies being many times larger (and more populous) than the motherland. Dutch merchants were spurred on when barred from Lisbon, which made them determined to create their own trading empire. They were so successful that in time they took over from the Portuguese the trade in oriental spices as well as silk and porcelain from China. Early VOC strategy was to attract shipping that had been using Malacca – still under Portuguese control – since Batavia was closer to the source of spices and had an easier nautical trajectory towards Europe.

THE CLOVE ISLANDS

Before the arrival of Europeans, only trade connected the islands of the Malay archipelago as they were individually governed by a sultan or village headman. Pepper grew in Sumatra, but the more valuable spices of cloves, nutmeg and mace grew in two distinct volcanic sub-archipelagos known informally as the Clove and Nutmeg Islands, collectively part of the thousand Moluccas islands lying between the larger islands of Celebes and New Guinea, some distance east of Batavia. The Chinese were the first to realise the attractive qualities of these spices, followed by traders from Arabia; but it was a major challenge for the Europeans to find these remote islands, from whichever direction they arrived. The Portuguese arrived from the West in 1511, as did the Dutch much later in 1594. The Spanish and English both made their first visits from the east after sailing across the Pacific Ocean: Magellan's Spanish sailors in 1521 (led after Magellan's death by Sebastian del Cano) and England's round-the-world voyager Francis Drake in 1579.

The Clove Islands straddle the Equator on the western side of the larger island of Gilolo or Halmahera. They are (from north to south) Ternate, Tidore, Motir, Makian and – just south of the Equator – Bacan (also spelt Batjan or Bachian). Wild clove trees of the genus *Syzygium aromaticum* were prolific on the most northerly islands of Ternate and Tidore, which had a combined population of about 25,000 when Europeans first arrived. Cloves also grew on adjacent islands, including Gilolo, but nowhere else in the world. By the time William Blaeu's map (in Chapter 6) was produced in Amsterdam

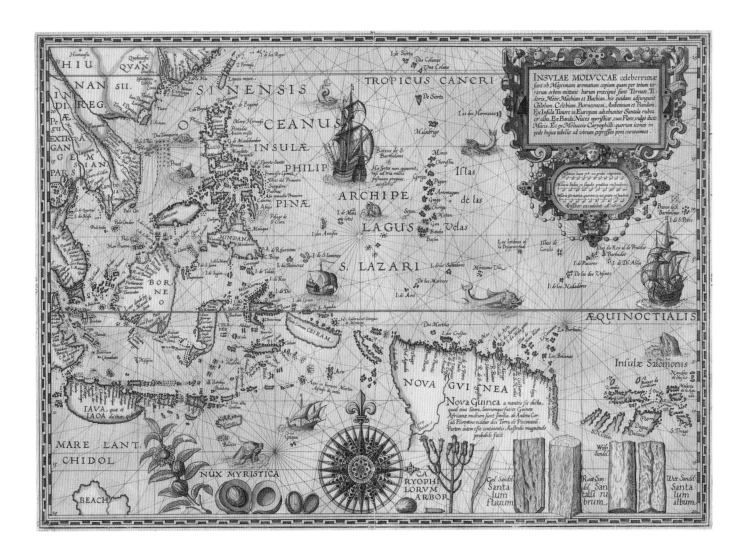

in 1650, the Dutch controlled all the Clove Islands; they had taken over the defensive forts built by the Portuguese, giving them Dutch names.

The Moluccas lie close to the 127° E line of longitude, near where the Indian Ocean gives way to the Pacific Ocean. Their precise location was relevant because, under the Treaty of Tordesillas, the pope had divided the world between Spain and Portugal. The line was drawn across the Atlantic at 46°30′ W of Greenwich, and there was an assumption that it continued on the other side of the world. But since there was at the time no means of measuring longitude, it was impossible to know whether the Moluccas fell within Spain's or Portugal's pope-ordained domain.

Linschoten wrote in *Itinerario* that the clove is so named because its shape resembles a bird's claw (*klauw* in Dutch). An alternative theory is that it comes from *clou*, the French for nail. The clove, which Dutch historian John Northrop Motley called 'this oderifous pistil', was popular in Europe for flavouring dishes, promoting appetite, aiding digestion and as a preservative; also for medicinal purposes, not least of which was the numbing quality of its oil. Linschoten wrote 'the water of green Cloves distilled is very pleasant of smell, and strengthens the hart' and is also used to treat 'the Pox'. He said that Indian women chew a clove 'to have a sweete breath', a practice being copied by 'Portingales wives that dwell there'.[5] The clove was also used for incense, to make perfume and as an aphrodisiac.

Tomé Pires reported that the islands produced a remarkable six crops of cloves each year. They were shipped to Java or Malacca from Ternate, or to the port of Machian under the control of the sultan of Tidore. He said that Mohammedanism was well established throughout the islands, and the sultan of Ternate 'has 400 women within his doors'. He said that the rulers of all the islands 'are at war with one another most of the time'.[6] The main 'war' was between the rulers of Ternate and Tidore, the chief clove-producing islands, who fought each other for control of the other islands. The Portuguese befriended the sultan of Ternate and the Spanish cultivated his enemy on Tidore, giving a European commercial dimension to their rivalry.

The Portuguese dominated the Clove Islands through the sixteenth century, until ousted from Ternate by the sultan in 1575; whereupon the Spanish attempted to take over the clove monopoly from settlements on Tidore and Gilolo, and from their new regional capital of Manila in what would become the Philippines. Although the Portuguese never made a formal claim to the Clove Islands, the viceroy in Goa appointed a succession of governors in a not entirely successful effort to ingratiate themselves with the Ternate sultanate; meanwhile they expanded their influence to Ambon, which under the Portuguese became the dominant centre of the Moluccan archipelago.

Curiously for rulers of such small and seemingly insignificant islands, the sultans of Ternate and Tidore addressed letters pledging their allegiances to King João III of Portugal or King Charles V of Spain – and to Queen Elizabeth I of England when her envoy, Francis Drake, called at Ternate in 1579 on his round-the-world voyage. Drake loaded his vessel, the *Golden Hind*, with cloves on top of the valuables he had plundered from the Spanish off the coasts of Peru and New Spain (Mexico); but he had to throw much of it overboard when the vessel foundered on a reef, though the ship's more valuable cargo of gold and silver reached Plymouth safely. Drake had left an English 'calling card' in the Moluccas, which was capitalised on twenty years later when the English East India Company came expecting a share in the spice trade.

The Clove Islands fell under Dutch control around the turn of the seventeenth century. The Dutch built their own fort on Ternate, named Fort Malayo and later Fort Orange. In 1606 the island became the seat of the first Dutch governor-general of the East Indies, Pieter Both. It was one of his successors, Jan Pieterzoon Coen, who transferred the trade headquarters and seat of government to Batavia in 1619. A twelve-year truce in Europe between the Dutch Republic and Spain helped the VOC see off Spanish competition

This 1525 image of a clove tree growing in the northern Spice Islands appeared in a French version of the book by the Magellan voyage's chronicler, Antonio Pigafetta.

from the Spice Islands. The VOC had taken control from the Portuguese of what would become the Moluccas' administrative centre, the central island of Ambon (or Amboyna), around three days' sailing south of Ternate; they built their own stockade, Fort Victoria, in the large west-facing bay. Ambon town, which grew up around the fort, dates its foundation from 1575.

The VOC insisted that growers sell their entire clove production to the company and not allow any cloves to reach their European rivals. Enforcing the monopoly was made easier by the small number of islands on which cloves grew, enabling their 'business model' to work. And they were learning that another economic principle, the law of 'supply and demand', came into play. Prices in Europe – and thus profits – would fall when the fleet came in and supply was plentiful; the 1,000 per cent profit margin then rose back to a staggering 3,000 per cent when cloves were scarce. The clove story has a curious outcome, in that seedlings the Portuguese planted in Ambon and the large adjacent island of Ceram grew to maturity after the Dutch had taken control; so although the monopoly of source was breached, it was to the Dutch advantage. They no longer had to deal exclusively with the quarrelsome sultans of Ternate and Tidore, since greater volumes of crop were available in territory they controlled.

THE NUTMEG ISLANDS

Two days' sailing south of Ambon and a little further east, at around 130° E, lie the Banda or Nutmeg Islands, the native home of the tree *Myristica fragrans* whose fruit produces both the nutmeg and mace. It is described here by the British naturalist Alfred Russel Wallace: 'Few cultivated plants are more beautiful than nutmeg-trees. They are handsomely shaped and glossy-leaved, growing to the height of twenty or thirty feet, and bearing small yellowish flowers. The fruit is the size and colour of a peach, but rather oval.' Wallace explains how the ripe fruit splits open exposing the crimson-coloured mace within which lies the hard seed or nut, 'a most beautiful object … the nutmeg of commerce'.[7] A Spanish traveller wrote that the oil the Bandanese make from nutmeg can be used 'to cure all Distempers in the Nerves, and Aches caus'd by cold … correct stinking Breath, clear the Eyes, comfort the Stomach, Liver, and Spleen, and digest Meat. [It is] a Remedy against many other Distempers, and serves to add outward Lustre to the Face.'[8]

The 1727 map by Pieter van der Aa (page 151) shows the eight Banda Islands: Rozengain, Kapal, Pisang (meaning 'banana'), Lonthor (also known as Banda Besar or Great Banda), Neira, Gunung Api ('volcano'), Pulau Ai (or Way) and Pulau Run (or Rhun). (*Pulau* means island in the Indonesian language.) Nutmeg grew on several of the islands. Situated far from any larger landmass, the islands were hard for early explorers to find. From the 1652 map of the Malay archipelago by the French cartographer Nicolas d'Abbeville Sanson, you understand why Linschoten told sailors from Europe to aim first for Java and continue east passing Bali and Timor on the right before turning northwards to cross the Banda Sea.

The Nutmeg Islands are smaller and less populous than the Clove Islands. They had no king or sultan, just village elders known as *orang kaya*

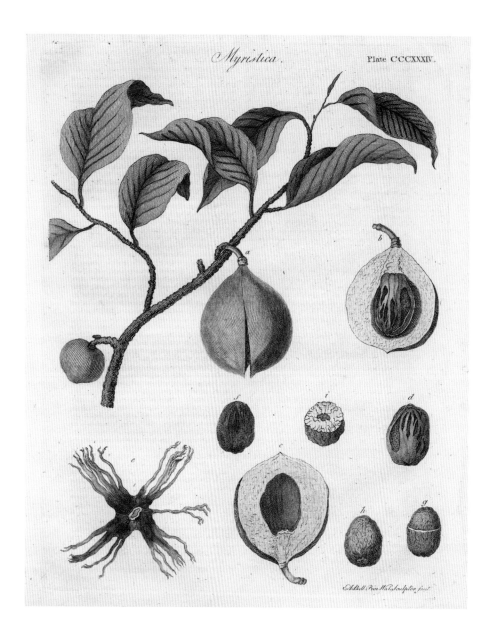

Myristica.   Plate CCCXXXIV.

– 'rich people' in the Indonesian language – making it harder for foreigners
to negotiate deals if they wanted to buy the entire crop. The islands had
plenty of nutmeg trees, but not enough other foodstuffs to feed their modest
population of fewer than 3,000 across all the islands when Europeans first
arrived, according to Tomé Pires. Inhabitants depended on selling nutmeg
and mace to buy rice and other crops brought from Java. The main nutmeg
plantations were on the largest island, Lonthor, as shown in the pictorial
map of 1702 by the Amsterdam artist Jacob van der Schley. Neira, the
administrative centre, also had plantations; to its west lay the active volcano
Gunung Api. The nutmeg tree typically grows in the shade provided by huge
kanari trees, which are themselves used for building *perahus*, simple rowing
boats, and as firewood for cooking.

Apart from volcanic soil, what these islands had in common with the
northern Moluccas was a tradition of welcoming visitors in their traditional
perahu kora-kora rowed by a team of men. The remarkable 1724 image by

*(opposite top) This 1727 map
by Pieter van der Aa shows
the Banda Islands where the
nutmeg tree grew. Pulau Run
(P. Rohn) on the left was the
subject of a power struggle
between the Dutch and English.*

*(opposite bottom) This earlier
map produced in Paris by
Nicolas d'Abbeville Sanson in
1652 locates the hard-to-find
Clove and Nutmeg Islands,
enlarging both groups in
insets. A century later another
Frenchman, Pierre Poivre,
succeeded in transplanting
both spices to Mauritius.*

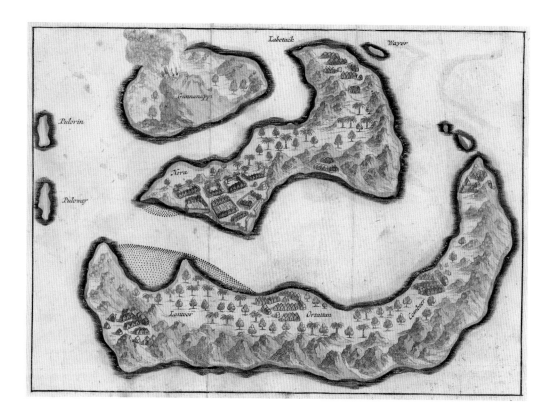

This graphic map of the Banda Islands in 1702 shows nutmeg plantations and the volcano on Gunung Api mid-eruption.

the VOC cartographer François Valentijn (page 153) shows how the Dutch lined up *kora-kora* boats in a strategy known as *hongitochten* to enforce their spice monopoly.

When the Portuguese first reached Banda, they found traders from China and Arabia buying spices from the islanders in return for textiles, porcelain and foodstuffs. Their attempt to take over the trade backfired since the islanders were content to sell to all comers. They started building a fort on Neira, but the islanders' hostility caused them to retreat to Ambon to buy nutmeg and mace there while concentrating their main effort on the Clove Islands.

The European battle for control of the Nutmeg Islands started in earnest with the coming of the Dutch in 1599 (before the VOC was founded), followed two years later by the English on an early venture by the East India Company (EIC). Both Dutch and English played on the fact that they were not Portuguese – not entirely successfully since the islanders were suspicious of the newcomers. In an attempt to impose their will, the Dutch built Fort Hollandia on Lonthor, Fort Nassau on the foreshore of Neira facing Lonthor, and later Fort Belgica on high ground overlooking Neira's main harbour. They tried to impose trading terms on the *orang kaya* with limited success and a great deal of hostility. A naval expedition sent from Batavia under Admiral Verhoeven was ambushed, the admiral and 26 other Dutchman being decapitated, an incident recorded in VOC annals as 'the Vile Bandanese Treachery of 1609'. One of the survivors was the young Jan Pieterzoon Coen, who had yet to make his mark in the company. This episode helped shape his 'might is right' philosophy.

After becoming the fourth governor-general of the Dutch East Indies and founding Batavia as the VOC's eastern headquarters, Coen returned to the

Banda Islands intent on enforcing the spice monopoly. He wanted everything for the Dutch, and ignored an agreement previously reached in Europe between Dutch and English: this was to share military and administrative costs and the spice produced, in a two-to-one ratio in favour of the Dutch, while excluding Spanish and Portuguese traders from the Moluccas. Coen treated the English as almost as much of an enemy as the Bandanese in his ruthless struggle to buy up all available nutmeg and mace. His motivation was clear: the price received from selling nutmeg in Amsterdam represented a vast profit over what the company paid for it in Banda.

Coen's tactic was to take over the Banda estates by force, killing or expelling their owners. He brought in Dutch managers as *perkeniers*, or leaseholders, to manage individual plantations or *perkens*, of which there were 68 across the islands. The company provided their food, imported from Java, and brought in forced labourers from other islands, including Ceram and Buru in the Moluccas, and Papuans from New Guinea. The *perkeniers* were required to maximise output from the estates and sell it to the company. Failure to do so risked a *perkenier* losing the privilege of working the estate. It was a harsh and brutal regime based on enforced labour, run by the Dutch. Coen's pogrom in the early 1620s massacred the islands' population: only about a thousand survived of a population ten times that number. The *Heeren XVII* stood behind his campaign, which delivered great quantities of spices; but there was considerable unease, indeed revulsion, in the Dutch Republic when the extent of his brutality became known.

A war of attrition between the two European powers continued through the first half of the seventeenth century: the Dutch trying to enforce a

The Dutch used local kora-kora boats to defend their spice monopoly, as graphically pictured here off the island of Ambon by François Valentijn around 1724.

monopoly, while the English demanded a share in the trade. The English occupied the outer islands of Pulau Ai and Pulau Run, while the Dutch controlled the main nutmeg-growing islands of Neira and Lonthor. The islands controlled by the English had no indigenous water source, so were dependent on rain and imported food. The English maintained a presence on the main islands from where they shipped supplies, fighting for control of the island group as they had over Batavia. Pulau Ai and Pulau Run changed hands several times.[9]

The most serious clash between the Dutch and English took place in 1623 on the island of Ambon, between the clove and nutmeg groups of islands; it was nominally over the terms of the 1619 agreement which granted both companies access to spices. The Dutch accused the English of trying to capture the strategic Fort Victoria. On the orders of the Dutch governor, ten Englishmen, nine Japanese and a Portuguese were tortured and executed, an incident that poisoned relations between England and the Dutch Republic and their trading companies. That the Spanish, Portuguese, Dutch and English all tried to reach and trade with the islands' rulers demonstrates just how great was the demand for cloves, nutmeg and mace in Europe at the time.

The English pulled out of Pulau Run in 1628, tiring of the constant battle with the Dutch for access to nutmeg, giving the Dutch effective control of the entire Moluccas and enabling them to enforce their spice monopoly as far as European markets were concerned. They also controlled the cinnamon trade with Ceylon and trade in pepper from India's Coromandel coast. Pulau Run came back into English hands briefly in 1665, and again in later centuries. To avoid falling foul of the Dutch in Bantam, the English shipped spices to the port of Makassar in south-west Sulawesi, a few days' sailing west of Banda. This blatant breach of their monopoly led the Dutch, in alliance with the Bugis, to take control of that city in the 1660s, in a battle witnessed by VOC surgeon Wouter Schouten.

Anglo-Dutch rivalry then moved to Europe, with naval confrontations in the North Sea. After their second trade war ended in 1667, following a daring

Dutch vessels in Ambon Bay with Fort Victoria, headquarters of the VOC in the Moluccas, and Ambon town on the right, in this 1708 view.

Ambon in the central Moluccas was captured from the Portuguese by the Dutch VOC under Admiral Steven van der Hagen in February 1605. The map, commissioned by the first Dutch governor, Frederik Houtman, pictured, shows Fort Victoria prominently and clove trees throughout the island.

Dutch raid on the English fleet on the River Medway, the English and Dutch negotiated and signed a peace treaty at Breda, Holland, on 31 July 1667. This resolved the issue of the Banda Islands in favour of the Dutch, forcing England to give up its claim on Pulau Run. The islands were not specifically mentioned, but the treaty provided that each nation hold onto territory it then controlled, a provision that would have implications for the island of Manhattan on the other side of the world.

THE DUTCH EAST INDIES

Back in Java, Coen successfully defended Batavia from attacks by the dominant Mataram kingdom of central Java, before succumbing to cholera in 1629 at the age of 42. He is remembered as founder of the Dutch Republic's East Indies colony, though hardly revered given his role in the massacre of the Bandanese. Batavia, the port city he created, would during the course of the seventeenth century become one of the most spectacular and significant in the East, nicknamed 'Queen of the East'. As well as being the gateway to the source of spices, it was a fulcrum of trade between Europe, China and Japan, as the eighteenth-century economist Adam Smith noted. Smith wrote that Batavia's pivotal location between East and West and the splendour of the city helped its European inhabitants 'surmount the additional disadvantage of perhaps the most unwholesome climate in the world'.[10]

Coffee was introduced to Java in the 1690s. A Dutch merchant trading in Arabia brought coffee cuttings to Amsterdam, where they were cultivated under glass, producing seeds which were then sent out to Batavia. An alternative version suggests that a pilgrim returning to India from Arabia

A graphic portrayal of the capture by the Dutch of the town of Makassar on Celebes (Sulawesi) in the 1660s. The victory helped the VOC protect its spice monopoly.

taped coffee seeds to his stomach to evade controls on plant exports and cultivated them near Mysore, from where they were subsequently taken to Java. Both accounts may be true. Either way, coffee took to Java's volcanic soil and in due course became the mainstay of Dutch Indies trade as demand for coffee overtook that for spices and Java coffee became the beverage of choice in European salons and coffee houses. According to the German coffee historian H. E. Jacob, Java coffee was so popular that 'from 1700 onwards, for many, many years, the Dutch East Indies controlled the price of coffee in the world market'.[11]

The Dutch would lose that dominant market position when a French naval officer smuggled the plant to Martinique in the Caribbean, from where it was transplanted to Brazil; this was the location that then overtook Java in the early eighteenth century as the world's major grower of coffee beans. Portugal controlled Brazil following its accidental 'discovery' by Pedro Álvares Cabral and the pope's sharing out of territory; so while Portugal lost the sixteenth-century fight to control oriental spices, it won the eighteenth-century battle to provide Europe's supply of coffee. Brazil would subsequently become the main supplier to Europe of sugar as well. At least temporarily the Dutch had achieved with coffee exactly what they had tried to prevent with cloves, nutmeg and mace: a diversification of sources

of supply leading to a fall in the price charged to consumers, and that paid to growers. Adam Smith, who deplored the use of monopoly powers by European trading companies, would have approved the end of monopoly in the supply of both coffee and spices.

The VOC was dissolved at the end of the eighteenth century after going bankrupt, its trading and administrative roles being taken over by the Dutch government. The trade that had started with spices and expanded to tea, coffee, sugar, quinine and palm oil had delivered significant profits to the traders, but fared less well after the Dutch monopoly was formally ended in 1864. By then the East Indies were firmly under Dutch rule. While the Dutch Republic's brutal rule over their newly colonised subjects was indefensible, its by-product was to unite the nation we now know as Indonesia.

MAX HAVELAAR AND THE CULTURE SYSTEM

There emerged in the East Indies a writer whom many regard as the greatest Dutch novelist, though his most celebrated book, *Max Havelaar*, was more a satirical exposure of colonial injustice than a novel. Eduard Douwes Dekker wrote under the Latin pseudonym *Multatuli* – meaning 'I have endured much' – which signified the bitterness he felt at his fruitless attempt to be reinstated in the administrative service of the Dutch East Indies after an enforced resignation. Today he might have brought an action for 'constructive dismissal'.

When *Max Havelaar* was published in the Netherlands in 1860, it shook the Dutch establishment; they saw it as an indictment of colonial rule, in particular of the so-called 'culture system' (*cultuurstelsel*, more accurately rendered in English as 'cultivation system') by which the rulers determined what crops should be cultivated, riding roughshod over local landowners and giving enormous power to the Dutch-appointed regents who enforced the system. Dekker regarded the system as tantamount to forced labour. Here he is at his most indignant:

If anyone should ask whether the man who grows the products receives a reward proportionate to the yields, the answer must be in the negative. The government compels him to grow on *his* land what pleases *it;* it punishes him when he sells the crop so produced to anyone else but *it;* and *it* fixes the price it pays him.[12]

He could have been writing about Banda, but his book was in fact based on Java where, from the company's point of view, the culture system was a success. Exports soared after it was introduced in 1830, and by mid-century much of the company's budget derived from the cultivation of crops under the culture system. Two years after *Max Havelaar* was published, the system started to be abolished – initially for pepper, cloves and nutmeg, crops no longer vital to Dutch profits. Subsequently the system was ended for the crops which had taken over as the mainstay of Dutch colonial rule: sugar, tea, coffee and tobacco. The book *Max Havelaar* was at least partly responsible for this change of policy. However, Dekker was not reinstated, although this was his ostensible purpose in writing the book. He became and remains something of a Dutch national hero: with a statue and commemorative museum in Amsterdam, and a plaque on the office he fictitiously represented as that of 'Last and Co, Coffee Brokers'. Decker is more highly regarded today than Jan Pieterzoon Coen, the man who colonised the East Indies for the Dutch.

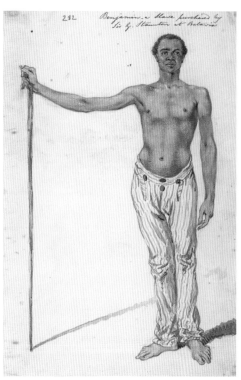

(above) Benjamin, a slave purchased by Sir G. Staunton at Batavia, from an album of drawings by William Alexander made during Lord Macartney's embassy to the Emperor of China, 1792–4.

WALLACE AND RUMPHIUS

Nobody ever sorted out the projection into the eastern hemisphere of the line determined by the Treaty of Tordesillas, because lines of longitude were not accurately measured until the 1770s, by which time the competition for the Moluccas was long over. But another line drawn through the archipelago by the British naturalist Alfred Russel Wallace was more real and bears his name. Wallace was an ally of Charles Darwin in the sense that both were working on the theory of natural selection independently of each other; they did not meet until Wallace returned to Britain in 1862, after several years in the East Indies.

Wallace devised what became known as 'the Wallace Line' separating the continents of Asia and Australia based on organic life. It runs through the Malay archipelago, modern Indonesia, between Borneo (Kalimantan) and Sulawesi and between Bali and Lombok. He had observed that several species of the marsupial possum family were found in the Moluccas and Sulawesi but not in Borneo or Java, concluding that the former islands were once land-linked to Australia while the latter were once joined to the Asian landmass. He also showed that there was a preponderance of bats and exotic birds to the east of the line, and that mammals were distinctive in belonging to one side or the other but seldom both, all of which supported his theory. There were far fewer mammals in the Moluccas than on Java. The distinctiveness was less evident with regard to flora, though one clear

(opposite top) Neira, the main island of the Banda group of Nutmeg Islands, viewed from the south, showing the Dutch-built forts, Nassau close to the shoreline and Belgica on the hill beyond, while Gunung Api at the left is erupting; depicted by Jacob van der Schley around 1752.

(opposite bottom) Ternate in the Clove Islands with Mount Gammalamma erupting, pictured by François Valentijn in 1725. The fort on the shoreline and shown in an inset was named after the volcano.

NEIRA.

TERNATE

de Fortres
Gamma-Lamma.

example was the eucalyptus tree of Australasia which was not found on Java or Borneo. Wallace wrote a ground-breaking book, *The Malay Archipelago*, on the flora and fauna of the islands around which he travelled.

While staying on the Banda Islands, Wallace witnessed the impressive volcano Gunung Api, rising to 640 metres (2100 ft), which rendered him philosophical: 'A volcano is a fact ... of so awful a character that, if it were the rule instead of the exception, it would make the earth uninhabitable; a fact so strange and unaccountable that we may be sure that we would not be believed on any human testimony, if presented to us now for the first time, as a natural phenomenon happening in a distant country.'[13] Wallace was not in Banda while the volcano was erupting, depicted in a 1752 view by Jacob van der Schley; but he would certainly have heard tales of the many eruptions on the adjacent island of Neira, which caused loss of life and damage to dwellings. Wallace was less inspired by the perfectly conical and more menacing volcano on Ternate, Mount Gammalamma, rising twice as high to 1715 metres (5626 ft), pictured by François Valentijn (both on page 159).

Indonesia contains around one tenth of all the active volcanoes in the world today, which form a so-called 'Ring of Fire' at the western end of the Pacific Ocean. The largest number of active volcanoes are on Java. The volcanic soil of the Moluccas provides a clue as to why nutmeg and clove grew there in the first place.

Another European naturalist who made his name in the Moluccas was Georg Eberhard Rumphius, known as Rumpf. Born in Hesse, Germany, he learned Dutch from his mother who had lived near the Dutch border and signed up to serve the VOC in the East Indies in the 1650s. He was posted to Ambon where he met the VOC cartographer, author and artist François Valentijn. Rumphius' research on the plant life of the Spice Islands led to his monumental work *Herbarium Amboinense* cataloguing more than a thousand plants which grew on the main islands and earning him the nickname *Plinus Indicus,* or 'Pliny of the Indies'. Echoing Tomé Pires, Rumphius believed that God had given spices to the Spice Islands and that plants grow where they are biologically suited and cannot be transplanted elsewhere. This theory, which would later be disproved, discouraged attempts to transplant spices, thus inadvertently supporting the Dutch monopoly.

Rumphius had a tragic life, losing his wife and daughter in an earthquake, going blind in his forties and twice losing his extensive manuscript, once in a fire and again when a ship carrying the lavishly illustrated work to Europe sank. After he had laboriously repeated his work with the help of family members, the VOC withheld publication because, they said, it contained sensitive information. The six-volume book was eventually published nearly forty years after his death. Rumphius is credited with founding the science of ethnobotany in which plants are classified by their species and genus,

Onshore view of the town of Batavia, by the English engraver Emanuel Bowen in 1748.

preparing the ground for the Swedish botanist and zoologist Carl Linnaeus, and influencing the work of later naturalists such as his fellow German Alexander von Humboldt[14] and Britain's Charles Darwin.

NAPOLEONIC TIMES

The East Indies were under Dutch control from the 1667 Treaty of Breda onwards, subject to efforts by such as the sultanate of Aceh in the north of Sumatra to retain their autonomy. Also the British – following the union of England and Scotland as one country in 1707 – maintained trading bases on Sumatra, shipping goods through the port of Bencoolen (now Bengkulu) on Sumatra's west coast, where they built Fort Marlborough. They made two further attempts to take control of the Spice Islands under the pretext of saving them from the French, after the Dutch motherland was occupied by the army of Napoleon Bonaparte.

In 1796 they seized Ambon and the Banda Islands without a shot being fired; they stayed until 1803, long enough to ship and sell plenty of spice, giving London a commercial advantage over Amsterdam. The 'occupation' also gave Britain an opportunity to transplant nutmeg plants to territories they controlled: Bencoolen in Sumatra, Penang (or Prince of Wales Island) off the Malay peninsula and the island of Ceylon off southern India. Nutmeg arrived on the London market early in the nineteenth century from these territories, which would eventually ship more nutmeg than the Banda Islands. But the British were not the first transplanters of nutmeg; this honour belongs – as we shall see in the next chapter – to a Frenchman.

A painting of 'A Market Stall in Batavia' displaying local fruits such as pineapple, jackfruit and durian, by Andries Beeckman who served as an artist for the VOC, c.1640–66.

A second opportunity for the British to ship nutmeg from Banda came when, on the same pretext of protecting the East Indies from the French, an East India Company official based at Malacca, Stamford Raffles, took control of Java and the Indies with Dutch agreement, though without the endorsement of his own London-based directors. This seizure, which started in Banda in 1810 before Raffles arrived on Java in 1811, suggested that the British still regarded spices as the most valuable crops the Dutch shipped.

For five years Raffles ruled the East Indies as lieutenant-governor on behalf of the English East India Company, continuing the reforms to agriculture prompted by the book *Max Havelaar*. He also pursued personal interests, for example presiding over the discovery of the remarkable Buddhist monument of Borobudur in central Java and writing a magisterial and prodigiously researched book, *The History of Java*. This includes the instructive observation that 'the women alone attend the markets, and conduct all the business of buying and selling. It is proverbial to say the Javanese men are fools in money concerns.'[15] Even back in the thirteenth century, the Chinese traveller Zhou Daguan noted that 'in Cambodia it is the women who take charge of trade'.[16] In these matrilineal societies, land could usually only be inherited through the female line. At his subsequent posting in Bencoolen, Raffles would have become familiar with one of the region's proudest matrilineal traditions, that of the Minangkabau, whose women are very much in charge of agricultural and trading matters and prevail over the male line in the inheritance of land. By the twentieth century, Indonesia overall still had a female participation rate in trade that was about ten times as high as the average for Arab countries.[17]

After Napoleon's defeat at Waterloo and the restoration of sovereignty to the Netherlands, Raffles was ordered by EIC directors in London to hand back power in the East Indies to the Dutch. He took up the less powerful role as lieutenant-governor of British-controlled Bencoolen, which he described as 'the most wretched place', overseeing trade there in pepper, and adding to his scientific achievements by having the world's largest and smelliest flower, *Rafflesia*, named after him. For his zoological and botanical work Raffles was elected a fellow of the Royal Society in London. One curious legacy of the British period of rule is that Indonesians still drive on the left, as in other former British territories. From Bencoolen, Raffles would set off on an expedition to claim Britain's final territorial conquest in south-east Asia, the island of Singapore.

Dutch rule of the East Indies lasted into the 1940s, with a further interruption when the Japanese seized the islands as part of their Second World War attempt to capture sources of supply; not so much spices this time as rubber and mineral oil, though they also benefited from coffee and sugar production. The Japanese changed the capital city's name, dropping the colonial 'Batavia'. Allegedly they found 'Jaccatra' difficult to say so they simplified the former name to that which the city bears today, Jakarta. Natives of the city are still known as *orang Betawi* or *Betawi* people, a curious linguistic link with the *Batavi* tribe who first settled the Netherlands.

When the Dutch regained control in 1945, they had a war for independence on their hands. They had earlier sent two nationalist leaders, Mohammed Hatta and Sutan Sjahrir, into prison exile on one of the islands which had brought the Dutch so much profit, Banda Neira. The country declared its independence immediately after the Japanese surrender in August 1945, but it took four years of fighting before the Dutch conceded and the independent nation of Indonesia emerged. Its name, attributed to British sea captain and writer George Windsor Earl in the 1850s, is derived from the Greek words *Indus*, meaning India or Indies, and *nesos* meaning islands.[18]

During four centuries of colonial rule, many Dutch words were incorporated into *bahasa* Indonesia, the *lingua franca* of modern Indonesia, as well as some words of Portuguese and English origin. The Indies gave Dutch or English words such as cockatoo, which comes from *kakatua,* and *orangutan* – literally 'forest person'. The name the Dutch gave to a Second World War spy, Mata Hari, comes from the Indonesian word for the Sun which combines *mata,* meaning eye, and *hari,* meaning day, so 'the eye of the day'. *Cajeput* oil – and the tree it comes from which is also known as the 'tea tree' – means the oil of white (*putih*) wood (*kayu*). The port of Makassar traded in another vegetable oil mixed with fragrant *ylang ylang* oil, known as Makassar oil, which was much used in Victorian England as

Rafflesia arnoldi, *the large flower nicknamed the Stinking Corpse Lily, 'discovered' by Raffles in Sumatra, drawn and engraved by E. Wedell, c.1825.*

hair oil, including by the poet Lord Byron. It became so popular that people started placing a small cloth square on the back of chairs to prevent the oil transferring to the chair – and that is the origin of the 'antimacassar'.

Bantam, the port where the European adventure began and hinterland of western Java, is the source of the breed of small chicken known by that name and the bantamweight category in boxing. The technique of *batik*, using wax to dye textiles, is of Javanese origin; that of *ikat*, meaning to bind or tie, hails from the islands of Borneo and Sulawesi. Both styles are used for *sarongs*, wrap-around skirts.

Indonesia still produces more nutmeg than anywhere else, the second largest source being Grenada in the Caribbean. Indonesians are also the world's largest consumers of cloves, an ingredient of the popular *kretek* cigarettes, but ironically cannot produce enough cloves to meet their needs so they import from Zanzibar. A Dutch company based in Rotterdam is the world's major trader in oriental spices, including cloves, nutmeg, mace and pepper.

Aspect du Fort

Montagne de la Table

Cap de bone Esperance

Fort

OCEAN MERIDIONAL

'The Cape may, with propriety, be ſtyled an inn for travellers to and from the Eaſt Indies, who, after several months' sail, may here get refreshments of all kinds, and are then about half way to their deſtination, whether homeward or outward bound.'

SWEDISH BOTANIST AND TRAVELLER C. P. THUNBERG, 1772[1]

8/ CAPE TOWN, MAURITIUS AND OTHER TAVERNS OF THE SEAS

An exaggerated view of Table Mountain towering over the fort which the Dutch built to protect their settlement of Cape Town, depicted by French artist and cartographer Alain Mallet in 1683.

In the early days of long-distance sea travel, it took many months to reach destinations like Malacca and Batavia from Europe. Sailors needed to be prepared for long stretches of open ocean with no opportunities to take on fresh water or food. Typically it took as much as nine months to reach India, while a voyage to Batavia could take over a year, with sailors away from home for three years in total. Uncertain navigation, currents and weather conditions meant that ships often sailed way off course, so the length of a voyage could only be assessed in the vaguest way.

The French writer Bernardin de Saint-Pierre described a journey from Lorient in France to Port Louis, Mauritius, of at least 12,000 km which took 4 months and 12 days 'without touching at any port'. On the journey they lost eleven of their 146 men: three were washed overboard and eight died of scurvy. Many became ill with scurvy from lack of fresh vegetables and fruit, or with dysentery from the poorly preserved meat onboard.[2] It was easy to break a mast in a fierce storm, like those routinely encountered off the Cape of Good Hope or the Mozambique Channel, while another risk came from attacks by pirates or by sailors of another nation. Sailors were always looking for opportunities to stop and refresh their water and food supplies to supplement what rainwater and fresh fish they could catch en route, or to make emergency repairs to ships after storm damage; but this was only possible if a port was in their nation's hands or was considered neutral.

CAPE TOWN

In 1652 Jan van Riebeck planted the Dutch flag in the shadow of Table Mountain near the Cape of Good Hope, at the behest of VOC directors. It was a strategic move to upstage the Portuguese and the English and to maintain the company's monopoly of the spice trade by creating a 'halfway house' at one of the most clearly identifiable stretches of coast. The large, flat-topped mountain, which sailors likened to a table top, was visible from afar; and Table Bay was easy to enter and provided protection from the winds.

The fortified settlement commanded the Cape for a century and a half, giving the Dutch a navigational advantage. For sailors it was a provisioning point known as 'the tavern of two seas'. For some it also became a graveyard, though it was considered healthier than Batavia from where patients were brought to recover. Cape Town prospered as a transit stop in Dutch hands, but was deemed unfriendly to English ships which instead used St Helena as their 'tavern', while the Portuguese used a base in Mozambique. A stop at Mauritius in the Indian Ocean depended on whether friend or foe was in charge at the time, though the American pepper traders of Salem – not seen as trading rivals – used all ports regardless of who controlled them. Without the search for spices and attempt to monopolise the trade, Cape Town would never have come into being. An image by Pieter van der Aa from around 1690 shows an active Table Bay, though still with a distorted representation of Table Mountain.

Pieter van der Aa's view of the Dutch settlement at Cape Town, looking east from Table Bay, 1690.

The area had its native inhabitants, the *Khoikhoi*, whom the Dutch called *Hottentots* from their word for 'stammerers', which was how they sounded to Dutch ears. The word came to have pejorative overtones. Europeans depended on the *Khoikhoi* to provide them with meat, while shipping rice and corn from the motherland and later from Java. When the colony prospered, the grains were exported to the Dutch settlements of Ceylon and Batavia. Migrants from Holland, many of French Huguenot origin, arrived to take up work as farmers or *boers*. This was the origin of the Afrikaner people and their language *Afrikaans*: Dutch mixed with languages spoken by enslaved manual workers brought from Madagascar and Java. The VOC forbade enslavement of *Khoikhoi* people.

Van Riebeck had instructions to fortify the port: not to make it a colony but merely a victualling station. He developed a market garden producing vegetables and fruit to provision vessels and authorised the planting of wheat beyond the town's confines, which brought the VOC into conflict with the *Khoikhoi*. The Cape Colony (as it would later be known) was self-sufficient in foodstuffs by 1684, and in due course vines were planted creating the Cape's wine industry and adding to the commodities on which the VOC claimed a trading monopoly. For all intents it was a Dutch colony, no different from Java and Malacca though with the additional role of sustaining and repairing long-distance vessels at around the halfway point on their long voyage. By the time van Riebeck left the Cape in 1662, the non-native population had grown to nearly four hundred, half of whom were indentured labourers, tantamount to slaves. The *boers* were 'free-burghers' – they chose which crops to grow, but had to sell them to the VOC at prices determined by the company.

When French forces under Napoleon invaded the Dutch Republic (renaming it the Batavian Republic) and Dutch-ruled territories technically fell under France, the British took control of what had become a colony at the request of the last *stadhouder,* Willem V, Prince of Orange (who fled to London); this was firstly from 1795 to 1803 and again in 1806, after which Cape Town was permanently ceded to Britain in the Anglo-Dutch treaty of 1814 – by agreement rather than by battle. The VOC was in significant decline by this time. Britain continued to expand the Cape Colony introducing new crops, encouraging self-government under a parliamentary system and ending the trafficking of enslaved people. Railways were built in the 1850s and the discovery of diamonds in the 1860s and gold in the 1880s encouraged a flow of migrants seeking work in the new mines. By the end of the century Cape Town's population had grown to 170,000 – around double that when the British arrived a century earlier.

A west-facing map of 1683 by the Dutchman Johan Nieuhof shows the Cape on the left and Table Bay in the centre. A line shows a canal the Dutch envisaged digging to connect Table and False Bays so that vessels could avoid rough seas around the Cape itself. The canal was never built, though False Bay became the alternative victualling point when the harsh north-westerly winds were blowing in the winter months. A 1754 sketch by Thomas Salmon shows Table Bay and its fort (see pages 170 and 171).

Cape Town prospered as a result of the Asia-to-Europe trade in spices and other goods. The South African nation was founded on this trade and

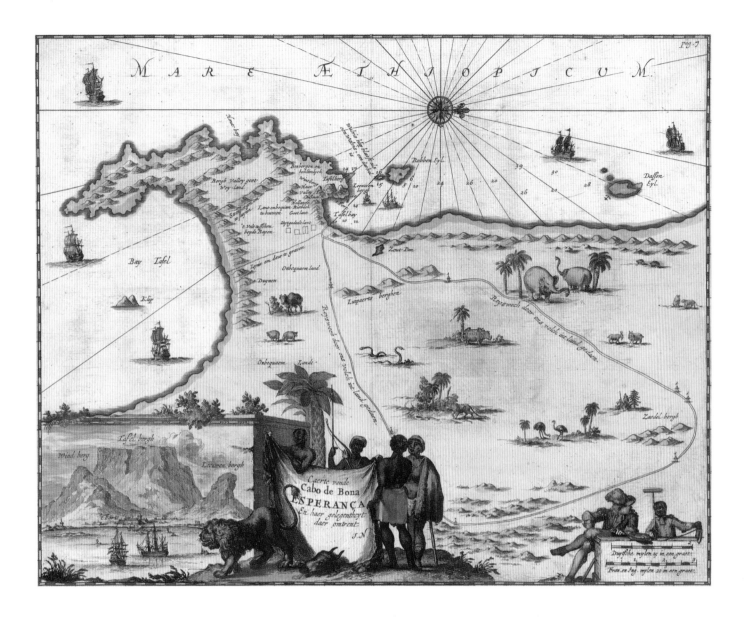

MARE ÆTHIOPICUM.

peopled by those attracted there from Europe, south and south-east Asia and the African hinterland. Then in 1869 the dreams of emperors were realised when vessels were able to use a quicker and cheaper route to and from the East with the formal separation of Africa from Asia following the opening of the Suez Canal. For Europeans this was a return to an earlier route to the East which had pre-dated passage around the Cape.

Cape Town lost its advantage, but could stand on its own feet as the main port of a prosperous new nation, albeit it not an independent one until the Cape Colony merged in 1910 with Natal and the Boer republics as the Union of South Africa. Cape Town with the parliament became its legislative capital, Pretoria the seat of its government, and Bloemfontein of its judiciary, while Johannesburg in the gold mining interior is the largest city. The British fought two wars against the *boers* and the country was ruled by white Afrikaners under apartheid, or separate development for different races, from 1948 before emerging as a proud black-ruled nation in 1994.

This west-facing map of 1683 by Johan Nieuhof shows Table Bay, where the Dutch established their settlement, and False Bay. A plan to build a canal between the bays, enabling ships to avoid the fierce winds around the Cape of Good Hope, at left, was never realised.

Another depiction of the settlement and fort at Cape Town by an artist who had never been there and was relying on mariners' descriptions, attributed to Thomas Salmon, 1754.

THE ATLANTIC 'TAVERNS'

The uninhabited South Atlantic island of St Helena was discovered by Portuguese mariner, João de Nova, on St Helena's day, 21 May 1502. It lies 15° south of the Equator, 1,950 kilometres from the coast of Africa and nearly twice as far from Brazil. It was a good source of water and enjoyed a climate that – despite its location – was more temperate than tropical because of currents and altitude. Most of the island is over 450 metres high. A drawback was that it had no harbour.

By the time Jan Huygen van Linschoten called there in 1589, the Portuguese had introduced livestock and edible plants and there was a 'great abundance of fish' making it a useful 'tavern' for sailors. He wrote 'it is a verie high and hillie country, so that it commonly reacheth unto the cloudes' and when discovered there were 'not any beasts, nor fruite'. Linschoten called St Helena 'an earthly Paradise for ye Portingall shippes ... [which] seemeth to have been miraculously discovered for the refreshing and service of the same'.[3] He told how sick sailors were disembarked to

recover there, which they usually did rapidly, enabling them to be picked up by a later ship.

The Dutch settled St Helena in 1633 but did not stay long, abandoning it in favour of the Cape, which provided better shelter from fierce storms in the southern winter. After the Dutch settled the Cape, the English East India Company took over St Helena. The island's forbidding aspect is evident from a 1752 view of Jamestown, the main town. The steep rocky hillsides are emphasised and there is nowhere for large East Indiamen vessels to tie up, so we see sailors rowing themselves ashore in smaller boats.

St Helena is best known for Napoleon Bonaparte being exiled there for five and a half years after his defeat at Waterloo in 1815.[4] It was a 67-day voyage for him from Plymouth on HMS *Northumberland*, and he described the island as 'a vile rock in the midst of the Ocean'. But in fact by the time of his arrival there it was a busy settlement with as many as three ships arriving each day and a population of several thousand. Napoleon had designs on India and set out to challenge its possession by the English,[5] so it was ironic that he should find himself in conversation with servants of the English East India Company, rivals of the French *Compagnie des Indes Orientales*, returning from postings in India and south-east Asia. Fearing that Napoleon might repeat his feat of escaping, as he had done from a previous exile on the Mediterranean island of Elba, the British fortified the island to a fastidious degree and gave orders that passing vessels were to take on fresh supplies speedily with passengers and crew not permitted to land. An exception was made when a particularly distinguished officer of the company passed by – as we learn in Chapter 12. A map of 1816, with Georgetown at the bottom, marks 'Buonaparte's Residence' on the left.

A view of St Helena from the north-west, showing the main town of Jamestown. Mariners had to be rowed ashore as there was no harbour. Painted by French artist Jean François Daumont, published in London around 1760.

In the early years of Napoleon's exile, the English admiral Sir Pulteney Malcolm had regular meetings with him. From the diary kept by his wife, we learn that the deposed emperor was against the trading of African people as 'slaves' and took the moral high ground in telling the admiral that 'the English ought to have made the Portuguese relinquish it entirely'. Admiral Malcolm replied that it was English practice to seize Portuguese ships 'to put [the slaves] on shore at Sierre Leone, where we had an establishment', feed them for one year and then give them lands and implements of husbandry, to which Napoleon nodded approvingly saying 'that was good, very good, for it might be the means of civilising Africa':[6] an interesting debate between these two colonialists.

Ten years before Napoleon's defeat, Arthur Wellesley, a military officer who distinguished himself in battle in southern India, spent three weeks on St Helena while his ship's supplies were replenished. Wellesley subsequently led British forces in defeating Napoleon, for which he was ennobled as the first Duke of Wellington. We may assume that the Waterloo victor had a say in determining the former emperor's place of exile, recommending the island because it is so remote. Napoleon's adversary at the Battle of the Nile, Horatio Nelson, also called at St Helena as a young naval lieutenant returning from India in 1776, though he may not have set

The victualling station of St Helena, depicted by Robert Read in 1816 from the north-west. 'Buonaparte's Residence' is marked amid trees on the left.

foot on the island. Napoleon's 'vile rock' would again be used as a prison at the start of the twentieth century, when Britain confined several thousand prisoners from the second Boer War there.

Some 1,300 kilometres north of St Helena lies Ascension Island, which was first sighted by the Portuguese navigator Afonso de Albuquerque on Ascension Day, 1501, naming it in Portuguese *Ilha da Ascensão*.[7] Situated 8° south of the Equator and 1,650 kilometres from the coast of Africa, Ascension is almost as isolated as St Helena, though would nonetheless have been a welcome stop after a long voyage. Initially its only value was as a source of fresh water, green turtles and their eggs.

Linschoten's 1596 Atlantic Ocean map shows grim images of Ascension Island and St Helena.

After the Dutch took control of Cape Town and denied access to its trading rivals, Ascension became popular with the French and English, who introduced other plants and livestock. Such was the hit and miss state of navigation at sea that ships hoping to put into St Helena on the homebound journey sometimes veered too far into the Atlantic and came across Ascension instead. Writer Bernardin de Saint-Pierre called at Ascension Island on his return from Mauritius in 1771 and reported that, despite the relative absence of vegetation, a few days ashore here was effective in relieving the symptoms of scurvy; though he complained on the subsequent journey back to France that 'one is soon tired of turtle, palatable and nutritive as it is – the flesh is very tough, and the eggs but of an indifferent taste'.

A third initially uninhabited South Atlantic island was Tristan da Cunha, named after the Portuguese explorer Tristão da Cunha who first sighted it in 1506. Tristan is the remotest of the three Atlantic 'taverns', lying at 37° S, 2,000 kilometres south of St Helena and 2,400 kilometres west of South Africa. Over the centuries it became a transit stop for Dutch and French sailors who had strayed too far westwards in their voyage around the Cape. It was annexed by Britain in 1816 to prevent any attempt by the French to free Napoleon from St Helena.

As with Cape Town, these Atlantic islands lost their relevance for the eastern trade with the opening of the Suez Canal in 1869, returning to relative obscurity although all are inhabited. Despite the decolonisation

These views of Ascension Island and St Helena were included as insets to Linschoten's 1596 map of the Atlantic Ocean, reproduced in Chapter 4.

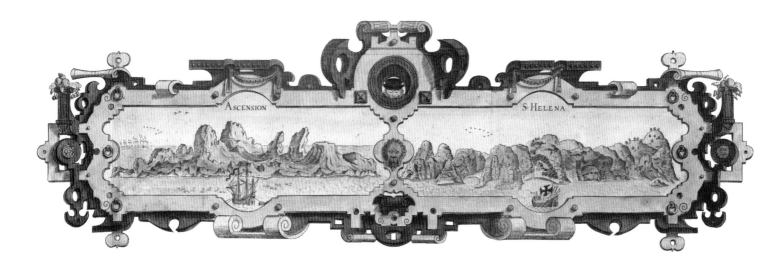

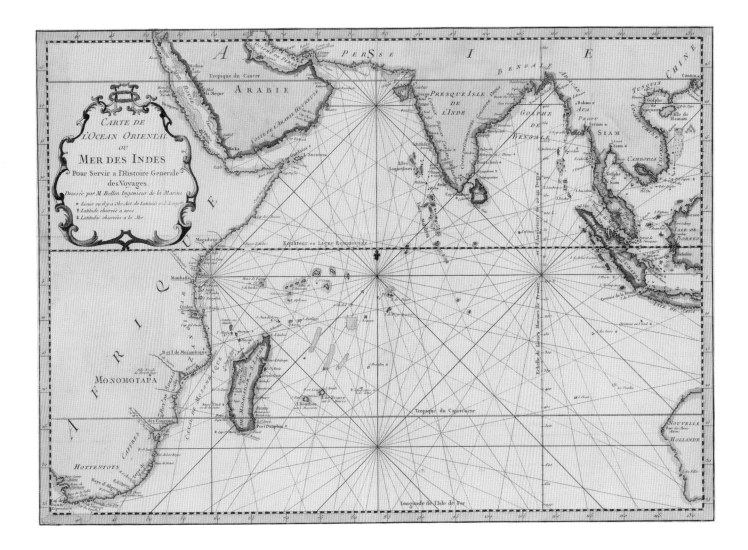

This 1754 map of the Indian Ocean by Jacques-Nicolas Bellin shows how Île de France (Mauritius) and Île Réunion (Bourbon) provided convenient 'taverns' for vessels heading to Malacca or Batavia.

of most of the former British Empire, they remain today within the British Overseas Territory of Saint Helena, Ascension and Tristan da Cunha.

THE MASCARENE ISLANDS OF THE INDIAN OCEAN

Rounding the Cape marked the end of the first leg of a long journey from Europe. Ahead lay the crossing of the Indian Ocean, which could take a further three to nine months depending on the destination: India, Malacca, Batavia or a more distant Chinese port.

On his first voyage Vasco da Gama hugged the east African coast, sailing through the channel that separates Madagascar from the mainland and putting into port at Mozambique, Mombasa and Malindi (see map on page 85); from here his crossing to India followed the well-tried route of Arab traders using the seasonal winds first recorded by Hippalus. Da Gama encountered animosity at some African ports, making subsequent captains nervous about calling for fear of receiving a hostile reception.

Later, the Portuguese king instructed his sailors to take a more direct route from Africa to India, which led to the discovery of the uninhabited Mascarene Islands. Réunion, previously known as *Île Bourbon*, Mauritius, known as *Île de France*, and Rodrigues were 'discovered' in 1512 by the Portuguese sailor

Dom Pedro Mascarenhas, from whom the archipelago takes its name. Other versions, however, say that the largest island, Mauritius, was discovered in 1507 by Diego Fernandez Pereira, who called the island Cirné after his caravel; or in 1511 by Domingos Fernandez, whose name is attached to the island on some early maps. It hardly strengthens Pereira's claim that Pliny in the first century referred to an island 'opposite Ethiopia' called Cerne.[8]

Whichever Portuguese sailor arrived first, the sixteenth-century discovery was 'for Europe', since the islands were already known to Arab traders and may have been visited by Admiral Zheng He's treasure fleet which called at Zanzibar and the coast of Africa between 1417 and 1431. Neither Arabs nor Chinese established settlements and nor did the Portuguese, who felt safer keeping closer to the African coastline; they set up bases at Quiloa (Kilwa) and Sofala in Mozambique, Malindi and Zanzibar. The Dutch arrived in the Mascarene Islands in 1598. Chancing upon the central island of the group, they named it for Maurits of Nassau, Prince of Orange, who had inherited the Dutch Republic role of *stadhouder* from his father, Willem the Silent.

Mauritius (to use the island's Anglicised name) is an atoll surrounded on three sides by coral reefs. Lying at 20° S, it was well placed for ships making the long voyage to Batavia and keeping south of the Equator, as is clear from the 1754 map of the Indian Ocean by the French map-maker Jacques-Nicolas Bellin.

In Europe, the Dutch had broken free of Spanish control and King Philip II of Spain had inherited Portugal. Dutch ships were no longer welcome in Spanish or Portuguese controlled ports, so the Dutch needed to create settlements of their own if they were to dominate or monopolise the spice trade, as was their aspiration. They built a settlement on the south-east corner of the island, variously known as Mahébourg Bay, Port Sud-Est or Port Bourbon, and nowadays as Vieux Grand Port; they named their fort Frederik Hendrik after Prince Maurits' half-brother.[9] They then exploited the island's plentiful supply of ebony wood, which they shipped to Europe for furniture making, and ambergris, a product of the sperm whale found washed up on beaches, which they used to make perfume. A raucous image of Dutch mariners shows them gorging on local foodstuffs: they brought to extinction the dodo, a flightless bird, though rats they inadvertently carried in their ships played a role too. The native turtle also became extinct, but has been reintroduced from other Indian Ocean islands. More positively they introduced deer and other animals from Java, as well as the cultivation of cane sugar.

The Dutch stayed from 1638 to 1710 (with a six-year break from 1658). Negotiations leading to the 1667 Anglo-Dutch Treaty of Breda provided that each nation hold onto territory they occupied, so the Dutch wanted to be in possession of this important 'tavern' protecting their lucrative trade in East Indian spices; just as importantly, they wanted to keep it out of the hands of the English and French. The Dutch hold on both Mauritius and Cape Town made it harder for ships of these rival trading nations to reach the Indies.

The Dutch settlement in Mauritius never exceeded 300 Europeans and a small number of indentured labourers. There were many reasons for their departure in 1710. By then they were making big profits shipping spices from the East Indies, while supplies of ebony on Mauritius had been exhausted. Although Port Sud-Est provided good protection for ships and was easy to enter, it was hard to sail out of the bay during the south-westerly winds that blow from April to September, so ships often stayed longer than intended waiting for the wind to turn.

The major factor influencing the withdrawal was that Cape Town was a going concern in Dutch hands. After refuelling there, Dutch vessels would make the long crossing to Java without any further need to stop, reducing the risks of bad weather and attacks from pirates then operating around the Mascarene Islands. By taking the so-called 'Brouwer Route' which benefited from the 'Roaring Forties' winds around latitude 40° S, they could halve the time taken to reach Java from Europe, though since there was as yet no accurate way to determine longitude, the option was a bit hit and miss.[10]

THE FRENCH

The French had already settled the smaller adjacent island of Bourbon (named for their Bourbon dynasty), so now seized their chance, though it cannot have been difficult after the Dutch departed. Mauritius had better

Dutch mariners feasting in Mauritius, as shown in this 1598 image by Theodore de Bry, contributed to the extinction on the island of tortoises and the flightless dodo bird.

ports than Bourbon and allegedly a better climate. After a particularly severe storm on Bourbon they pounced on Mauritius, planting a flag there and establishing a settlement from 1721; they renamed it *Île de France*, and the south-eastern port favoured by the Dutch they named *Port Bourbon*. They chose for their settlement a port in the north-west which the Dutch had called Port Moluccas, which was both larger and easier to navigate in and out.[11] They named it *Port Louis* for their king, Louis XIV, and it became the base for the governor-general of *Île de France* and *Bourbon* during France's 90-year rule. Another map, by Pieter van der Aa, shows the island in 1714, when the south-eastern port was still in use.

France's strategic plan was to build a naval base at Port Louis from which to protect trading settlements in Arabia, Persia and especially India, where England's establishment of a base at Madras in 1639 threatened French settlements on the Malabar coast and in the Bay of Bengal. They aimed to make the two islands productive, succeeding where the Dutch had failed, and to create a storehouse for goods on their way to and from settlements in India.

French rule is remembered for two towering figures. The fifth governor, Bertrand-François Mahé, Comte (Count) de La Bourdonnais, presided for eleven years 1735–46 and is credited with developing both islands. A former trader who had served with the Portuguese in India before becoming an officer of the *Compagnie des Indes Orientales*,[12] he understood the importance of a forward defence position to protect France's trade with its settlement at Pondicherry on India's Coromandel coast. He created a naval base at Port Louis which could repair vessels damaged on the India run and build its own ships.

La Bourdonnais developed the sugar industry, opening the first refinery at Pamplemousses, north of Port Louis.[13] The Dutch had introduced cane sugar from Java but it was not a commercial success, or may just have been eclipsed by spices. Responding to the growing popularity of tea and coffee in Europe in the late seventeenth century, La Bourdonnais helped Mauritius become the major sugar producer that it remains today. Coffee grew well on Bourbon (which La Bourdonnais also governed), having been introduced from Mocha on the Arabian peninsula in 1718. Sugar from Mauritius and coffee from Bourbon were in even greater demand in France when the Napoleonic Wars cut supplies from Java and the West Indies.

La Bourdonnais introduced cotton and indigo as well as wheat, rice and cassava. To run new farms he brought experts from France and enslaved peoples from Madagascar and west Africa, so the population climbed sharply from the 300 or so inhabitants when he arrived. But these particular slaves were supposedly treated more as migrant labourers, enjoying a gentler regime in these islands than their countrymen taken to the West Indies.

The importance of the new naval base at Port Louis was demonstrated when the Pondicherry-based governor of French India summoned help from La Bourdonnais, who immediately led a naval squadron to defend French interests in India. They attacked the English off the Coromandel coast, besieging their trading base at Madras 160 kilometres north of Pondicherry, capturing Fort St George and taking the English governor hostage. The French also took control of the old Portuguese settlement of *São Tomé*

This 1714 map of Mauritius by Pieter van der Aa shows the south-eastern harbour by Fort Fredrik Hendrik, and on the opposite side of the island the north-western harbour, later Port Louis.

with its cathedral, in whose vault it is said lies the body of St Thomas. This struggle between European powers resonated beyond the coastal ports, since the English and French had allied with different rulers in the south and east of India.

The Treaty of Aix-la-Chappelle in 1748 brought peace and the return of Madras to the English after nearly three years' occupation, a turning point in the colonial history of India. England's rivalry with France for control of Madras, as well as Palashi or 'Plassey' in Bengal, was as much a war for control of the spice trade as those between the English and Dutch the previous century.

The siege of Madras and its outcome had a costly impact on the career of Mahé, Comte de La Bourdonnais, who quarrelled almost as much with the French governor in Pondicherry, Joseph François Dupleix, as with the British. Voltaire called La Bourdonnais a bold genius who was 'the avenger of France and the victim of envy'.[14] He is regarded as the man who made the island matter in a strategic and military sense and viable in a commercial sense. His statue stands in front of the harbour he developed at Port Louis and he gave his name to Mauritius' southern port city (Mahébourg) near where Europeans had first landed on the island; also to Mahé, the largest island of the Seychelles archipelago north of Mauritius, which came under French control during La Bourdonnais' term. La Bourdonnais was responsible for bringing indentured labourers from India to give Mauritius a non-European population. One of his successors, David Charpentier de Cosigny, wrote that 'the Île de France will one day astonish Europe and Asia by its riches ... in the course of time it will have great influence on the commerce of Europe in the Indies, and incalculably extend the advantages of the nation who possesses it, in that quarter of the globe'.[15]

PIERRE POIVRE

The second Frenchman associated with Mauritius and the history of spices is Pierre Poivre, who broke the Dutch monopoly of clove and nutmeg cultivation.[16] Poivre spent his early life as a trainee missionary in China, before fate led him in a different direction as a botanist and ultimately a colonial administrator. Returning from China his ship, the *Dauphin*, was attacked by the English as it passed through the Bangka Straits off Sumatra. Poivre was hit by a cannonball in the right arm and put ashore at Dutch-ruled Batavia to have his arm amputated.

This ended his ambition to become a missionary and gave him a chance to research the prized spices under Dutch control while recovering in

The inner harbour at the French settlement of Port Louis, in a photographic print by Frederick Fiebig, c.1853.

hospital at Batavia. It is not clear whether he set out to disprove the theory of the German/Dutch botanist Georg Eberhard Rumphius that plants grow where they do for a reason and cannot readily be transplanted elsewhere. Poivre may have felt that France deserved as much as the Dutch to prosper from the spice trade. He believed that both the volcanic soil and the tropical heat of Mauritius were sufficiently close to those of the spice-growing islands around Ternate and Banda, and became determined to take seedlings from the Spice Islands to cultivate elsewhere – at risk of death if the Dutch were to catch him violating their monopoly.

In 1751 he sailed to Manila in an attempt to reach a northern spice island not closely watched by the Dutch, supported by the Spanish governor of the Philippines. The Spanish had no love for the Dutch who had ousted them from control of the United Provinces. Poivre was dependent on financial support from the *Compagnie's* governor in Pondicherry, Joseph François Dupleix, who was not persuaded by his argument that transplanting spice seedlings was the path to profit; hence the first mission was cut short when the funding ran out.

For Poivre's second mission he sailed via Timor, an island to the south of Banda which was partly under Portuguese control. The sympathetic Portuguese governor gave him a number of clove and nutmeg seedlings which he took back to Mauritius, but they did not flourish or – Poivre suspected – may have been destroyed on the orders of Dupleix. He returned to France unable to fulfil a promise to present France's king with 'a French nutmeg'.

When the French government took over administration of Mauritius and Bourbon in 1767, ending the trading privileges of the *Compagnie des Indes Orientales* and appointing its own administrators, Poivre was surprised to be appointed deputy governor responsible for finance. It was exactly a hundred years since the Anglo-Dutch treaty signed at Breda had shored up the Dutch spice monopoly by giving them control of Pulau Run.

Poivre took his family to Mauritius and purchased Monplaisir, the home built by La Bourdonnais at Pamplemousses, and developed there extensive botanical gardens, planting crops introduced from other lands including breadfruit, mango, durian, avocado and mangosteen. He had not lost sight of the plan to cultivate spices on the island. His financial responsibilities prevented him from leaving the islands, so he sent a trusted aide, Povost, to the Spice Islands. Povost collected clove and nutmeg seedlings with the assistance of a sympathetic village headman. Narrowly escaping inspection by a Dutch patrol boat, he dispersed his precious cargo between two vessels for safety and sailed via Portuguese-ruled Timor to reach Mauritius in June 1770 with 400 rooted nutmeg plants and 70 small clove trees.

Poivre planted these at Monplaisir to produce the first 'French' cloves and nutmegs. After Poivre left Mauritius neither spice flourished, but he had taken the wise precaution of sending plants to Madagascar, Zanzibar (now the world's main clove producer) and Martinique in the Caribbean. Poivre had broken the Dutch spice monopoly before the British. But he was not the first to disprove Rumphius' 'native plants' theory: Asian ginger had already been successfully cultivated in Jamaica in the late sixteenth century, while tea, coffee and sugar had all been transplanted away from their

An illustration from an early edition of the French novel, Paul et Virginie, *1806.*

original habitats. Later vanilla and chocolate from the Americas would be successfully introduced to Mauritius.

A third French figure who put Île de France on the map, at least in a literary sense, was Bernardin de Saint-Pierre who arrived on the island in 1768 and whose account of the journey, *Voyage à l'Île de France*, has already been cited. Some years after returning to France, de Saint-Pierre wrote a novel based on events in Mauritius that captured the popular imagination and earned a respected place in French literature. *Paul et Virginie* is a love story based around the *Saint Géran*, one of four ships wrecked off Port Louis in 1615 which claimed many lives including that of Pieter Both, the first governor of the Dutch East Indies. Among those drowned were three young women due to be married at Mauritius.

De Saint-Pierre's novel was a satire on the class structure of eighteenth-century France which he compared unfavourably with the social equality of Mauritius, whose inhabitants shared possessions and cultivated land together. When enslaved people were mistreated in this account, the book's heroes confronted their cruel masters. De Saint-Pierre's arguments for social equality and against slavery chimed with those advanced by the French philosopher Jean-Jacques Rousseau and other 'prophets' of the European Enlightenment and led to changes in France's colonial policy. Mahé de La Bourdonnais, a friend of De Saint-Pierre, appears in the novel as a force for good.

THE BRITISH

France held onto Île de France through the eighteenth century, regarding it as an important plank in the defence of its territories in India. In 1766 William Pitt the Elder became prime minister of Britain. His personal wealth and parliamentary seat derived from his grandfather's trade in India, so he was acutely conscious of the importance to Britain of India. He presided over the defeat of allies of the French at Plassey in 1757, causing him to declare that 'as long as the French have Île de France, the English will not be the masters of India'.[17] France may have felt that control of Mauritius secured its factories in India, but Britain felt they threatened its own command over a much greater part of India.

Another British victory, over France's ally Tippu Sultan at Seringapatnam in southern India in 1799, increased rivalry between the two European powers, though events in Europe also played their part. Napoleon became emperor of France in 1804 and fought a series of battles against Britain and other European powers – the Napoleonic Wars. France's last Mauritius-based governor, Captain General Charles Decaen, found himself starved of resources to defend the island when all available men were committed to delivering the Napoleonic victory at Austerlitz in 1805. Decaen engaged in a bit of flattery on the emperor's birthday in 1806 by renaming Port Louis *Port Napoleon*; Port Sud-Est became *Port Imperial*; and the island of Bourbon became *Île de Bonaparte*. Napoleon may already have given up hope of retaining Mauritius, as a conversation with the brother of the island's governor suggests. Napoleon told René Decaen: 'I have never been able to understand why they [the British] didn't take it. It's sheer idiocy on their part.'[18]

The remark was prophetic. A blockade by British ships caused food shortages. In desperation the governor encouraged pirates based in Madagascar to raid British ships heading to or from India. Lord Minto, Britain's governor-general in India, sent a large fleet from Bombay supplemented by vessels from Cape Town, which the English had retaken in 1806. It captured Rodrigues without difficulty in 1809, then Réunion the following year. The main target though was Île de France, the French seat of government and the only one of the three islands with decent ports.

An attempt to land a small force from Réunion in the south-west was a failure, resulting in a resounding victory for the French; all four English battleships were captured or run aground on the tricky coral protecting the port, with many soldiers and sailors taken prisoner. The Battle of Grand Port is regarded as Napoleon's final naval triumph after his defeats at the hands of the British at Aboukir Bay (1798) and Trafalgar (1805).

In a second assault, the English landed without opposition on the north of the island and marched overland to Port Napoleon, the seat of government. Decaen's forces were outnumbered and the French surrender came swiftly on the morning of 3 December 1810. It was said that French settlers loyal to the former monarch Louis XVIII, who by then was in exile in Britain, were not unhappy at the British conquest which brought an end to the island's blockade. Under the terms of the surrender, the inhabitants could keep their religion, their laws and their customs, including use of the French language. At formal peace negotiations in Paris in 1814, Britain agreed to return Réunion to France but retained control of Île de France, which it renamed Mauritius, as well as Rodrigues. France retained control of Pondicherry and other coastal enclaves in India. But neither country any longer threatened the other in the Indian Ocean.

CHARLES DARWIN AND OTHER VISITORS

A prominent Dutch visitor to Mauritius in the 1640s was Abel Tasman, who sailed there from Batavia on a journey that would 'discover' the Australian island which took his name, Tasmania, as well as New Zealand and Fiji, territories previously unknown to Europeans. The French explorer Louis Antoine de Bougainville called at Mauritius on his return from a two-year circumnavigation during which he claimed for France several Pacific Ocean islands including Tahiti and Bougainville, which stills bears his name. In Mauritius he was presented with a purple flower brought from Brazil by a botanist friend of Poivre, who named it as a tribute to 'this great navigator'. The colourful *bougainvillea* flourishes in Mauritius and much of the tropics.

The British naturalist Charles Darwin visited Mauritius in 1836, as well as St Helena and Ascension. This was his famous voyage on HMS *Beagle*, collecting evidence for the theory of evolution that he was to expound twenty-two years later.[19] By this time all three islands were occupied by Britain. Darwin noted that in Mauritius even the English spoke to their servants in French; he described labourers brought from India to work the plantations as 'noble-looking figures'; and he suggested that the excellent state of the island's roads was the reason for its prosperity. He was impressed by the brilliance of the green fields, a result of extensive cultivation of sugar cane, and noted that sugar production had increased 75-fold since the English took control: 'considering the present large export of sugar, this island ... when thickly peopled, will be of great value'.

After a brief stop at Cape Town, which was also under British control, Darwin arrived at St Helena, which he recorded 'rises abruptly like a huge black

A watercolour portrait of Charles Darwin on the occasion of his marriage, in 1840.

castle from the ocean'. He spent several days wandering across the island; he was fascinated to find a total of 746 species of plant, of which only 52 were indigenous to the island, the remainder having been introduced mainly from England. He was intrigued to find in the soil some shells of several extinct sea creatures. He concluded: 'There is so little level or useful land, that it is surprising how so many people, about 5000, can subsist here.' He commented on how well fortified was Jamestown, with small forts and guns 'filling up every gap in the rugged rock'. This may have given an impression that there was something worth defending fifteen years after Napoleon's death, though more likely these measures were designed to keep out Britain's trading rivals, the Dutch and the French.

Darwin then called at Ascension, an arid island entirely without trees and 'very far inferior to St Helena' in this and every other respect. There he encountered plenty of rats and mice, which he believed were imported, but no native birds, only the abundant guinea fowl imported for food from the Portuguese-ruled Cape Verde Islands. Cows and horses had joined the goats introduced earlier by the Portuguese, and the island's springs were well managed for the benefit of its residents and visiting sailors. Later Darwin and another British naturalist, Joseph Hooker, instituted a programme of tree planting on the island with the help of the Royal Botanical Gardens at Kew.

Darwin refers to both Ascension and St Helena in his ground-breaking *Origin of Species* when discussing the naturalisation of plants. The barren island of Ascension, he says, 'aboriginally possessed under half a dozen flowering plants; yet many have become naturalised ... In St Helena there is reason to believe that the naturalised plants and animals have nearly or quite exterminated many native productions.' He concludes that oceanic islands often have a high proportion of endemic species found nowhere else, and that without certain natural species they have often been 'more fully and perfectly' stocked by human visitors. Darwin never visited Poivre's botanical gardens at Pamplemousses in Mauritius, or if he did he does not mention it. There he would have found extensive evidence for the cultivation and naturalisation of non-native plant species, including those previously endemic to the Spice Islands.

9/

BOMBAY, GATEWAY OF INDIA

Bombay grew from humble origins to be one of the most important ports in Asia. Its vast natural harbour provided shelter to wind-blown vessels arriving from the Arabian Sea. Before European traders arrived in the early sixteenth century, vessels from Arabia made use of the inner shore of its harbour. The novelist Salman Rushdie was born in the city and tells rhapsodically of its origins in his 1981 novel *Midnight's Children*:

> The fishermen were here first ... before the East India Company built its Fort ... at the dawn of time when Bombay was a dumbbell-shaped island tapering, at the centre, to a narrow shining strand beyond which could be seen the finest and largest natural harbour in Asia ... when Mazagaon and Worli, Matunga and Mahim, Salsette and Colaba were islands too— in short before reclamation, before tetrapods and sunken piles turned the Seven Isles into a long peninsula like an outstretched, grasping hand, reaching westwards into the Arabian Sea ... the fishermen—who were called Kolis—sailed in Arab *dhows*, spreading red sails against the setting Sun ... and before you could blink there was a city here, Bombay.[1]

The court of Mughal emperor Akbar I meeting at his Delhi durbar, c.1820. The British resident is prominent on the left.

Was Venice the inspiration? One writer calls the Government Secretariat completed in 1874 'a textbook translation of the Doge's Palace'.[2] In fact it was London that inspired the remarkable development of Bombay, as the Victoria Terminus and the Prince of Wales Museum testify, and the presence of a cricket pitch near the heart of the city. Yet the number of Catholic churches – allegedly one on each of the original islands – demonstrate that the city also has a Portuguese past. It seems remarkable that three European nations – Portugal, the Dutch Republic and England – fought for control of this harbour, to which none of them had any entitlement. Just as remarkably, the port which initially offered nothing but a safe haven for sailing vessels should 'before you can blink' have grown into one of the world's largest and most prosperous trading cities.

A view of the islands that make up Bombay, looking east in 1803 before they were joined up to enclose the large natural harbour beyond.

THE GEOGRAPHY

Tradition has it that Bombay was created by the merger of seven islands, though it is by no means certain that they were true islands in the first place rather than parts of the mainland disconnected at high tide. Nor is it clear which the original seven were. Rushdie includes Salsette, not generally regarded as one of the originals. What is clear is that the islands

were connected to each other and then to the mainland through a process of drainage and land reclamation that continues to this day. If Bombay was originally made up of seven distinct islands, most sources list them, from south to north, as: Colaba, Old Woman's Island (sometimes known as Little Colaba), Bombay (Rushdie's dumbbell), Mazagaon, Worli, Parel (also known as Matunga) and Mahim. These may have been the *Heptanesia* referred to by Claudius Ptolemy in his *Geographia* written around AD 150, or the *Sesecreienæ* mentioned in *The Periplus of the Erythræan Sea*.[3]

We get an idea of how the area may have appeared before all the islands were joined from the imagined 'aerial view' in 1803, looking eastwards. At the front centre is Bombay island, already merged as one landmass with Mazagaon, Parel, Worli and Mahim. To its south (right) is the spur of Colaba island, as yet unconnected. To the north (left) of Bombay island are Bandra, and beyond it Salsette and Trombay, islands later incorporated into the city. The hills in the distance are on the mainland beyond the harbour. A 1756 image by the French hydrographer Jacques-Nicolas Bellin, also looking eastwards, gives a clearer depiction of the relationships between islands before Colaba and Old Woman's (or Women's) islands to the south (right) and Salsette to the north (left) were merged with the landmass at the centre.

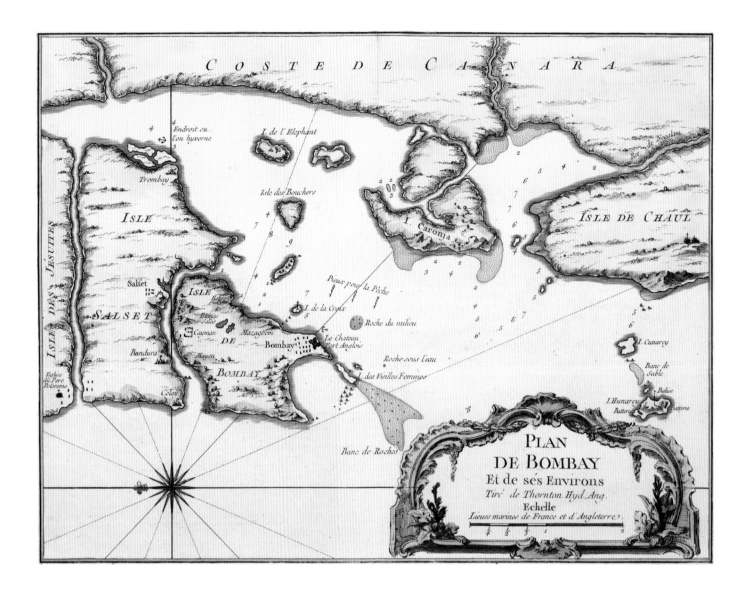

Within the map:

COSTE DE CANARA

Endroit ou l'on hyverne

I. de l'Elephant

Trombay

Isle des Bouchers

ISLE DES JÉSUITES

ISLE

Saliet

ISLE

DE

Mazagéem

Bombay

BOMBAY

Bandura

Colay

Balize du Pere Poloremo

I. Caronja

ISLE DE CHAUL

Pieux pour la Pêche

I. de la Croix

Roche du milieu

Le Chateau Fort Anglois

Roche sous l'eau

I. des Vieilles Femmes

Banc de Roches

I. Cunarey

Banc de Sable

Balise

I. Hunarey Batterie

Batterie

PLAN
DE BOMBAY
Et de ses Environs
Tiré de Thornton Hyd. Ang.
Echelle
Lieues marines de France et d'Angleterre

Neither image bears much resemblance to the shape of the city today, but both give an indication of the large natural harbour which was the port's chief attraction, though not of its scale. Cave temples on Elephanta island are the earliest evidence of habitation in the region. At the harbour mouth are the islands of Henery (Hunarey) and Kenery (Cunarey), once inhabited by pirates.

A Portuguese expedition to Bombay in 1529 named it *ilha da bôa vida*, the island of good life, reflecting the pleasant time the sailors spent there. The name 'Bombay' may be an English corruption of the Portuguese for 'good bay' – *bôa báia* – though another theory suggests that the name derives from the *bombil*, the Marathi name of a tasty fish found in Indian waters, curiously known in its dried form as 'Bombay duck'. The Hindu goddess Mumbadevi is the nearest the city has to a patron saint, at least as far as its Hindu population is concerned. They campaigned for the city to be renamed Mumbai, which happened by an act of the Indian parliament in 1995. *Mumba* means 'mother' in Marathi, the language of the city and its surrounding state of Maharashtra.

Jacques-Nicolas Bellin's map of Bombay and its harbour in 1756, before Salsette was linked to Bombay island by causeways.

THE HISTORY

Early Bombay is the story of the Koli community, who made a living by fishing and rice farming and cultivated the palm tree from which the alcoholic beverage toddy is fermented. As Salman Rushdie writes, they 'caught pomfret and crabs and made fish-lovers of us all'. They gave their name to Colaba, the most southerly district of Bombay which retains a small fishing harbour. When English traders came, Kolis were hired to load and unload their ships. Later, Kolis were transported as far afield as Mauritius, Réunion and the West Indies to work on sugar and coffee estates, reversing the Portuguese practice of enslaving people in Madagascar and bringing them to India.[4]

The Romans never came to Bombay, their focus in India being on the spice ports of the south. The Venetian explorer Marco Polo visited Thana on the mainland opposite Salsette island in 1292 and reported a lively seaborne trade. He says the area was ruled by a king who was 'tributary to none'. Noting there was no pepper to be found there, Polo describes it as 'a busy centre of commerce and a great resort of merchant shipping, exporting leather goods worked in various styles of excellent quality and design ... plenty of good buckram[5] and cotton as well'. Merchants from Arabia brought gold, silver, brass and other goods 'which the kingdom required in exchange for such wares as they hope to sell profitably elsewhere'.[6]

Bombay island and its surroundings were captured in 1348 by the Muslim king of Gujarat, who defeated a Hindu rival from southern India. Its trade with Arabia increased during this period and may have eclipsed that with Surat, Gujarat's main port 500 kilometres to the north, closer to the Red Sea. The Goan author of *The Origins of Bombay* writes that the kings of Gujarat 'did nothing to improve the condition of the island, except, if tradition speaks truly, [by] the plantation of some fruit trees at Mahim'.[7] Gujarat ruled the area until 1534 when its king, Bahadur Shah,[8] signed the Treaty

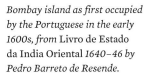

Bombay island as first occupied by the Portuguese in the early 1600s, from Livro de Estado da India Oriental *1640–46 by Pedro Barreto de Resende.*

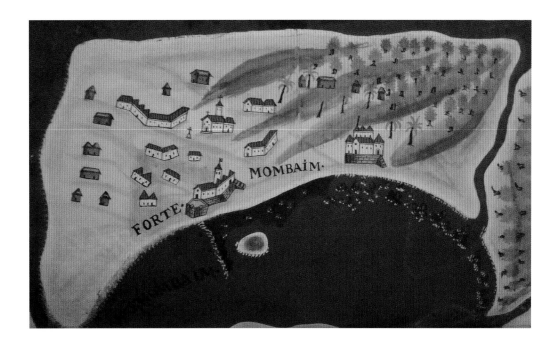

of Bassein with the Portuguese governor, Nuno da Cunha, putting the islands together with the mainland settlements of Chaul, Bassein, Daman and Diu Island under the control of the Portuguese king.

A slightly earlier map by Bellin (see page 195) shows the key European settlements at that time (with minor variations in their spelling): from Cochin and Calicut on the Malabar coast in the south, through Goa on the Konkan coast, to Chaul, Bombay, Salsette, Bassein and Daman, to Surat, Swally and Baruch on the coast of Gujarat. Across the Gulf of Cambay lies the island of Diu where the Portuguese built a fort. Possession of Bassein gave the Portuguese control of shipping between India and the Red Sea with the power to collect customs dues and engage in that long-established tradition of the coast, piracy.

Bassein's proximity to Goa meant that they did not give serious consideration to using Bombay's sheltered harbour as an alternative base, despite one viceroy, Antonio de Melo e Castro, writing to his king: 'I see the best port your majesty possesses in India, with which that of Lisbon is not to be compared … [is] treated as of little value by the Portuguese themselves.'[9] A map of Bombay island in 1646 looking west shows a mole, or quay, stretching into Bombay harbour and the Portuguese fort in the position where the English would later build theirs.[10] The grand house on the right is probably the Manor of Mazagaon, where an agreement would be signed to hand over the island to the English.

Surat Castle, built by the English as their first trading post in India, shown in a picture by French cartographer Alain Mallet around 1690.

A MILITARY ALLIANCE MASQUERADING AS A ROYAL DOWRY

The English were latecomers to the trade in Asian spices, joining long after the Portuguese and just behind the Dutch. They came first to Surat near what is now the frontier between Pakistan and India, establishing a trading base there in 1612 after defeating the Portuguese at the sea battle of Swally (properly called Suvali) off the Gujarat coast, thereby ending Portugal's monopoly of European trade with India. Surat, lying on the Tapi River which discharges into the Gulf of Cambay, provided a good anchorage. They chose it as much because the Portuguese had not settled there, though the English also saw an opportunity to trade with Arabia and Persia for which Surat was well suited, though it was not close to the spice-producing region of Malabar. By the 1670s, Surat was trading silk and satin cloth from Ahmedabad, indigo dye from Agra, woven cloth from Baruch (Broach) as well as calico and chintz, different qualities of cloth from southern India; also goods brought from Bantam in Java and China, such as sugar, tea, porcelain, lacquerware, quicksilver, zinc and copper, elephants' teeth from Sumatra, seashells from Siam and fine wool and coffee from Persia.[11]

The English built a fort at Surat, pictured here by Alain Mallet, and described in a later publication as 'a great City of Indostan, commonly called the Mogul Empire in India'.[12] They were, however, most attracted by the protection afforded by Bombay harbour. India's west coast is notorious for the severity of its monsoons, so the prospect was appealing of a haven where ships could anchor until the wind changed direction to favour the home-bound voyage.

Initially the Portuguese presence at Bombay deterred the English from settling there; however, with their Dutch allies, they made an attempt to take the harbour in 1626, which failed. Instead they took control in 1639 of an area of south India on the east-facing Coromandel coast, the first part of India over which the English claimed sovereignty, a more fully 'colonial' occupation than at Surat. It was close to São Tomé, the settlement founded by the Portuguese a century earlier to mark the alleged martyrdom of St Thomas. There the English built Fort St George and – as later would be the case at Bombay – the city grew around the fort, becoming known as Madras, later Chennai. Wars between the English and the French would be fought off India's Coromandel coast.

Bombay remained an English target, and in 1652 the council of the East India Company in Surat sent a recommendation to London that negotiations be opened for the purchase of the island. By that time the English were at peace with the Portuguese, but had embarked on a series of wars with the Dutch over rival claims to trade with 'the Indies'. Now the Portuguese invited the English to help protect their establishments from attack by the Dutch.

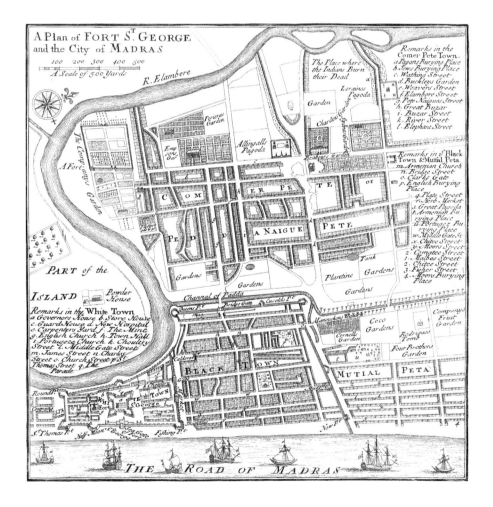

Fort St George, which the English built on the east-facing Coromandel coast at the port of Madras, known now as Chennai, shown in around 1800.

Events in Europe brought Bombay into English hands as part of a royal dowry. King Charles II was restored to the English throne in 1660 after an eleven-year interregnum. The following year it was agreed that he would marry the daughter of the Portuguese king, João IV, Doña Infanta Catarina de Bragança or Catherine of Braganza.[13] The deal, which was hardly a love match, was sealed in the Treaty of Whitehall of 23 June 1661, strengthening an Anglo-Portuguese alliance concluded nearly three centuries earlier; this was when King João I married the sister of King Henry IV of England, Philippa of Lancaster, becoming in due course parents of Henry the Navigator who first started the competition between European nations to control the trade in spices.

The 1661 treaty provided that for 'the better improvement of the English interest and trade in the East Indies ... the King of Portugal ... gives, transfers, and by these presents grants and confirms unto the King of Great Britain, his heirs and successors for ever, the Port and Island of Bombaim in the East Indies with all its rights, profits, territories and appurtenances whatsoever thereunto belonging, and together with all income and revenue, as also the direct and absolute Dominion and Sovereignty of the said Port and Island of Bombay'.[14] Was there ever a more blatant case of a nation giving away territory which did not belong to it in the first place?

A secret article of the treaty obliged 'His Majesty of Great Britain' to restore to the Portuguese any 'Dominions and Conquests of the King of Portugal' which might subsequently fall into Dutch hands, thus creating an alliance against the Dutch. Yet seven weeks later Portugal would sign a trade treaty with the United Provinces (forerunner of the Netherlands), and six years later Britain signed its own peace treaty with the Dutch.

The actual handover of Bombay took some years to come to fruition, because a vital map showing which islands were to be ceded went missing. The terms of the treaty were in any case ambiguous since, as we have seen, what constituted 'the Port and Island of Bombaim' depended on whether it was high or low tide. The fleet that King Charles sent to take possession of the 'gift' was forced to retreat to the uninhabited island of Anjediva[15] off Goa, where many of the soldiers perished. Eventually a deal for the transfer was signed at a manor house overlooking Bombay harbour in 1665. Possibly the Portuguese only intended giving away the unprofitable parts of their colony while retaining the places from which they derived an income, such as Bassein with its plentiful supply of teak.

Portuguese officials in India remained unhappy with the gift. The viceroy who told his king that he was giving up 'the best port your Majesty possesses in India' predicted that 'India will be lost [to Portugal] the same day in which the English nation is settled in Bombay'.[16] The Portuguese may have regretted making the gift, yet the English king felt he got a bad deal. We learn this from the diarist Samuel Pepys who wrote in September 1663 of 'the disappointment the King met ... by the knavery of the Portugall Viceroy, and the inconsiderableness of the place of Bombaim'. Pepys had spoken to the captain of one of the ships sent to take possession of the 'gift', and formed an impression that the Portuguese had swindled the English by misleading them as to its true worth. He continued:

Bellin's map of the west coast of India in 1747. The Vengurla rocks off Goa may have been the heptanesia *or seven islands referred to by Claudius Ptolemy.*

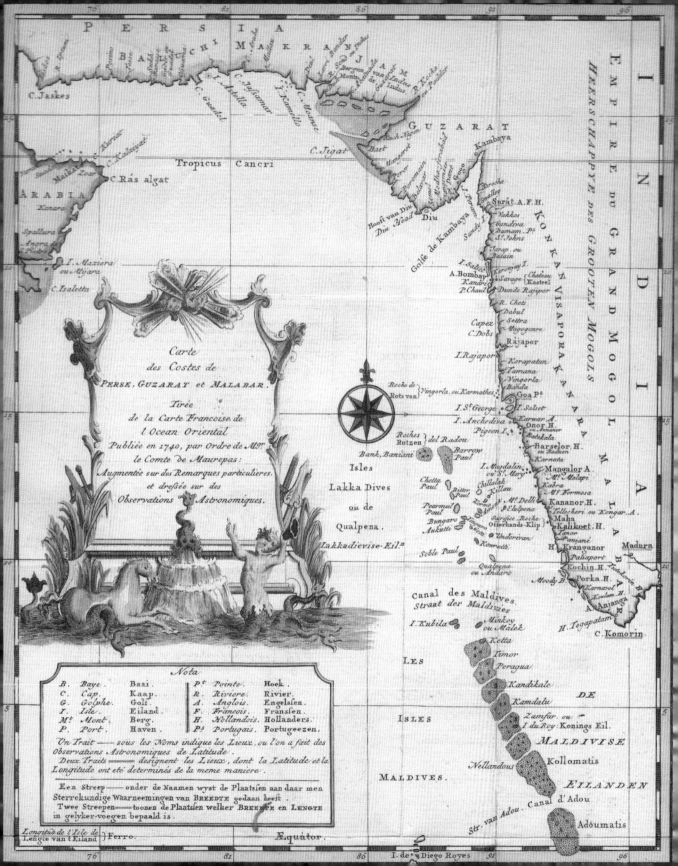

P E R S I A

BALOCHI   MAKRAN   I A M

C. Jaskes

ARABIA

Tropicus Cancri

GUZARAT

C. Jigat   Kambaya

I N D I A

EMPIRE DU GRAND MOGOL

HEERSCHAPPYE DES GROOTEN MOGOLS

KONKAN VISAPORA KANARA MALABAR

Carte
des Costes de
PERSE, GUZARAT et MALABAR.

Tirée
de la Carte Françoise de
l'Ocean Oriental
Publiée en 1740, par Ordre de M.r
le Comte de Maurepas:
Augmentée sur des Remarques particulieres,
et dressée sur des
Observations Astronomiques.

Isles

Lakka Dives

ou de

Qualpena.

Lakkadievise-Eil.ⁿ

Canal des Maldives.
Straat der Maldivies

Goa P.ᵗ

Surat A.F.H.

Madura

C. Komorin

LES   ISLES   DE   MALDIVISE   EILANDEN

MALDIVES.

Canal d'Adou

Adóumatis

Longitud de l'Isle de Ferro.
Lengte van 't Eiland

Æquator.

I. de Diego Royes

It seems strange ... that such a thing as [Bombay], which was expected to be one of the best parts of the Queene's portion, should not be better understood, it being ... but a poor little island, whereas they made the King and Lord Chancellor, and other learned men about the King believe that that, and other islands which are near it, were all one piece, and so the draught was drawn and presented to the King, and believed by the King and expected to prove so when our men come thither, but is quite otherwise.[17]

If the king did not get what he expected in Bombay, the same appeared to be the case with regard to his wife. Catherine's failure to produce an heir and Charles's dalliance with Nell Gwyn and other ladies suggest that he may have been more interested in the promise of the place than of the princess. As Rushdie tells it, 'Catherine ... would all her life play second fiddle to orange-selling Nell'. On 21 September 1668 the cash-strapped king presented his 'poor little island' to the East India Company for the modest consideration of £10 per annum, paid in gold. He probably thought it a bargain to be paid to rid himself of a disappointing 'gift'.

EAST INDIA COMPANY RULE

The inland city of Delhi on the banks of the River Yamuna was the seat of the Mughal rulers who had arrived in India in the 1520s from central Asia. When the Mughals tightened their grip on Surat, the East India Company decided to transfer its main operations to Bombay, which in 1686 became

Part of a panorama from the top of the Lahore Gate of the Red Fort, Delhi, 1846, by artist Mazhar Ali Khan.

one of the company's three 'presidencies' alongside Madras in the south and Calcutta in the east. Early years were spent developing Bombay's trade with the Red Sea and Persian Gulf ports, with China and the East, and with London and Liverpool. A company doctor in 1754 wrote 'when this island was first surrendered to us by the Portuguese, we hardly thought it worth notice'. Now it is 'perhaps the most flourishing of any this day in the universe … the grand storehouse of all the Arabian and Persian commerce'.[18]

In charge in Bombay were company governors (later presidents), of whom Gerald Aungier is regarded as founder of the British city. As Bombay's governor from 1670, he established a mint and a printing press – as the Portuguese had done at Goa – and began developing the city into a commercial centre. Chief trading commodities at first were salt, coconuts, betel nut, rice, ivory, cloth and lead, mostly destined for Persia or Arabia rather than England. Aungier was reminded by East India Company headquarters in London that 'our business is to advantage ourselves by trade and what government we have is but the better to carry on and support that'.[19]

Aungier recognised a need for shipbuilding facilities to provide warships for the company's young navy, the Bombay Marine (forerunner of the Indian Navy), which clashed with Portuguese, French and Dutch vessels as well as well as the notorious Malabar pirates. Also needed was a dry dock to repair sailing ships before they made their long journey homewards around the Cape. The recommendation was first made in 1673, yet it was 77 years before the first dry dock was completed.[20] A hundred years later a British admiral

described Bombay as 'the only Port in the East Indies where a ship of the line can be docked and effectively repaired'.

The word 'bunder', meaning a dock or quay, derives from the Persian – as in *shahbunder* which means 'harbour master' in several languages. Bunder remains in current English usage in Bombay, in the port district of Apollo Bunder for example, and also in Karachi. The name Apollo, one of the original gates of the fort,[21] is thought to come from the palla (or palva or hilsa) fish which was landed at the Koli fishing dock; it is unconnected with the Greek god of that name.

Most credit for shipbuilding and dock construction in Bombay belongs to various Parsi families. The Parsis, more formally Zoroastrians, were followers of a religion that respected fire as a creative, life-giving source. Originally from Persia, hence Parsi, they settled in Gujarat and played a role in developing Surat's ship-constructing business to the satisfaction of both the company and the Mughals, many subsequently migrating with the English to Bombay to develop similar craft skills there. Pioneer shipbuilder Jamshetji Bomanji Wadia, who has been described as 'the real creator of Bombay', was one of several members of the Wadia family to hold the post of Master Builder at the Bombay Dockyard. The first British ship built in Bombay was completed in 1736. The company recorded that 'experience has convinced us that vessels built here of teak timber … are far more durable and proper for the climate than any that can be sent from Europe'. Subsequent output was prolific, and many of the British frigates which fought at the Battle of Trafalgar in 1805 were built in Bombay's dockyards.

In the early eighteenth century the British built a fort adjacent to the harbour which enclosed the governor's residence, the barracks, a hospital and a prison as well as warehouses for the main products, including cotton and opium, that were exported from the nearby quay. An area to the west of the fort known as the Esplanade was cleared of buildings in the 1770s to provide a range of fire: by this time it was an attack by the French that was most feared.[22] A view of the harbour in 1754 by Jean François Daumont shows the customs house prominently, with the mole where vessels would tie up for unloading and loading. The most heavily fortified part of the fort was Bombay Castle, seen on the right in this picture, flying the flag of St George. English defenders came under pressure from the navy of the Mughal Empire; and on the landward side from the Marathas, who took control of Bassein from the Portuguese in 1739. A view of the harbour and castle just over a hundred years later (page 200), looking east from the island, shows that by this time the city was enjoying a commercial boom.

A prominent Parsi was the 'venture capitalist' Sir Cowasji Jehangir Readymoney, whose surname came from his readiness to invest in a variety of projects; Parsis often chose surnames to reflect their profession. A pioneering Parsi in the cotton industry was Jamsetji

Jamshetji Bomanji, the Master Builder at the Bombay dockyard, in an oil painting of 1836.

A hand-coloured print looking west towards the customs house and fort at Bombay, with St Thomas church in the distance, by Jean François Daumont, 1754.

Tata who set up Alexandra Mills. This was the origin of Tata Industries which in modern times have been major players in chemicals, steel, vehicle production and airlines, among other industries.

Another community attracted to the rapidly industrialising city were the Jews, of whom the best known was David Sassoon. He arrived from Iraq following a wave of anti-Jewish persecution there, part of a third influx of Jews to India following those who arrived on the Malabar coast. David Sassoon invested in carpets and cotton, wool and wheat; with his son Abdullah, he is also remembered for building the city's first wet docks, Sassoon Docks, on reclaimed harbourside land. The Sassoon family endowed schools, hospitals and synagogues, making the Jews important players in the city's commercial and social development, alongside Hindus, Muslims, Parsis, Jains and Christians.

The East India Company began the process of linking the islands together more solidly by building embankments and causeways and filling in the mud flats, constructing so-called 'Hornby vellards', named for the British governor who ordered them. The word 'vellard' is derived from the Portuguese *vallado* meaning mound or embankment. Another typically Bombay geographical usage is 'breach' to describe the areas where the sea intruded onto the land separating the original 'islands', as at Breach Candy where the islands of Bombay and Worli were joined. Closure of this gap and the ensuing reclamation of swampland nearly doubled Bombay's area.

Bombay's original islands were linked together by 1838. The much larger island of Salsette[23] to the north, separated from the merged landmass by a

channel half a kilometre wide, was connected in 1845 by the Sion Causeway, enlarging the city further. A second causeway carried India's first railway, completed in 1853, from Bombay to Thana. An important moment for the city was the railway crossing of the Western Ghats, the previously impenetrable mountain range on the mainland; this achievement connected Bombay to the rest of India through a railway network that would eventually reach 68,000 kilometres, giving rise to a steady migration of Indians to the city in search of work.

These labourers needed somewhere to live, so the authorities built residential blocks, tenement homes known as *chawls,* a word of Marathi origin that was later applied to any form of housing. The density of low-cost housing led British town planner Patrick Geddes to remark that inhabitants of the *chawls* were not so much housed as warehoused. Other words to have entered English usage from Bombay include *lascar,* a soldier or sailor, which is of Hindi/Urdu origin. The Maharashtra town and military base of Deolali, which included a mental asylum, gave rise to the expression 'to go doolally', meaning 'to go crazy'. Hindi words incorporated into English include jungle, loot, shampoo – and pukka, meaning genuine.

The gaps between islands had been filled, but the city was not a salubrious habitat. Visitors said it smelled strongly of the fishmeal used to enrich the palm trees which grew coconuts and toddy for making liquor, and whose leaves were used for thatching. Bombay was an unhealthy place to live, and settlers were prone to gastroenteritis, scurvy, malaria, cholera and bubonic plague. An especially severe bout of the plague in 1896 claimed an estimated 56,000 lives. Life for European settlers tended to be short and infant mortality high. The city was densely populated, indeed overcrowded,

A view east of the fort and harbour at Bombay by Thomas Allom and Arthur Willmore around 1850.

and so began a further programme to reclaim land from the sea. Over two centuries Bombay increased its land area considerably, while 'sea bridges' improved north–south communications along the peninsula.

COTTON, TEA AND OPIUM

Bombay traded in goods which previously flowed through Surat, but three additional commodities made Bombay rich: cotton, tea and opium. The company used Bombay as a base from which to penetrate China, which resisted European traders as much as it could. When the company learned that China was short of cotton, it seized the opportunity to ship India-grown cotton, developing Bombay as a milling centre. Mills were built in the area later known as Girangaon (meaning 'mill village') and at Dongri on Bombay island, which gave its name to the coarse cotton known as *dungaree*.[24] By 1900 there were more than 130 mills employing several thousand workers. Initially they were meeting a demand from China, but later they supplied the looms of Lancashire in Britain.

The British developed a taste for the tea that China exchanged for cotton, so company ships returned from China laden with tea which was shipped onwards to Britain. Throughout the eighteenth century the tea drunk in Europe came exclusively from China, some being shipped onwards to Britain's North American colonies. It was Chinese tea that colonists threw into Boston harbour as a protest when the British prime minister, Lord North, imposed a tax on sales of tea. Tea was only cultivated in India from the 1830s, originally from seeds smuggled from China, and developed into an indigenous variety. Indian tea was grown in Assam and Darjeeling in the mountainous north-east and traded through Calcutta (Kolkata) rather than Bombay.[25]

The third commodity of which India had a seemingly unlimited supply, and for which China had a voracious appetite, was opium. In the 1750s

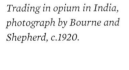

Trading in opium in India, photograph by Bourne and Shepherd, c.1920.

opium grown in Bihar and Bengal constituted nearly half of all Bombay's exports. It made both Britons and Indians wealthy, but led to war between Britain and China's Qing dynasty over trading rights; one outcome was the granting to Britain of sovereign rights over Hong Kong.[26] Cotton then opium were the bedrocks of Bombay's wealth.

The 1850s and 60s were a boom time for Bombay, seeing the first railway (1853), first cotton mill (1854), development of financial, insurance and shipping companies, a chamber of commerce (1836), a stock exchange (1875), and India's first trade union (1884). Bombay University was founded in 1857 and many schools, libraries and hospitals were built around the same time. The Municipal Corporation and the Bombay Port Trust came into existence in the 1870s and a City Improvement Trust in 1898. Bombay was linked to London by electric telegraph in 1870, by which time it was the second city of Britain's empire, larger than Manchester, Glasgow or Dublin. The Reserve Bank of India was founded in the 1930s, close to the site of the original mint, cementing Bombay's position as the commercial capital of India.

Historical chance again intervened to give Bombay an opportunity, when the outbreak of the American Civil War in April 1861 halted the export to Europe of cotton from the southern US states. The millers of

The coastline of Bombay in 1860, looking towards Colaba and the port area of the harbour beyond, by the French artist Isidore-Laurent Deroy.

Lancashire turned their attention to the readily accessible, though inferior, Indian cotton to keep their looms shuttling. Since textiles woven on the Lancashire looms were often shipped back to India, it is likely that this trade retarded industrialisation in India while contributing to Britain's industrial revolution, though at the time it seemed as if both countries benefited. Bombay's industrial progress in the mid-nineteenth century was fuelled by the extension of British rule in India, as it took control of the Deccan plateau, Bihar and Maratha regions, giving it access to cotton- and opium-growing regions.

A British governor of the time, Sir (Henry) Bartle Frere, another titan of the city's development and of the cotton trade in particular, wrote to a business associate in Britain in 1861: 'Cotton has always been a special hobby of mine. The capacity of India to supply cotton is absolutely unlimited ... we can supply you all you want.'[27] The Jain merchant, Premchund Roychund,[28] known as 'the cotton king', suffered financially when the American Civil War ended in May 1865, though the decline was short-lived. For in 1869 Bombay benefited from another event far away: the opening of the Suez Canal made it the most accessible Asian destination for ships arriving from Europe via this 'short cut'.

We get an idea of how the city looked in 1860 from a view south-east from Malabar Hill. It shows the long curve of Back Bay and the burgeoning English settlement around the fort and harbour entrance beyond. Malabar Hill, named for the pirates who used to pay their respects at the Mumbadevi temple there, was still outside city limits. The British governor's residence moved from the fort to Malabar Hill, and many of India's maharajahs or princes built themselves bungalows in the same area.[29]

The events in 1857 known to the British as the Indian Mutiny and to Indians as the First War of Independence had relatively little impact on Bombay, where commerce and the availability of jobs made the population more accepting of British rule: not just manual workers in the docks and mills, but the Parsi, Jewish, Muslim, Hindu and Jain bosses who ran the city's industry. Caste and national and religious differences mattered little in cosmopolitan Bombay, where the main purpose in life was to make money. More than in other British settlements, Indians thrived, not just their foreign overlords.

When in 1858 the whole of India was handed over to the British government, those who made their money by trading may not have remembered that two centuries earlier Bombay had been gifted in the opposite direction, from the king to the company. There was no longer any question of the British monarch, Queen Victoria, treating India as a personal fiefdom, even after she was granted the title Empress of India by Prime Minister Benjamin Disraeli. Running India was too much for one company, which needed to maintain an army and a navy to protect its investment. Arguably the British had already outstayed what welcome they may once have had, though that argument was heard less in Bombay than in other parts of the Queen-Empress's domain.

When the movement against British rule gathered momentum, Bombay played its part. The Indian National Congress, the political party that would

Gengibre.

Dela Nuez Moſcada.

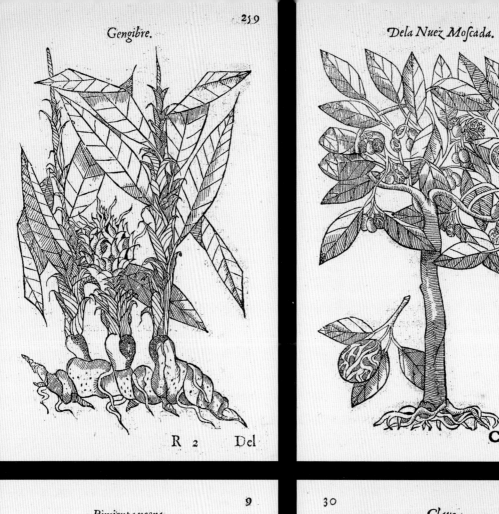

R 2   Del

C 2   De

Pimienta negra.

Clauo.

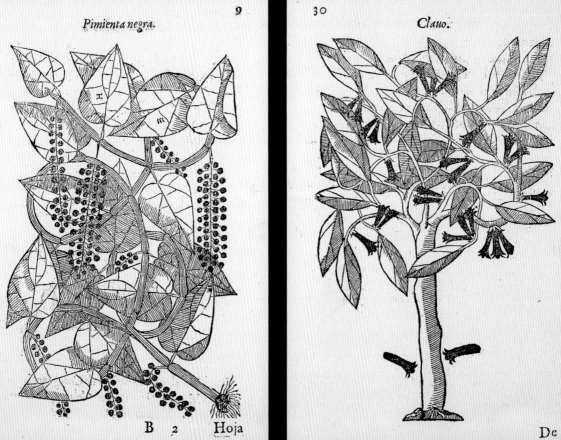

B 2   Hoja

De

Illustrations of spices from
Garcia da Orta's Colloquies,
published in Goa in 1563,
featuring clockwise from top
left: ginger, nutmeg, clove
and pepper.

lead India to independence, convened in the city in 1885. India's chief 'freedom fighter', 'Mahatma' Gandhi, tested philosophies such as *satyagraha* (non-violent resistance) and *swadeshi* (dependence on home-produced products) in Bombay.

GARCIA DA ORTA

In 1548 the king of Portugal granted land on Bombay island to the eminent doctor and herbalist Garcia da Orta, whom we previously encountered in Chapter 3 when he lived in Goa. Da Orta took a lease on the *quinta*, or 'estate', overlooking Bombay harbour on condition that he improved the place. There he created a botanical garden to continue his research on the medicinal properties of plants and completed his famous book on the subject, *Colloquies on the Simples and Drugs of India*.[30] He drew on classical sources, such as the Roman authority Pliny, the Greeks Dioscorides and Galen and the Persian Avicenna, though was not afraid to correct them where he felt they made mistakes.

As well as medicinal plants, da Orta pontificated on fruits such as the durian from Malacca, which he had never seen but had heard it could help treat asthma; those who ate too much could 'lose their heads'. Cannabis, he wrote, helps a man 'to be raised above all cares and anxieties' while women take it 'when they want to dally and flirt with men'. Opium is a good painkiller or relaxant that is also 'efficacious for the work of Venus', but taken in too great quantity can cause impotence. More salaciously, da Orta, who married his cousin and sired two daughters, wrote: 'As those who take opium are beside themselves, the act of Venus comes more slowly ... when the man is slow, the female also reaches the act of Venus more slowly, so that they both complete the act at one time', an intriguing insight into the sexual mores of the time.

Da Orta wrote of the medicinal properties of the spices that first attracted his countrymen to the East. He says cardamom 'draws out inflammations from the head or stomach' while cinnamon is 'used to warm the stomach and the nerves'. He says the best cinnamon comes from Ceylon, but has been transplanted 'from one land to another', an early acknowledgement of a spice being moved from its native place. Root ginger, he says, is good 'against the plague and against poisons' while tamarind infusion has the effect of discharging choleric and phlegmatic humours. Da Orta identifies three varieties of pepper growing in India: black, white and long. White pepper is 'good against poison and for the eyes' and all types are good for cooking.

Of spices from further afield, da Orta says cloves have both medicinal and culinary purposes and are found only in five islands of the Moluccas, where the Spanish and the Portuguese rival each other to gain access. He takes a dim view of his countryman, Magellan, for trying to upstage Portugal for access to cloves: 'The devil entered into a Portuguese, who, because the king would not grant him an unjust favour for which he asked, went over to Castile, fitted out armed ships, and discovered a strait, before unknown, which led by another route to Maluco.' He quotes the sultan of Ternate: 'The clove was given by God to the Portuguese, because each clove contains the five *quintas* (estates) of the Kings of Portugal.'

He says mace, the red-coloured covering of the nutmeg, 'is good for dysenteries' and for 'issues of blood'; made into an oil, it is 'a very good medicine for the nerves' and 'worth three times as much as the nutmeg'. The fleshy outer part of the nutmeg fruit can be mixed with sugar to make a sweet-smelling conserve which is 'very good for the brain and for nervous complaints'. He mentions the unhealthiness of the Banda Islands, adding – reassuringly to his fellow Portuguese – that 'Banda, the native place of the nutmeg, belongs to the King our Lord'.

His account of this 'holy trinity' of clove, nutmeg and mace will have benefited those hoping to find their source. Da Orta, the exiled Portuguese Jew, showed the Dutch and English where to go and look for the spices that were contributing substantially to the wealth of Venice and Lisbon. His book was printed in Goa in 1563 and revised and translated many times. It is not clear how much of it he wrote in Goa and how much in Bombay, where he maintained an extensive library. Da Orta's house, the Manor of Mazagaon, gained its own place in history a century later when the treaty by which Bombay was transferred to the English was signed there on 18 February 1665.

FAMOUS VISITORS

In 1774 the eighteen-year-old British sailor Horatio Nelson visited Bombay. He saw the lights of Old Woman's Island as his ship entered the harbour at two o'clock in the morning.[31] Then 24 years later, after Admiral Nelson defeated Napoleon's navy at the Battle of the Nile, he wrote to the governor of Bombay to say that 40,000 French forces had arrived in Alexandria and he feared they were planning to embark at Suez for India. Nelson wrote: 'I have Bonaparte's dispatches before me ... Bombay, if they can get there, I know is their first object; but, I trust, Almighty God will in Egypt overthrow these pests of the human race ... I am confident every precaution will be taken to prevent, in future, any Vessels going to, Suez, which may be able to carry troops to India.'[32] This was long before the opening of the Suez Canal, at a time when it was widely believed that Napoleon's aim was to capture India for the French.

Nelson's contemporary, Arthur Wellesley, was a British soldier who won his reputation serving the East India Company in India. While his brother Richard (later Lord) Wellesley served as governor-general, Arthur Wellesley helped extend Britain's Indian domain. He led the company's army against Tipoo Sultan who ruled Mysore in the south, and subsequently helped defend Bombay and its hinterland from the Marathas. Britain believed it was protecting native rulers from dominance by the powerful Marathas, while Indians are more inclined to see British policy as one of 'divide and rule': making alliances with some rulers in order to resist others. Arthur Wellesley would later return to Europe to fight Napoleon's forces in Denmark and Portugal, before defeating the French emperor at Waterloo. He was ennobled by his country as the first Duke of Wellington and subsequently held office as prime minister.

The writer Rudyard Kipling was born in Bombay in 1865. His father taught at the School of Art founded by the Parsi, Sir Jamsetjee Jejeebhoy, the son of a cotton merchant who made a fortune trading opium. Rudyard would

later recall early morning walks to the Bombay fruit market with his *ayah*, or nanny, 'a Portuguese Roman Catholic'. He was proud of the city of his birth, and as an adult wrote an ode to Bombay, part of which goes:

> Mother of Cities to me,
> For I was born in her gate,
> Between the palms and the sea,
> Where the world-end steamers wait.

Mumbai, as it is now known, is today one of the most densely populated cities in the world. Its shape bears little resemblance to that of the original islands as a result of extensive reclamation that continued into the twenty-first century; a third of the city area has been reclaimed from the sea. The business of making money still drives the city. From its humble origins, which the Portuguese called 'the island of good life', the British built it into '*urbs prima in Indis*', the first city of India; it became known as the 'Manchester of the East' on account of its cotton processing, and 'City of Gold' because so many fortunes were made there. It is now better known for the song and dance tradition associated with its 'Bollywood' film business.

Clemens et Regni moderatrix iusta Britanni
Hac forma insigni conspicienda nitet.

Tristia dum gentes circum omnes bella fatigant,
Cæciq; errores toto grassantur in orbe.
An:Dñi pace beas longa, vera et pietate Britannos: 1579
Iusticia moderans miti sapienter habenas.
Chara domi, celebrisq; foris, longævaq; regnũ
Hic teneas, regno tandem fruitura perenni.

'*To this city from every nation under heaven merchants delight to bring their trade by sea; the Arabian sends gold; the Sabaean, spice and incense; Scythian, weapons; from its rich soil, Babylon sends palm oil; the Nile, precious stones; Norwegian and Russian send furs such as sable; Seres, her purple clothing; Gaul, her wines.*'

WILLIAM FITZSTEPHEN, C.1175

10/ LONDON, WAREHOUSE OF THE WORLD

The monarch who started England's maritime quest, Queen Elizabeth I, from the atlas of England and Wales by Christopher Saxton, 1579, which pre-dated that produced by John Steed in 1610.

The settlement at a crossing point on the River Thames that we now know as London may date back three millennia, though its foundation as a city is usually linked to the arrival of the Romans around AD 47. They turned the river crossing into a prominent trading centre long before settling Lisbon. Using its name in Old English, the Roman poet Tacitus writes that *Londinium* is much frequented by merchants and trading vessels.[1] The Roman city was burned to the ground in around AD 61 by Boudicca and her Iceni followers from East Anglia, but the Romans restored it in around AD 100 as the capital of their province of Britannia. They built a defensive wall around the city on the northern bank of the River Thames. Roman London grew to have a population of around 60,000.

The departure of the Romans in AD 410 was followed by a period of decline, interrupted by the arrival of other invaders from Europe: the Anglo-Saxons in the seventh century, the Danish king Canute (Knut) early in the eleventh century and William 'the Conqueror' from Normandy later the same century. William was crowned king of England in London's newly completed Westminster Abbey on Christmas Day 1066 and subsequently

209

built the city's fortress, the Tower of London. In 1209 the River Thames was bridged in stone when London Bridge was constructed near the Tower, an act of penitence by King Henry II following the murder in 1170 of Archbishop Thomas Becket of Canterbury. A church on the bridge was dedicated to the archbishop, whom the pope canonised as St Thomas. The bridge was 282 metres long, had nineteen arches and a wooden drawbridge to allow tall vessels to pass. London's main trading areas were the City north of the bridge and Southwark on the south bank. A map from 1541 of Albion (England), Caledonia (Scotland) and Hibernia (Ireland) gives a distorted view of the islands. It shows Londinium's position on the River Thames, which appears to enter the North Sea near the Wash.

   In the late twelfth century, William Fitzstephen, a clerk to Archbishop Becket, wrote of the city's extensive trade links. The Arabians, Scythians and Sabaeans inhabited Arabia; the Seres or 'silk people' are from China; while his reference to the Norwegians and Russians implies trade with the Baltic Sea. London's waterfront was a marketplace for spices, incense and others goods, while grains, hides and metals were the main exports. In his 1598 Survey of London, John Stow chronicles the early years of 'the principal storehouse and staple of all commodities within this realm' and its 'fishful river of Thames' leading to 'the French Ocean'. Stow writes of

German cartographer Martin Waldseemüller's depiction of the British Isles, based on Ptolemaic calculations, first published in 1513.

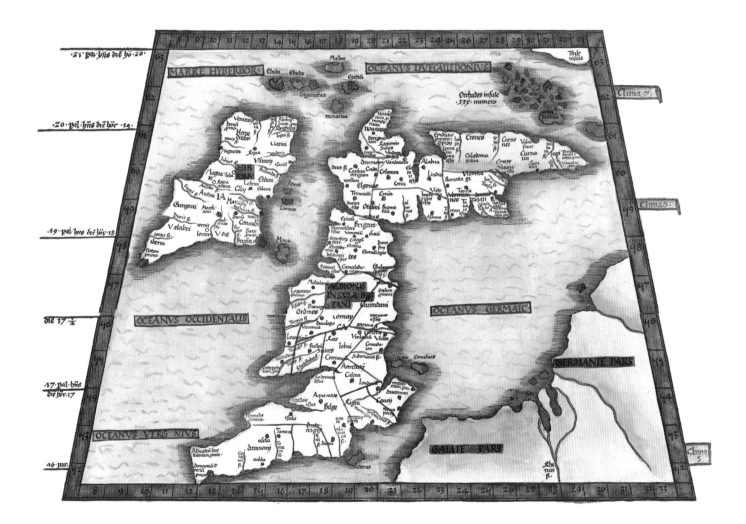

Geoffrey Chaucer, 'the most famous poet of England', whose stories were
published by the English printing pioneer William Caxton in 1476. Another
contemporary of Stow was the map-maker John Speed, who produced a
collection of 54 maps of England, Wales, Scotland and Ireland.[2]

In the mid-sixteenth century so-called 'legal quays' were created on the
Thames to regulate trade, or rather to tax it. Duty on imported goods was
collected at the Customs House, pictured in a view of the Thames in 1770
by Jean François Daumont. Sir Thomas Gresham gave a boost to London
as a trading centre by building the Royal Exchange where merchants could
meet and trade goods. Another view of the city before the Great Fire of 1666
by Joseph Leopold (pages 212–13) looks north to show the original stone-
built London Bridge. Old St Paul's Cathedral stands prominently as does the
Tower of London, while the Royal Exchange is seen in the distance. On the
nearside river bank is Shakespeare's Globe Theatre. Ships' masts around
St Olaf's Church suggest that quays in the area were busy.

THE ELIZABETHAN ERA

The first recorded long-distance voyage from England took place in 1497,
the year Vasco da Gama discovered a route to the East. King Henry VII
sponsored a voyage by a Genoa-born citizen of Venice, Giovanni Cabotto
or John Cabot. Following the example set by Columbus five years earlier,
he tried to find a route to the Spice Islands by sailing west. He set sail from
Bristol in western England and reached the large island we now know as
Newfoundland in Canada, one of the first Europeans to set foot in North
America. The straits between Newfoundland and Cape Breton Island are
named after him.

LONDINUM

1. S. Paul. 2. S. Brides/Bainurds Castle 4. Arondel hause.
5. Sanay. 6. Borley House. 7. Dioham House.
8. Iack House. 9. Kiings Pallast. 10. Cheap Crosse.
11. Bon Churche. 12. Te Gulliarde 13. Cole harbour.
14. S. Laurent. 15. Child Hall. 16 S. Antonius.
17. S. Lorenz Pudney. 18. The Eschange.

Die

LONDON

19. The Dutch Church. 20. S. Mich. 21. S. Peter. 22. Le
aire Hall. 23. Fischmongers Hall. 24. S. Helen. 25. S.
Andrew. 26. S. Dunstand Eart. 27. Lion Kay. 28. Te Bridge.
29. Hackney. 30. Alhalewes. 31. Stepney. 32. The Tour.
33. S. Katharine. 34. S. Olass. 35. S. Mary overus.
36. Vinchester House. 37. The Globe. 38. The Bear.
39. The Sain. 40. The crusch ipes. 41. de Gally Ki.
Ster. 42. Harowe ou the Hill. 43. Hamsted.

Cabot's expedition did not inspire the king to invest in further voyages, so there was a lull in exploratory activity of well over half a century until Henry VII's granddaughter Elizabeth I acceded to the throne in 1558 after a tumultuous period for England's monarchy. Elizabeth's father, Henry VIII, quarrelled with the pope for refusing to grant him a divorce. Henry's response, in line with the religious Reformation sweeping Europe, was to break with the Catholic church and create the Church of England with himself at its head. Henry's elder daughter, Mary, married Philip II of Spain (and later Portugal) in a diplomatic match. The marriage treaty provided that Philip was to share the role of monarch with his wife, notwithstanding that he spoke no English.[3] An act of the English parliament gave him the title 'King of England' though in reality Mary ruled as sole monarch. On her death in 1558, her half-sister Elizabeth took over. Philip never renounced his claim to the English throne, so Elizabeth began her reign with an urgent need to raise money for ships to enable her to fight off the Spanish monarch, who had designs on conquering England and restoring it to Catholicism.

FRANCIS DRAKE

Long-distance sailing with a money-making motivation took off under Elizabeth, who was inspired by the successes of the Portuguese and Spanish. A sailor who came to her attention was Francis Drake, a buccaneer – in other words, a pirate – from Plymouth in Devon who had made a fortune preying on the cargoes of gold and silver that the Spanish brought from Peru and shipped to Spain from *Nombre de Dios* bay on the Panama isthmus. The Spanish Main, as the area was known, was from 1510 under the control of Spain, the most powerful nation in the Western world. Drake, a Protestant, was motivated by greed but justified his bounty-hunting in terms of a religious war against Catholics. His success at plundering ships earned him the nickname among Spanish mariners of *El Draco*, the dragon.

Elizabeth relished the thought of financing a navy to fight the Spanish monarch with the proceeds of pirate raids on Spanish ships; so when Drake moved to London to seek funding for a round-the-world voyage, she became one of the chief financiers. Drake's vessels sailed from Plymouth in December 1577. Following Magellan's lead half a century earlier, he sailed through the straits that bear Magellan's name to enter the Pacific Ocean, the first Englishman to do so. He attacked Spanish treasure ships off the western coast of America before taking the long route home across the Pacific, pausing at the Spice Islands. English mariners had already reached the Nutmeg Islands, but Drake was the first to land on the Clove Islands.

Drake returned from his circumnavigation in 1580 after nearly three years. His ship, the *Golden Hind*, was laden with Spanish gold and silver and a modest amount of cloves from the call he made at Ternate. He had to offload some cloves after running aground on leaving the Clove Islands. The voyage was highly profitable and Drake made a significant return on investment to his queen. According to the twentieth-century economist John Maynard Keynes, Elizabeth used her share of the proceeds to pay off her debts; she invested the balance of £42,000 in the Levant Company (which received its charter in 1592), whose profits were subsequently used to fund the East India Company (EIC), England's main vehicle for overseas expansion. Thus there was a direct link between Drake's plunder of Spanish gold and the formation of the EIC. Keynes calls this 'the origin of British Foreign Investment'.[4]

Drake became a national hero through having triumphed over the Spanish, rather than gaining success in any conventional trading sense. He was considered to have 'captured' the Pacific Ocean, affirming the dictum of another great Elizabethan explorer, Walter Raleigh, that 'Whosoever commands the sea commands the trade; whosoever commands the trade of the world commands the riches of the world, and consequently the world itself.'[5] Raleigh, another Devon-born Protestant, also earned his wealth (and knighthood) preying on Spanish vessels off America, and later established

A broadsheet showing Francis Drake plundering goods on the Spanish Main of central America.

England's first North American settlement which he named Virginia – for his 'virgin' queen, Elizabeth – before pioneering the planting of tobacco there.

Drake's next mission on behalf of his queen – now as Sir Francis Drake – was to lead her naval force in 1588 in resisting Philip of Spain's attempted invasion of England with his fearsome Spanish Armada of 130 ships. He helped precipitate the Armada's sailing by a daring raid on Spanish treasure ships in Cadiz harbour which sank 25 vessels, a raid known as 'the singeing of the king's beard'; he then captured a Spanish galleon carrying funds to pay the Spanish army who were fighting to retain hold of the United Provinces. England's success in defeating the superior Spanish Armada was attributed to the speed and manoeuvrability of its vessels and the prowess of Drake compared with the less experienced Duke of Medina Sidonia who commanded the Spanish fleet. With the Dutch Republic supporting the

East India House in Leadenhall Street, headquarters of the East India Company, pictured in 1817 by Thomas Shepherd.

English, the defeat was a decisive victory by Europe's newly Protestant powers over the Catholic nations that had until then dominated global trade. It also marked England's emergence as a naval power.

THE EAST INDIA COMPANY

England grasped the nettle of international trade with both hands as trade took over from piracy as a means of enrichment. On the last day of 1600, Queen Elizabeth granted a charter to the East India Company 'to break the Dutch monopoly on the spice trade', awarding it exclusive rights to trade in 'East India'. This was more than a year before the VOC was formed in Amsterdam, though the Dutch were ahead of the English in shipbuilding, cartography and finance and had already made trading voyages to the East Indies. Like its Dutch counterpart, the English company had quasi-governmental powers, including rights to enforce laws and maintain an army. As the Dutch were jealous of the Portuguese, who had held similar feelings towards the Venetians, so it was the turn of the English to harbour feelings of avarice towards their Protestant neighbours, the Dutch, who seemed to be ahead of the game.

The East India Company traded initially in spices, then cotton, indigo (a plant dye), tea, silk, sugar and opium. It would soon become the most profitable of several chartered trading companies based in London, laying the building blocks of what would become the British Empire: operating from trading bases in India such as Surat, Bombay and Madras and later

William Daniell's 1808 view of
the newly constructed docks
downriver from the City of
London at Wapping.

Calcutta. The company's transition from trader to ruler dates to 1757, the
Battle of Palashi (or Plassey) in Bengal, not far from Calcutta, when the
company's army defeated the Nawab of Bengal, who was allied with the
French East India Company. The English forces were led by Robert Clive,
who had served his apprenticeship with the company in Madras.

Company rule of India lasted exactly a hundred years until 1857, the
year of the uprising known either as the Indian Mutiny or First War of
Independence; the result was that the British government took over the
task of ruling India. Like the Portuguese in Goa and the Dutch in the East
Indies, another small seafaring European nation had used force to assume
responsibility for administering a much larger Asian territory, enriching
itself handsomely in the process.

Senior East India Company officers like Robert Clive and Warren
Hastings retired to large stately homes in England, with titles or seats in
parliament. Prime ministers were among those who grew rich on trade with
India. Britain's mercantilism was complicit in the buying and transporting
of people as slaves from west Africa, especially after 1713 when it won the
contract or *asiento* to ship enslaved people from Africa to Spanish colonies
in Latin America. In Asia the practice of shipping indentured labourers to
work overseas was already prevalent, but colonisation generally implied
strong European powers exercising control over weaker subject peoples.
Much later, in 1936, the India-born colonial policeman and writer George
Orwell deplored the resulting inequalities. In his *Road to Wigan Pier* about

the state of Britain, he wrote that 'the high standard of living we enjoy in England depends upon our keeping a tight hold on the empire ... In order that England may live in comparative comfort, a hundred million Indians must live on the verge of starvation – an evil state of affairs.'[6] It was as powerful a sentiment as those expressed by Multatuli of the Dutch East Indies and de Saint-Pierre of Île de France or Mauritius. Eleven years after Orwell wrote those words, India gained independence with the end of British colonial rule.

The East India Company's grand headquarters in London's Leadenhall Street boasted of a company confident in its ability to turn a profit through trade and to administer distant territory based on instructions sent out from London. Goods from the East arrived at quays or docks on the River Thames, some of which – like the Tea Trade Wharf and the Tobacco Dock – were named for the commodity being traded. As ships became larger and could no longer easily sail to the 'Pool of London' in the middle of the City, so large docks were built, or rather excavated, downriver where there was more space. In the early nineteenth century the company constructed the vast East India Docks at Blackwall. The magnificent depiction by William Daniell in 1808 (page 217) shows the import dock in the foreground and the export dock beyond. The larger docks also allowed space for ship maintenance.

From the company's foundation, London was engaged in a competition to succeed Amsterdam as the European centre of trade. As the two cities rivalled each other for dominance in global trade, they both created the infrastructure to support a busy port. In many respects London followed the Dutch capital city: banks took over from goldsmiths as keepers of valuables. The Bank of England – headquartered near the East India Company – was founded in the late seventeenth century to serve the government. Tea and coffee both reached England in the 1650s and London coffee houses – like Jonathan's in Change Alley – became places where shares in the chartered companies were bought and sold, before the first purpose-built stock exchange opened in 1773. Lloyds Coffee House, opened in 1686, gave rise to London's first insurance market, Lloyds of London. It would become the centre of the global insurance business from new headquarters built on the site previously occupied by East India House. Ships' cargoes were among the first to be protected by insurance, and the Great Fire of London in 1666 boosted property insurance. London's first newspaper, the *London Gazette*, appeared in the plague year of 1665. The stately view of the River Thames by the French artist Daumont in 1770 shows the grand panorama of buildings at London in 1770, before the docks were built.

CONSTITUTIONAL TURMOIL AND TRADING WARS
On Elizabeth's death in 1603, the accession to the throne of England by James I brought England and Scotland under one monarch; he had ruled Scotland as James VI for 36 years, since well before Elizabeth's defeat of the Spanish Armada and the formation of the East India Company.[7] While the company gained strength and wealth in the East, other chartered companies traded with Africa, the West Indies (or Caribbean) and America. The trading companies of London reached all parts of the world. Trade was not always

the principal motivation. Soon after London started to trade with India, English pilgrims wanting to practise a purer form of Christianity – known as Puritanism – created pioneer settlements on the north-eastern seaboard of America, the first Europeans to settle in the northern part of the continent.

Meanwhile England went through a constitutional crisis following disagreements between parliament and James I's son and successor, Charles I, over the wielding of power and tolerance of religious freedom. Charles dismissed parliament and attempted to rule arbitrarily according to 'the divine right of kings', a concept that was going out of favour in continental Europe. This led to a civil war of royalists (Cavaliers) battling against parliamentarians (Roundheads), and ultimately the execution of the king. During the interregnum which followed, from 1649 to 1660, England's de facto ruler Oliver Cromwell embarked on the first of a series of wars with the Dutch. Unlike wars with Spain and Portugal which were mainly about religion, the Anglo-Dutch wars of the seventeenth and eighteenth centuries were about control of trade, territory and the oceans, with each country trying to enforce a monopoly on trade with the territories it controlled. The first such war lasted two years and failed to resolve anything.

Cromwell's death in 1658 paved the way for the restoration of the monarchy. And this is the moment to introduce an important figure in Restoration England in the person of Samuel Pepys. His *Diaries*, an account of the Restoration period, which were discovered only in the nineteenth century, revealed that as secretary to the Navy Board and later president of the Royal Society Pepys played an important political role. Wearing his naval hat, Pepys sailed to the Dutch Republic to bring back the son of the executed king from exile: he acceded to the thrones of England and Scotland as Charles II.

The Restoration was an eventful period in British history, not just because it included the Plague of 1665, which killed a quarter of London's population, and the Great Fire which destroyed most of the city the

The Pool of London before the building of the docks, by the French artist Jean François Daumont around 1770. From left to right, note London Bridge; Wren's St Paul's Cathedral; the tall Monument built to commemorate the Great Fire, not far from the East India Company headquarters in Leadenhall Street; and the Tower of London.

following year. Charles's reign was a constant battle to restore royal finances to pay for his army and navy. The king saw the expansion of the country's overseas reach as a means towards wealth, and so he did more to advance that cause than any monarch since Elizabeth. Soon after he became king, parliament passed the first Navigation Act to protect English shipping against the Dutch, essentially ensuring that English trade was carried in 'English bottoms'.

In 1662, Charles married the Portuguese princess Catherine of Braganza. It was a diplomatic alliance concluded in a treaty rather than a love match, a marriage that produced no children; but Charles acquired the moniker 'the Merry Monarch' for his dalliances with other women, with whom he sired sixteen offspring. He seems to have regarded the marriage as a business venture, since from the princess's dowry he was to receive half a million pounds (not all of which was paid) as well as the ports of Bombay and Tangier. He leased the spice port of Bombay to the East India Company for £10 a year, and in return received a £50,000 loan from the company. King Charles spoke of the company as 'the true and absolute Lords and Proprietors of the Port and Island'. The company used Bombay to expand its commercial grip on India. Tangier, a port on the northern coast of Morocco close to the Straits of Gibraltar, provided a base to protect English trade in the Mediterranean; it was put under the control of the navy – incidentally resulting in a visit there by Samuel Pepys.

Two years after acquiring Bombay and Tangier, Charles decided to take the North American colony of New Amsterdam from the Dutch. He chose Richard Nicolls, a poet and editor who also had experience as a sailor, to lead a fleet of four vessels. They sailed into New York harbour and took over the settlement without a shot being fired. Charles presented the captured territory to his brother, James Duke of York (later King James II), renaming both the small settlement on the island of Manhattan and its northern hinterland in his honour. New York would become a spice port in its own

The Royal Exchange in an engraving by Wenceslaus Holler, 1647.

right, though for rather different reasons from Bombay, a story we follow in the next chapter.

Charles would have preferred to entrust the takeover to his favourite buccaneer, Admiral Robert Holmes, but he was preoccupied in attacking Dutch shipping off the coast of Guinea in west Africa. This also concerned James Duke of York, who was Lord High Admiral of the navy as well as a director of the Royal African Company, which made much of its income by enslaving Africans. So James, and hence Charles, had direct personal interests in the 'mountain of gold' reported to lie in the territory of Gambia (page 83) waiting to be collected. James and Holmes arranged to plunder it, with the king's connivance, ignoring the fact that much of the Guinea coast was already under the control of the Dutch.

Holmes performed the task too well by claiming for his king an exclusive right of trade and navigation along the entire west African coast, from Cape Verde to the Cape of Good Hope. He caused havoc on a second Guinea coast expedition by capturing Dutch forts and ships; he was accused on his return to London of overreaching his instructions, for which he was detained in the Tower of London. England was forced to disavow his territorial claims after the Dutch took reprisals on English ships, recovering most of their forts in west Africa. Yet, after receiving a pardon, Holmes returned to naval duties and engaged the Dutch again. He destroyed 150 Dutch vessels by sending a fireship among them in 1665, off the West Frisian islands north of Texel where the Zuiderzee gives way to the North Sea, thus provoking another Anglo-Dutch naval war. The event, known as Holmes's Bonfire, inflicted a heavy blow on Dutch merchant shipping and briefly gave the English the upper hand. But in a reprisal attack nine months later, the Dutch Admiral Michiel de Ruyter destroyed six English vessels and captured the flagship of the English fleet at Chatham, concluding the second Anglo-Dutch war in favour of the Dutch.

At least the positive outcome for London was that the attack on Chatham led to peace talks at the Dutch city of Breda, which concluded with the important Treaty of Breda (1667) for 'the liberty of navigation and trade' between the two nations, reversing the impact of the navigation acts. There was tacit agreement that each retain control of overseas territories then occupied. This meant that the English could hang on to New York town and state, while the Dutch retained Suriname in South America (which the English had earlier occupied) as well as the Spice Islands, including Pulau Run in the Bandas, enabling the Dutch to enforce a nutmeg monopoly – in theory at least.

On Charles's death in 1685, his brother the Duke of York acceded to the throne as King James II of England, James VII of Scotland. Amid parliamentary opposition to James's attempt to restore Catholicism, a group of parliamentarians invited the Dutch *stadhouder,* Willem of Orange, a grandson of Charles I, and Willem's English wife Mary, daughter of King James, to take the throne and rule jointly. Willem was the great grandson of Willem the Silent who had led the Protestant revolt against Catholic Spanish rule in the Dutch Republic, so he was well qualified to shore up Protestantism in England and Scotland. In a largely peaceful transition

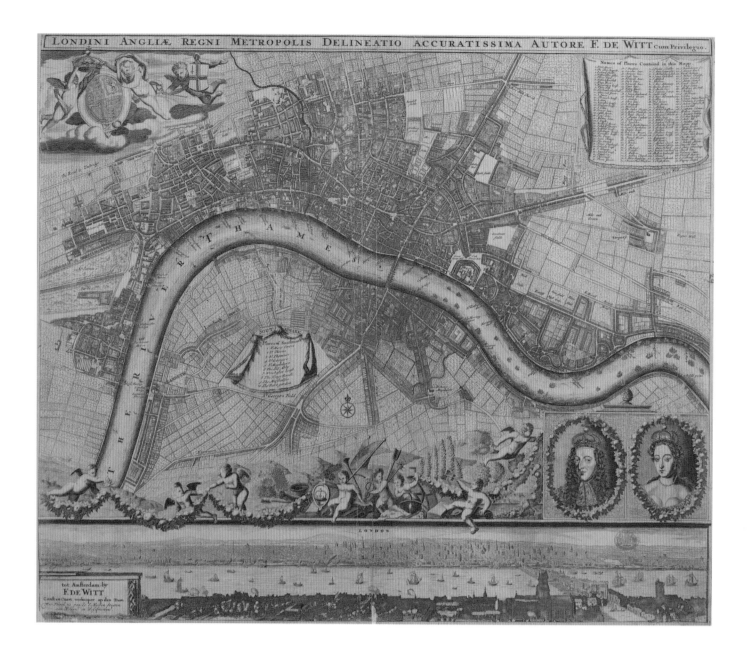

known as the Glorious Revolution of 1688, James was superseded by his daughter and son-in-law: they were crowned as King William III and Queen Mary II of England and Scotland. The accession is commemorated by a 1690 map of London picturing the new co-monarchs.

Once again, the naval board secretary Samuel Pepys was on hand, this time to arrange for the deposed king, James, to sail into exile in France. Had the Dutch opted to make Willem the Silent their king, instead of becoming a republic, this transition could have united the two Protestant nations as one, as Oliver Cromwell allegedly suggested after the first Anglo-Dutch war, though his motives in doing so were to prevent Willem acceding to the throne in either country. Cromwell's proposal was greeted with incredulity in The Hague.[8]

European rivalries over religion were not at an end. In the 1740s England was at risk of being invaded by France, which wanted to oust George II and replace him with a Catholic ruler. George survived, dying a natural death in

This special edition map of London with an elongation of the River Thames below was based on one first produced c.1689 by Dutch publisher Johannes de Ram to commemorate the crowning of Dutch Prince Willem and his English wife Mary (pictured bottom right) as king and queen of England.

1760, by which time Britain was on its way to dominating world trade with major settlements in India and North America – and was deeply involved in the transatlantic slave trade. Britain spent much of the eighteenth and early nineteenth centuries fighting its other main colonial rival, France, in a series of wars which would culminate in the defeat of the French emperor, Napoleon Bonaparte, in 1815.

The War of the Austrian Succession (1740–48), ostensibly about European alliances, was followed by the Seven Years War (1756–63) of Britain and France fighting for control of territory in Europe, North America and India. Britain's defeat of France at the Battle of Quebec ensured British supremacy in North America, while victory in India at Plassey over the Nawab of Bengal, with whom the French were allied, enabled Britain to take control of Bengal and its port city of Calcutta. Battles at Plassey and Madras were episodes in Anglo-French rivalry for control of the Asian spice trade, like the wars between the English and Dutch the previous century.

THE ROYAL SOCIETY, ROYAL OBSERVATORY AND DETERMINATION OF LONGITUDE

King Charles II's passion for science translated into patronage for all things – and people – scientific. He presided over the birth of a scientific revolution, granting a charter in 1662 to a London-based 'club' for intellectuals, the Royal Society 'for the promotion of Experimental Philosophy'. The all-encompassing study of 'natural philosophy' gave way to more precisely defined scientific disciplines, such as physics, astronomy and anatomy. Isaac Newton formulated his theory of gravity; Robert Boyle created chemistry out of ancient alchemy; Richard Lower performed the first blood transfusion between animals; and Edmund Halley correctly predicted the return of the comet that bears his name.

Astronomy was the most relevant and vital source of knowledge for long-distance trade and exploration, as no one had yet found a way to determine location by measuring longitude. The challenge to Aristotle's geocentric view, that the Earth was at the centre of the universe, originated by Copernicus in Poland and developed by Galileo in Italy (to the annoyance of the pope), then fell to Isaac Newton in Cambridge. Newton contributed immensely to an understanding of how the universe worked. His early experiments in optics and the colour spectrum, building on the work of Descartes in France, led him to develop a telescope with an internal mirror which provided greater magnification than that of Christiaan Huygens in the Netherlands.

At the Royal Society in London, astronomers Christopher Wren and Edmund Halley challenged Newton to explain how planets orbited the Sun. Newton gave his response in the book *Principia Mathematica*[9] with a series of laws of motion showing the relationship between mass, force and inertia. Out of this emerged the theory of gravitational pull, or gravity, for which Newton is best remembered. Newton explained that the theory occurred to him while watching an apple fall from a tree. President of the Royal Society at the time was Samuel Pepys, who had already supervised the arrival of one king and departure of another. No scientist himself, Pepys was guided

Map of the constellations of the Southern Hemisphere by J. G. Doppelmayr, c.1720. It features in the corners the astronomical observatories at Greenwich, Copenhagen, Cassel and Berlin.

by Wren, Halley and others who recognised the far-reaching significance of Newton's work. *Principia Mathematica* was published by the Royal Society with Pepys's name beneath Newton's on the title page.

The book had a profound impact on people's view of the solar system and earned Newton a place among the other greatest minds of the Enlightenment, setting a direction for scientific study which was not superseded until Albert Einstein advanced his theory of relativity in the early twentieth century. Einstein in turn described Newton as a 'shining spirit', saying his ideas about motion influenced physics, optics and the study of light, thermodynamics, heat, energy and gases, electricity and magnetism.

Newton moved to London to become warden and then master of the Royal Mint, responsible for producing the nation's coinage. He played a prominent role at the Royal Society, becoming president in 1703 and making

Enlargement of the top left corner, the Royal Observatory at Greenwich.

his famous remark: 'If I have seen further, it is by standing on the shoulders of giants', variously interpreted as either exhibiting his modesty, or else a cutting comment on his predecessor in the post, Robert Hooke, a scientist specialising in microscopy who was of short stature and with whom Newton did not get on. By this time Christopher Wren, one of the Royal Society's founders, was excelling in the field of architecture, overseeing the rebuilding of London after the Great Fire of 1666 with St Paul's Cathedral as its centrepiece. Newton took an interest in the voyages of exploration and commerce, but lost the money he invested in the South Sea Company; its share value at first rose rapidly and then collapsed in the 'South Sea Bubble', an episode reminiscent of tulip mania in Amsterdam.

Newton was a member of the Board of Longitude, set up by parliament to oversee a contest to find a way to determine longitude. The method of 'slicing' the world longitudinally from pole to pole was originated by the Greek Hipparchus in the second century BC and adopted by Claudius Ptolemy, the father of map-making. The problem for sailors was that there was no way of measuring longitude accurately to know exactly where they were at any particular time. If time could be measured at sea, then a ship's position could be determined; hence all maritime nations had an interest in meeting the challenge. Philip III of Spain in 1598 offered a handsome pension 'in *ducats*' to whoever could solve the problem. Galileo took up the challenge, initially based on the moons of Jupiter and subsequently by inventing a clock regulated by a pendulum; meanwhile kings Louis XIV of France and Charles II of England set up observatories in Paris and London to try to find a solution to the problem. The Royal Observatory at Greenwich was built by Christopher Wren, combining his roles as astronomer and architect. In 1627 the government of the Dutch Republic, the States General, offered a reward of 10,000 *guilders*, which encouraged Christiaan Huygens to enter what was becoming an international competition. He patented a pendulum clock which improved on the accuracy of an early design of Galileo's by adding spring balances. The English sailor Robert Holmes was assigned the task on his west African expeditions of testing the accuracy of Huygens' clock.

Britain entered the challenge with a competition of its own which would finally produce a result, though not during Newton's lifetime. Parliament offered a reward to whoever produced a maritime timepiece accurate within 1° longitudinal degree, and a higher reward if it were accurate within 0.5° of true. A Yorkshire-based carpenter and clock-maker, John Harrison, built a total of five timepieces over three decades, finally producing in the 1760s a clock – known as H5 – which met the most stringent test of accuracy. The Board was reluctant to give Harrison credit for what was undoubtedly a breakthrough, because he would not share his method and they considered it a lucky 'one-off'. But intervention by the king led to Harrison being rewarded and recognised as the true creator of what came to be called the 'chronometer', an accurate timepiece that enabled longitude to be determined at sea. The nation's legacy from the Yorkshireman's tribulations was that 0° longitude – from which all others would be measured – ran through Greenwich, where much of the research was carried out.

The nineteenth century brought more accolades for British scientific research when two naturalists reached conclusions which led to the postulation of the theories of evolution and natural selection. They were Charles Darwin and Alfred Russel Wallace, who had each travelled the world in search of evidence to support their theory. Darwin focused on South America, especially the Galapagos Islands where he studied finches, and also visited, among other places, the islands of Mauritius, St Helena and Ascension. Alfred Russel Wallace did his research in south-east Asia, especially in the Spice Islands. Both were elected fellows of the Royal Society and each published his findings independently. The theory of natural selection was outlined in Darwin's book *Origin of Species* in 1859 and the author was generous enough to share credit with Wallace. On his death in 1882, Darwin's body was laid to rest in Westminster Abbey, London, alongside that of Isaac Newton.

Apart from the Royal Society, several other scientific organisations grew out of London's links with Asia. The botanical gardens at Kew were founded in 1759 by the mother of George III. Seedlings were sent back from South Africa, the South Atlantic and South Pacific for propagation under glass, giving the gardens a reputation as a centre for transplantation. They would later play a pivotal role in propagating rubber in south-east Asia. The Linnean Society was founded in London in 1788, taking its name from the Swedish naturalist Carl Linnaeus who devised a system for classifying plants and animals. In 1828 London Zoo, the first urban collection of wild animals in the world, was founded under the auspices of the Zoological Society of London. It was intended as a place of scientific study of animals, equivalent to the Royal Botanical Gardens. Although he did not live to see the zoo's opening, the East India Company official Stamford Raffles – of Java, Bencoolen and latterly Singapore – was its principal benefactor.

Giving a foretaste of the coming industrial revolution, Britain pioneered steam-driven transport as the Dutch had harnessed wind power two centuries earlier. The Scottish engineer James Watt developed a way of using steam for traction, and the first steam-driven passenger railway opened in 1825 between the northern towns of Stockton and Darlington. In 1826 the steamship *Enterprise* sailed from Falmouth in Cornwall to Calcutta in India – using steam power initially and, when the coal ran out, more conventionally the power of the wind. Also, Dutch engineers used wind power to help drain the fens of eastern England.

LITERATURE

Another outcome of England's experience of competitive global trade was the flowering of English literature with a nautical flavour. Shakespeare was

an early example with *The Merchant of Venice* (1605). In the eventful year of 1667 John Milton made reference to Asian kings from India, the Golden Chersonese (Malaya) and the island of Taprobane, the classical name for Ceylon, in his epic poem, *Paradise Lost*. An anti-slavery novel by the female writer Aphra Behn, titled *Oroonoko* and set in Suriname, was published in London in 1688; it did not have as great an impact as did *Paul et Virginie*, by the French author Jacques-Henri Bernardin de Saint-Pierre and published in 1788, on life in Mauritius. In 1726 Daniel Defoe wrote the seafaring story of *Robinson Crusoe*, regarded as the English language's first novel; and in the same year Jonathan Swift published his political satire *Gulliver's Travels*. William Wordsworth wrote a triumphant sonnet in 1802 entitled 'On the Extinction of the Venetian Republic'; and in 1855 Charles Kingsley wrote *Westward Ho!*, a novel in which Francis Drake plays a key role.

Henry Newbolt romanticised Drake's exploits in an 1897 poem called 'Drake's Drum', after the drum that Drake allegedly carried on his circumnavigation. The poem begins: 'Drake he's in his hammock an' a thousand mile away, (Capten, art tha sleepin' there below?) Slung atween the round shot in Nombre Dios Bay, An' dreamin' arl the time o' Plymouth Hoe.' John Masefield built on the nautical theme in his poem 'Cargoes' (1902), with

The East India Company took over Brunswick Dock at Blackwall and expanded it to accommodate the larger number of vessels arriving from the East, pictured here by William Daniell in 1803.

a degree of poetic licence: cinnamon comes from the East not the isthmus. The second verse reads: 'Stately Spanish galleon coming from the Isthmus, Dipping through the Tropics by the palm-green shores, With a cargo of diamonds, emeralds, amethysts, Topazes, and cinnamon, and gold moidores'.[10]

The Anglo-Dutch wars inspired more literature, like John Dryden's play *Amboyna or the Cruelties of the Dutch to the English Merchants* (1673); while Rudyard Kipling, arch-imperialist that he was, wrote a deeply political poem in defence of empire, 'The White-Man's Burden' (1899) and a jingoistic verse entitled 'The Dutch in the Medway' (1911). William Whiting in 1860 wrote a poem which became a familiar hymn in church dedicated to 'those in peril on the sea'. And perhaps the best-known quote about London comes from Samuel Johnson, spoken to James Boswell in 1777 of the city where he spent most of his life: 'When a man is tired of London, he is tired of life; for there is in London all that life can afford.'

A popular nursery rhyme originating in Tudor times shows how the English were influenced by the nutmeg: 'I had a little nut tree, Nothing would it bear, But a silver nutmeg And a golden pear. The King of Spain's daughter Came to visit me And all for the sake Of my little nut tree.' It is thought to have been an allegorical reference to the betrothal of the daughter of King Ferdinand II and Queen Isabella of Spain to Prince Arthur, the elder son of King Henry VII of England. The line 'Nothing would it bear' may have been an allusion to Arthur's alleged impotence or the fact that the marriage was never consummated because Arthur died young. Instead, the daughter, Catherine of Aragon, married Arthur's younger brother soon after he ascended the throne as King Henry VIII of England. (A later line in the poem, 'Her dress was made of crimson', may have been a reference to the crimson-coloured mace covering the nutmeg 'nut'.)

LONDON'S DOCKLANDS

The volume of London's trade in the early nineteenth century was so great that the East India Company decided to build docks of its own. It took over and expanded the Brunswick Dock at Blackwall (also known as Mr Perry's Dock), building alongside it a larger dock for 'East Indiamen' returning from India with spices, textiles and all manner of goods. The larger basin was used to unload vessels, the smaller for loading outgoing ships. Together they could accommodate 250 vessels. A painting by William Daniell in 1803 (page 227) shows Brunswick Dock before the expansion, full of ships. Later, the East India and West India Docks were combined, allowing ships from the East to use the larger capacity of the latter dock at Wapping. The East Indiaman gave way to the 'clipper', a faster vessel with greater sail area especially associated with the tea trade. The once-prosperous East India Company was dissolved in 1874, having found it hard to remain viable after losing its trading monopoly earlier in the century, and with Queen Victoria and her government taking over its political functions.

The docks lay in rural surroundings outside the expanding city. Horses and carriages were used to haul goods the four miles or so to company warehouses in the city around Fenchurch Street and Cutler Street. With the coming of steam, these were the first docks to be connected to the city by

(top) The River Thames in 1845 jammed with vessels, from Greenwich (far right) to the Tower of London. The West India Docks are at upper right and beyond in the distance are the East India Docks. Also shown are railways connecting London to the docks, and to the south coast. Part of a wider panorama by William Little and Fredrick James Smyth published in the Illustrated London News *in 1845.*

(bottom) This magnificent view published by Rober Sayer shows Westminster Bridge the year after its opening in 1750. At the right is Westminster Abbey, which played an important role in London's foundation, and early buildings of the British parliament.

railway. When the seasonal fleets arrived from the East, there was a huge volume of goods to be transferred to city warehouses.

The location of the East India Docks was symbolic for several reasons: they straddled the 0^0 line of the meridian, measured from the Royal Observatory at Greenwich on the opposite bank of the River Thames. Greenwich has a long association with the sea through the pioneering work of the Royal Observatory in establishing and measuring longitude. Britain's Naval Academy also used to stand there – and the National Maritime Museum still does. Greenwich was the birthplace of Elizabeth I, the monarch who did more than any other to 'launch' Britain as a maritime nation. Brunswick Wharf, where ships once entered the East India Docks, was the point of departure in 1606 of the ships which established England's first colony at Virginia in North America. The East India Docks have now been partly filled in, as seen in the aerial view which also shows the arena built at Greenwich on the river's south bank at the turn of the twenty-first century.

By contrast, a bird's-eye view of London's dockland area in 1845 (page 229) shows what was by then the busiest and most important trading port in the world. Nearly a quarter of the inhabitants of the globe lived under British rule. The view, part of a panorama of the River Thames distributed with the *Illustrated London News*, shows the stretch of river between the Tower of London (extreme left, north bank) and Greenwich Hospital (extreme right, south bank). At the right is the Isle of Dogs, formed by the Thames making a sweep to the south on its way to the North Sea. A

Flying over London, a view down to the north of the site of the East India Docks in 2011, now mainly filled in and built over, including top left the Millennium or O2 arena at Greenwich on the South Bank. The Greenwich Meridian crosses the River Thames at this point. (Out of the picture to the right is the 2012 Olympic stadium.)

remarkable aspect of this picture is the number of sailing vessels queuing to offload their wares – almost certainly exaggerated by the artist – before taking on fresh cargoes for their return voyage. This was London at the centre of global maritime trade.

North of the River Thames is the new Blackwall railway, used to transfer freight from the East India Company docks (visible at top right) to warehouses in the City. South of the river, passenger railway lines from London Bridge terminus follow the route to Greenwich, and a southern line heads to Dover and to Brighton on the south coast. The small dock depicted on the south bank is the Greenland Dock at Deptford, built by an imperious master of the East India Company, Sir Josiah Childe, to fit out his vessels. By the time of this image, it was a base for whaling expeditions to the North Sea, hence its name.

In 1698 Tsar Peter the Great of Russia spent three months at Deptford near Greenwich at the invitation of the Dutch-born king William III, following the tsar's earlier visit to Amsterdam. Tsar Peter was determined to learn all he could about shipbuilding and how to create a navy, doubtless studying the role of Samuel Pepys who a generation earlier had managed the finance and logistics of the Royal Navy. He visited the nearby Royal Observatory and Woolwich Arsenal as well as the Royal Society, Royal Mint and Oxford University, though chose not to meet any of the great minds of the time, such as Isaac Newton, Edmund Halley or Christopher Wren. Within five years of Peter's return, Russia's first navy came into being at St Petersburg on the Baltic Sea. He hired craftsmen in London and Amsterdam to make this possible.

London's spice trade history is remembered in street names like Clove Crescent and Nutmeg Lane, and in the financial district of London where there used to be roads called after India, Rangoon and Muscovy, reminders of the foreign connections that made London the warehouse of the world. Not surprisingly immigrants from places served by shipping settled around the docks, notably *lascars* or sailors from India. Jews expelled from Spain and Portugal were welcomed to England by Oliver Cromwell during the interregnum, many settling in the East End of London where Britain's first synagogue was established. Muslims from Bengal, a region of India (and now Bangladesh) which provided much of the East India Company's profit, also settled in the East End, making the borough of Tower Hamlets one of the most ethnically diverse districts of London.

By the mid-nineteenth century, after some rivalry with Paris, London was recognised as the financial centre of the world, a position it held until the Second World War, after which a dynamic new city across the Atlantic took over.

To His Excellency
Sir Henry Moore, Bar.
Captain General and Governour in Chief
In and Over His Majesty's Province of
NEW YORK
and the Territories depending thereon in America,
Chancellor and Vice Admiral of the same.

This Plan
of the City of New York and its Environs,
Surveyed and Laid down,
Is most Humbly Dedicated by His Excellencys
Most Obedient Humble Servant,
B. Ratzer.

PORT OF NEW YORK

NORTH, OR HUDSON'S RIVER

EAST RIVER OR THE SOUND

LONG ISLAND

Salt Meadows

PAULUS HOOK

OYSTER BANKS

Buckings Island

Bedloes or Kennedy's Island

The Governor's or Nutten Island

PART OF THE BAY

Red Hook

The WALLABOUT BAY

Southward Boundaries

Magnetic Meridian

PLAN
of the
CITY of NEW YORK
in
NORTH AMERICA:
Surveyed in the Years 1766 & 1767

REFERENCES.

PART OF LONG ISLAND

Scale of 2000 Feet.
Scale of One Mile.
Scale of Yards.

A South West View of the City of New York,
Taken from the Governours Island.

11/

NEW YORK, SALEM AND THE MANHATTAN TRANSFER

A map or 'aerial view' of lower Manhattan in 1766–67 by Bernard Ratzer. It includes as an inset an onshore view from Governour's Island, from a watercolour by Thomas Davies, 1760.

New York is a creation of European colonial powers. Before the colonisers arrived, it was inhabited by 'Indians,' in the misnomer of Christopher Columbus who thought he had reached 'the Indies', or 'native Americans' in today's terminology. A much later map of 1909, showing human occupation in 1609 (overleaf) and overlaid with modern streets, suggests that the southern end of Manhattan Island was inhabited by the Warpoe, Nahtouk, Ishpetenga and Saponika 'tribes' or 'nations', while the northern end is labelled with settlements of the Muscota and Wickquaskeck (or Wecquaesgeek). Of early Europeans known to have entered New York harbour, both Giovanni da Verrazzano in 1524 and Henry Hudson in 1609 mention the Lenape, which may have referred to native Americans living along the Delaware River, an area known as *Lenapehoking*, or 'where the Lenape dwell'. Both travellers had the same mission: to find a route to the East Indies via the Pacific Ocean.

Giovanni da Verrazzano, a Florentine explorer in the service of the king of France, observed Lenape mariners using canoes to cross a large lake. He named the area *Nouvelle Angoulême* (New Angoulême) for his monarch,

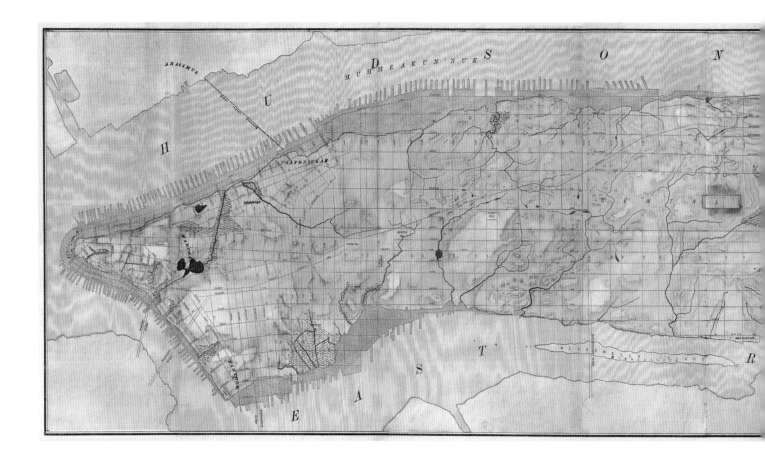

Francis I, Count of the French district of Angoulême, though the name
(sometimes recorded as 'New France') did not catch on. Verrazzano's
'discovery' was overshadowed by the return to Spain in September 1522 of
the crew of the circumnavigation led initially by Ferdinand Magellan, which
had succeeded in finding a route round the Americas to the Pacific Ocean.

Then 85 years later Henry Hudson, an Englishman in the service of the
Dutch East India Company or VOC, reported to his masters in Amsterdam
of an island known as *Manna-hata,* or hilly island. (The map also spells it
as *Mannahtin.)* Hudson found that there was more to Verrazzano's large
lake than the Italian realised when he journeyed 150 miles (240 km) up the
river that now bears his name. He wrote of favourable prospects for trading
in beaver pelts, a report that was promising enough for the Dutch to make
further voyages. They set up a small trading post near what is now the city
of Albany. The post was later taken over by the Dutch West India Company
who named it *Beverwyck*, meaning 'place of beavers'. There, on territory
inhabited by Mohawk people, they built Fort Nassau which became the hub
of their *Nieuw Nederland* or New Netherland settlement, a trading centre
for pelts which provided the felt hats popular in Europe.

Dutch settlers were threatened from the north by the French, who had
journeyed up the St Lawrence River and were also buying beaver pelts
from the Mohawk; and from the south by the English, who were making
territorial claims on the mouth of the Hudson River; and also by native
Americans on whose land they had trespassed. So in 1625 the Dutch fortified

*Manhattan (Mannahtin) in
1609, depicted in this 1909
image by Townsend MacCoun,
overlaid with streets existing
at the time of publication.
The map shows which native
American peoples were settled
on different parts of the island.*

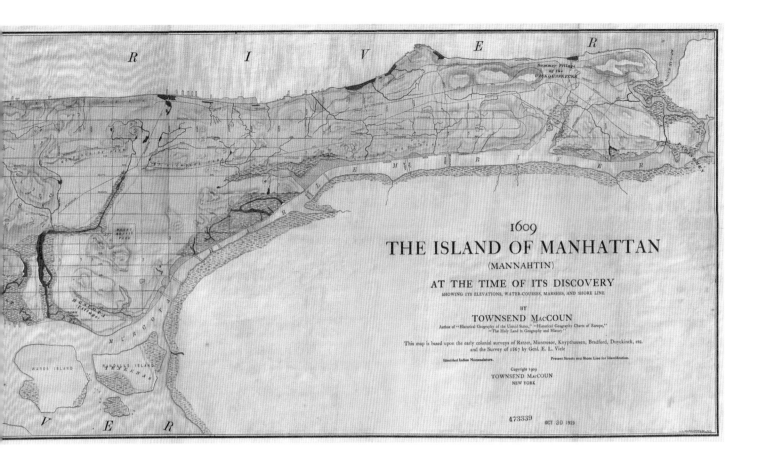

1609
THE ISLAND OF MANHATTAN
(MANNAHTIN)
AT THE TIME OF ITS DISCOVERY
SHOWING ITS ELEVATIONS, WATER-COURSES, MARSHES, AND SHORE LINE
BY
TOWNSEND MacCOUN
Author of "Historical Geography of the United States," "Historical Geography Charts of Europe,"
"The Holy Land in Geography and History"

This map is based upon the early colonial surveys of Ratzer, Montresor, Knyphausen, Bradford, Duyckinck, etc.
and the Survey of 1867 by Genl. E. L. Viele.

Identified Indian Nomenclature.   Present Streets and Shore Line for Identification.

Copyright 1909
TOWNSEND MacCOUN
NEW YORK

473339   OCT 30 1929

a settlement on the south of Manhattan Island, calling it *Nieuw Amsterdam*, and encouraged their settlers to occupy the surrounding areas of Long Island and (what would become) New Jersey. Six years after the founding of Batavia on the other side of the world, New Amsterdam – as it is usually remembered – became the Dutch trading headquarters in America, a centre for shipping beaver pelts to Europe.

A New York foundation myth tells how the following year the company's chief representative Peter Minuit purchased the entire island of Manhattan from native Americans for the princely sum of 60 *guilders*, equivalent to US$24. If true, and the story has been told often enough to be accepted as fact, this would make the island the best real estate bargain in history.[1] Settlers – Calvinists, Huguenots and Jews – flocked to New Amsterdam and its northerly hinterland of New Netherland. Following a pattern set in South America, enslaved labourers were shipped in from Africa. Early Dutch settlers had difficulty making the settlement pay its way.

They brought in Petrus Stuyvesant as director-general of New Netherland. Stuyvesant had previously served on the West Indian island of Curaçao, where the Dutch were having more success, and had lost his right leg to a Spanish cannonball in a battle for control of another West Indian island. He made Calvinism, the creed of the Dutch Reformed Church in which his father was a priest, the approved religion for Dutch settlers of New Netherland. He took a dim view of Quakers, Lutherans and Jews, though correspondence from the time suggests that New Amsterdam was a

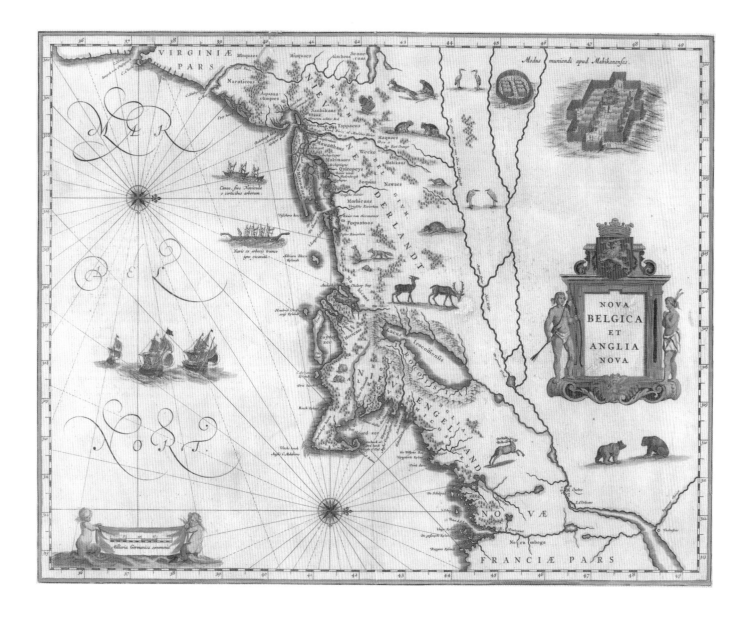

centre of religious freedom in line with the spirit of its namesake European
city, and in contrast to the less tolerant philosophy of early English settlers.
Enslaved labourers in Dutch-ruled areas had more rights than those in
English-controlled colonies.[2] In trade too the Dutch were more tolerant
of rivals, at least in this part of the world, embracing the philosophy of
the Leiden-educated jurist Hugo Grotius (or Hugo de Groot) who in 1609
outlined the principle of freedom of the seas in his book *Mare Liberum*, an
early draft of what would evolve into the laws of the sea.

English settlers regarded themselves as refugees escaping a religious
environment that was intolerant of their 'purer' form of Protestantism. A
group of English 'Puritans' had ventured west in search of a new homeland
aboard the ship *Mayflower* in 1620, landing north of New Amsterdam
at Plymouth in Massachusetts Bay, which is sometimes regarded as the
birthplace of the new American nation. A 1640 map by Willem Blaeu,
confusingly entitled New Belgium and New England, faces south to show
New Netherland nestling between New England on one side and the

*Territory defined by its
occupants as New England and
New Netherland, including parts
of New Belgium and French-
occupied territory, as drawn
by Dutchman William Blaeu in
1635 in this south-facing map.
New Amsterdam (top centre)
is marked on an oddly-shaped
Manhattan Island.*

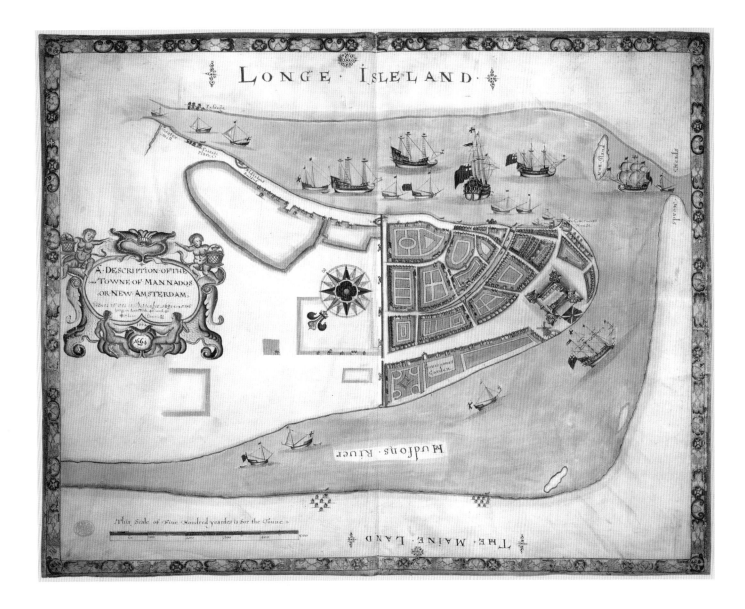

The map labels visible include: LONGE ISLELAND, A DESCRIPTION OF THE TOWNE OF MANNADOS OR NEW AMSTERDAM, 1664, Hudsons River, THE MAINE LAND.

The Duke's Plan by an unknown artist, held at the British Library, explained to James, Duke of York (the future King James II), the extent of his newly conquered territory on the south of Manhattan Island.

loosely defined Virginia colony on the other, both of which were controlled by English traders.

With the restoration of the English monarchy in 1660, Charles II became king and determined to take over the fur trade from the Dutch by seizing New Netherland. His determination may have arisen out of a dislike of the Dutch – notwithstanding they gave him a home during his years of exile – possibly dating from England's humiliation at the massacre of Amboyna in the East Indies in 1623, when Charles's father was on the throne, which continued to rankle with the English. He had acquired Bombay and Tangier from the Portuguese by marrying Catherine of Braganza and had an appetite to extend his country's trading empire further. He wanted to link up the English settlements of Massachusetts and Connecticut with Virginia to the south, for which he needed to take control of New Amsterdam.

Charles sent four warships under Richard Nicolls to seize New Amsterdam. Stuyvesant was outnumbered by military force but also by opinion among settlers, including his 17-year-old son Balthazar who thought they might gain commercial advantage under the English. There were almost as many English as Dutch settlers in New Netherland. Manhattan fell under English rule on 8 September 1664 without a shot being fired. New Amsterdam, with an estimated population of 1,500 – including a diminishing number of Lenape and a few hundred enslaved people brought from Africa[3] – was renamed New York, and the settlement up the Hudson River at *Beverwijck* was named Albany, in both cases for the king's brother, James, who held the duchies of York and Albany in England and Scotland respectively. The entire colony was also named New York. Fort Amsterdam in lower Manhattan became Fort James and the North River reverted to Hudson River, though the name of the river would chop and change. The Dutch had earlier named it River Mauritius, after Willem the Silent's son, Maurits.

Settlers were of many European nationalities, so it was only the overall command that changed. The Dutch West India Company lost out the most: after 1674 the Dutch language could no longer be used in New York courts. The English were less interested in the fur trade, and found sugar brought to New York from the West Indies more profitable, as well as tobacco from Virginia. Tobacco was also grown on Manhattan. As a trading port, New York was not subject to the vagaries of Anglo-Dutch relations and could trade freely with both London and Amsterdam. England's seizure of New York was one of the factors that led to war in Europe between the English and the Dutch the following year, during which the Dutch took their revenge by seizing the English-run sugar territory of Suriname in South America.

Charles II wrote enthusiastically to his sister in France of the seizure, in the words quoted on page 233, as if to say 'Look, we scored one over the Dutch.' His assertion that 'it did belong to England heeretofore' is open to question. Samuel Pepys might have been expected to be asked to administer the newly acquired port, as in the case of Tangier, but instead Charles immediately 'gave' the colony to the navy's Lord High Admiral, his brother James, who would accede in 1685 as James II of England and VII of Scotland. Richard Nicolls, who led the expedition which seized the town, became the first English governor of New York.

The Duke's Plan[4] is a famous map (see page 237) that was presented to James as a visible token of the territorial gift. Dated 1664, it describes itself as 'a description of the Town of Mannados or New Amsterdam' as it was under Dutch rule in September 1661, though ships shown are flying the English ensign. Features of the plan are the Dutch-built fort facing south-west, alongside a windmill and the governor's house (facing south-east) near the harbour; also a canal the Dutch built so that goods arriving at the harbour on the East River could be transported by boat into the residential area around the fort. The fort and settlement were connected to northern Manhattan and the hinterland by a north–south trail used by the Wickquaskeck people, which the Dutch knew as *brede weg*. They widened it and renamed it initially *Heeren Weg* or Gentleman's Way – like the canal and street in Amsterdam – but later it reverted to Broadway, an English translation of its Dutch name. Interesting mapping innovations on the Duke's Plan are the use of a scale (at bottom left) to give an indication of distance and the compass rose at the centre.

A street scene in lower Manhattan by Samuel Davenport 1860, with St Paul's chapel on the right and evidence of shipping on the lower Hudson River.

The wooden wall to the north of the governor's gardens, which linked the East and Hudson Rivers, was built by Petrus Stuyvesant in 1653 to protect the Dutch settlement from native Americans who claimed the territory as their own and resented the newcomers – or possibly to keep the English out. This became the site of a slave market, located where Wall Street reached the East River, established in 1711 as a place where enslaved black people and Native Americans could be hired or purchased. A trade in enslaved people had been conducted in Manhattan from 1626 and lasted until the trade was abolished in New York state in 1827. The English dismantled the wall in 1699, but the place where it had stood remained Wall Street, later the home of New York's first stock exchange at the street's junction with Broadway.

A street scene in lower Manhattan by British artist Samuel Davenport shows the view south down Broadway in 1860 towards Battery Park, with St Paul's Chapel on the right, built before independence and the oldest continuously occupied building in the city. Ships' masts suggest that the

Hudson River mouth (on the right) had become a more significant wharf area than the East River by this time.

Peter Schenk's view of New York harbour on lower Manhattan's east side during the *restitutio* period of 1673, with the Dutch-flagged vessel intended to reinforce the country's claim.

THE MANHATTAN TRANSFER

New York played relatively little role in the import of oriental spices to North America, so its inclusion in this review of spice ports needs an explanation. As mentioned, the port's seizure by the English helped trigger the second Anglo-Dutch war, fought in the English Channel and North Sea in 1665–7. The war ended when the Dutch caused substantial damage to the English fleet at Chatham on the River Medway, whereupon the two nations met at Breda in Holland to negotiate a peace. This resulted in the Treaty of Breda, signed at the end of July 1667, an important document in European and colonial history as much for what it does not say. Implicit was agreement by both nations that they retain control of territory then in their possession. England held onto New York town and state, while the Dutch retained Pulau Run in the Banda Islands, thus maintaining, at least in theory, their monopoly on the trade in nutmeg and mace.

The agreement was not final, however, and the Dutch seized control of New York once more in August 1673 while the two nations were engaged in Europe in the third Anglo-Dutch war, with consequent name changes to New Orange for Manhattan and Willemstad for Albany. The reoccupation lasted fifteen months, before the English took over again under a deal that also guaranteed Dutch control over Suriname.

Apart from that interruption, England held onto its newly conquered territory in North America, the former New Netherland and New Amsterdam now the English colony of New York. It would appear that the Dutch had swapped a substantial territory in America (59 sq km or 22.8 sq miles for Manhattan alone) for the insubstantial and waterless island of Run (barely 3 sq km or 1.16 sq miles) to secure control over the trade in nutmeg and mace, and that the English got by far the better bargain. This is not strictly true, since there was no overt swap in the terms of the treaty: territories simply remaining under the control of their possessor at the time. It nonetheless gives rise to speculation that had circumstances been different, Americans might today be speaking Dutch!

The Dutch Republic's forty-year occupation of Manhattan and adjoining territory left its mark in the preponderance of Dutch names still in use today: such as Brooklyn (*Breukelen*), Haarlem (*Harlem*), Hoboken, Yonkers (from *jong heer* meaning 'young gentleman', a title bestowed on landowner Adrien van der Donck), Catskills (*Kats Kil*), Coney Island (*Konijneneiland* or 'rabbit island'), Flushing (*Vlissingen*), Willemstad (after Willem the Silent), Staten Island (named for the Dutch States General), Bowery Street (from *bouwerie* meaning 'farm') and many more, while Lange Eylandt transmogrified into Long Island. Some American families reveal their heritage by their Dutch-origin names, ranging from those of historically prominent dynasties, like the Roosevelts, Stuyvesants and Vanderbilts, to the more ordinary but distinctive Jansens, Kuipers, Peters, Hoeks and Hendriksens. Other Dutch place names which have not survived but can be seen in Jansson/Visscher's map (page 243) include Texel and Zuiderzee. The American word 'boss' is derived from the Dutch *baas* meaning master.

The borough of Bronx was named for Jonas Bronck, a Danish settler at whose homestead the Dutch signed a peace treaty on 22 April 1642 with leaders of the Wecquaesgeek who had long occupied that area. Catherine of Braganza, who brought Bombay as dowry on marrying King Charles II of England, is the 'queen' who gave her title to the New York borough of Queens, while her husband is the king referred to in Brooklyn's official title of King's County, not that either of them ever visited the colony.

A view by German engraver Peter Schenk shows south-eastern Manhattan in 1673 during the *restitutio* (recovery) period after the Dutch reclaimed ownership, hence it is the Dutch flag atop vessels in the foreground. The scene shows the main quays abutting the East River. At the left the coastline bends round the famous southern tip. *Heere Gracht* or Gentleman's Canal (at the centre), flowing along what is now Broad Street, provided a means to ship goods into the heart of the walled town. No evidence of the waterway remains today. One of the waterfront houses alongside the canal would become New York's first City Hall. At the right of the scene is the start of the new settlement outside the wall, known as the *Voorstadt* or Suburb. The windmill is surrounded by gardens and orchards cultivated by the Dutch West India Company, reminiscent of those the VOC developed at Cape Town. The gardens were connected to the residential area around the fort by the *brede weg* or Broadway.

AMERICA'S PEPPER MILLIONAIRES

New York's prosperity was not built on spices, but to the north-east in Massachusetts Bay is a port whose wealth actually was: where America's first millionaires made their fortunes trading in pepper. Salem, founded in 1626 by Puritan settlers from England, was known originally by its Algonquian[5] name Naumkeag (or Naimkeck). In the map of 1656 by Jansson/Visscher, the original name can be found beside the lettering 'Massachusetts', though by then the port was known as Salem, meaning 'place of peace' in Hebrew, from the same root as the greeting words Shalom and Salaam.[6] The map is one of the earliest with a degree of geographical accuracy, and was part of a *remonstrance* or petition to the government in the motherland by New Netherland settlers, which led to reforms which were evidently not sufficient to save the colony from its subsequent takeover by the English.

Settlers at Salem initially made a living by fishing. That in turn gave rise to a boat-building industry involving carpenters and caulkers, sail, chain and rope makers and a variety of other crafts, who together transformed a small fishing port into a major centre for long-distance international trade. This was before Salem's southern neighbour of Boston joined the competition. Boston does not show on the 1656 map, though the point where the Charles River enters Massachusetts Bay is marked. Salem's trading vessel of choice was the schooner of 100 tons or more, slower than a Dutch *fluyt* but better at sailing into wind and so adept at crossing two mighty oceans. By the end of the eighteenth century, ships of up to 275 tons were being launched at Salem. The view of the harbour in 1780 (page 246) shows shipbuilding and goods being transferred into smaller vessels for onward travel; the same artist produced the slightly earlier view of New York.

Salem mariners copied Europeans in sailing past the Cape of Good Hope into the Indian Ocean, reaching the large East Indies island of Sumatra. There they found pepper, *Piper nigrum,* which had been traded from Venetian times for use as a preservative, a flavourer – in stews, for example – and an aphrodisiac. It was even used as a currency as in 'peppercorn rent', meaning a very low or nominal rent. But for Salem's sailors the value of pepper was closer to that of gold.[7]

Pepper grew on the western slopes of Sumatra's mountains, so Salem's sailors traded along what came to be known as the 'Pepper Coast'. They traded at Bencoolen, which was under the control of the British, and Padang, which was ruled by the Dutch, but their preference was to do business north of the Equator in Acheen (or Achem, now Aceh), which was inhabited by the

Piper nigrum, *or black pepper, from Sumatra, on which Salem's prosperity was based, in a Bengal-style watercolour collected by the Marquis of Wellesley, 1798–1805.*

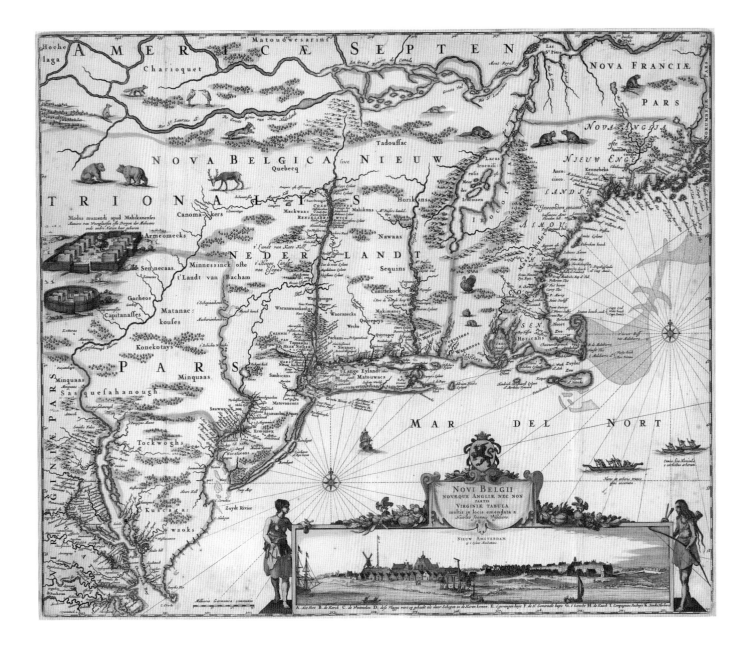

fiercely independent Chinese. There they could deal directly with local headmen (see map on page 258). This was not without dangers, as the region was rife with piracy. The Salem trade was very largely for pepper, though to make up a cargo they sometimes returned with cinnamon and camphor as well as nutmeg, mace and cloves trans-shipped in Sumatra or from nearby ports in Java. There was no attempt at colonisation let alone proselytisation by the Salem traders as there was with Europeans.

Shipping spices made millionaires of Salem's traders. The grand old man of the port's long-distance trade was Elias Hasket Derby – nicknamed King Derby – whose trading activity took off after the American Revolution ended in 1791. His ships were among the first to reach Sumatra and returned laden with pepper, helping Salem become one of the wealthiest ports in America: 'the most famous port in the New World', in the words of historian Ralph D. Paine.

Salem's first customs house was inaugurated in 1789 and was soon contributing 10 per cent of all the new nation's tax revenue. Salem's trade with Sumatra involved a round trip of at least 42,000 kilometres (26,000 miles), much further than for the Dutch or English and often in difficult sailing conditions, but the rewards in terms of profit made it worthwhile. Its ships had a good safety record: most of the hundreds of vessels despatched to Sumatra returned safely, a credit to the sturdiness of Salem-built ships. The Derby family were the first to make their ships 'copper-bottomed' for greater strength and to introduce the supercargo, a travelling business agent. Elias Hasket Derby is said to have controlled American trade with Bombay, Madras and Calcutta. Derby ships also called at Batavia, loading sugar, coffee and nutmeg, and at Manila and Canton.

Another Salem family to benefit from long-distance trade in spices were the Crowninshields, seventeenth-century immigrants from Saxony in Germany.[8] They were in competition with the Derbys, though also linked through marriages in the 1760s: Captain George Crowninshield, Senior, married Mary Derby, Elias Hasket Derby's sister, while Elias married George's sister, Elizabeth Crowninshield. The families maintained separate wharves, each about half a mile long, with a third, the Union Wharf, for general use. A painting by George Ropes Junior in 1806 shows the Crowninshield Wharf stretching into Salem harbour.

The pepper trade with Sumatra made millionaires of the Derby and Crowninshield patriarchs, America's first, while George Crowninshield, Junior, built and sailed America's first 'pleasure yacht', launched at Salem in 1816; it was named *Cleopatra's Barge* after the luxurious 'cloth of gold' canopy under which the Egyptian queen Cleopatra VII reclined, as featured in Shakespeare's play *Antony and Cleopatra*.[9]

The trade in spices was interrupted when America's third president imposed what became known as the 'Jefferson embargo' in 1807, ordering ships to remain in port in an effort to stay neutral in the Napoleonic Wars then raging in Europe, to prevent them falling prey to British or French vessels. Salem was badly affected, though the Crowninshields made money by resorting to 'privateering': sponsoring independent sailors to attack enemy vessels. The act introducing the embargo was repealed after fourteen months, though trade was interrupted again when Britain and America fought what amounted to a trade war in 1812.

By then Boston was taking over from Salem as Massachusetts' main trading port. Larger vessels needed deeper harbours. Boston had followed Salem's lead bringing tea from Canton – across the Pacific and round Cape Horn so as not to be in direct competition with Salem, whose traders by this time were carrying tea from Canton across the Indian and Atlantic Oceans, as well as sugar from Mauritius, cinnamon from Ceylon, ginger from Malacca and cotton from India. They brought wine from Madeira, salt from the Cape Verde Islands and pioneered trade with Denmark, Sweden and Russia on the Baltic Sea, while New York dominated trade with the 'parent' ports of Amsterdam and London. Within two decades of America gaining its independence, Salem had become the sixth largest city in the federated states; but Boston had overtaken it, taking fifth place.[10]

Salem historian James Duncan Phillips attributes Salem's rise to its having 'a greater number of intelligent, courageous, industrious people at that period than any other town in America ... These men believed they had the best ships in the world and they were largely right ... They could sail faster and closer to the wind than any ships then built.'[11] Phillips questioned what the traders did with the vast quantities of pepper and other spices reaching Salem in the peak period around 1810, and found that much of it was re-exported to Europe, taking on the Dutch and English at their own game, or shipped onwards to Boston, Philadelphia and Baltimore from where it may also have been traded with Europe. Salem had become 'the pepper mart of the world ... No port in America has ever dominated the trade in a single foreign commodity, or in a single part of the world, so

Crowninshield Wharf at Salem in 1806 when the pepper trade was thriving, painted by George Ropes Junior.

thoroughly as Salem did in pepper from Sumatra in the first fifty years of the [US] Republic.'[12] By 1846, when larger vessels needing larger ports took over the trade, Salem had received 179 shiploads of pepper.

Salem is better known for the trials of witches there in the 1690s when twenty men and women were hanged, a notorious case of mass hysteria. Also of note is its novelist, Nathaniel Hawthorne, whose book *The House of the Seven Gables* was based in Salem. Young Phœbe is asked by her maiden aunt Hepzibah to roast some coffee, 'which she casually observed was the real Mocha, and so long kept that each of the small berries ought to be worth its weight in gold', a reference to the fact that the Derby family were also the first to bring coffee from the Arabian peninsula; it was renowned at the

time as being the finest.[13] Hawthorne knew much about Salem's maritime tradition, having worked as a young man at the town's customs house, experience he features in an introductory chapter to his most celebrated novel, *The Scarlet Letter*.

The Dutch first brought tea to New York, but before long Salem and Boston became the choice port of entry for tea brought from the Chinese port of Canton by the English East India Company. An important date in America's bid for independence from England was 10 May 1773, when settlers protested at the imposition of a tax on tea by Britain's parliament. At what came to be known as the Boston Tea Party, they threw 342 chests of tea into Boston harbour, demanding that there be 'no taxation without representation'. Settlers in Britain's thirteen American colonies could not send representatives to the British parliament, which nonetheless imposed taxes on their trading activities.

The Boston Tea Party grew into the 'Revolution' when the government in London tried unsuccessfully to remove local control of colonies and close down Boston's commerce. This led to the American Congress's Declaration of Independence on 4 July 1776, which was eventually accepted by Britain in the Treaty of Paris of 3 September 1783. The Boston Tea Party is said to have weaned future US citizens off tea in favour of coffee drinking. For a time after the Tea Party, Boston harbour was closed as punishment; Salem, with a population of around 4,500, temporarily became capital of the new state of Massachusetts. But Boston overtook Salem as the dominant port, having deeper berths for larger vessels and the advantage of a river, enabling goods to be transferred up-state. The more populous city of New York was capturing business from Salem too.

Events in Boston may have sparked the Revolution, but the first blood was spilled in Salem; so American independence was more truly born in Salem. The maritime origin of Salem's wealth is commemorated in its motto 'To the Farthest Ports of the Rich East'. The port also engaged in the so-called 'triangular trade', by which European vessels shipped enslaved Africans to the West Indies, and sugar and molasses produced there by enslaved labourers were shipped to the North American colonies. This gave Salem an industry distilling rum, which was in turn shipped to Europe.

Leaving Massachusetts to return to New York takes us through New Haven, Connecticut, the home of Yale University, whose benefactor Elihu Yale earned his fortune working in India for the English East India Company. Born in Boston, Massachusetts in 1649, the young Elihu Yale was brought to England at the age of 3, attending school in London before gaining employment with the East India Company and sailing to India. He spent his working life at Fort St George, Madras, rising to become president of the company's south India operation which traded mainly in spices. In later years Yale was tainted by involvement in the slave trade and implicated in corruption scandals. It was alleged that he bought land for personal use with East India Company money.

After retiring to England, he made gifts towards the foundation of Yale College in response to two separate approaches; he then moved to Wales, having never seen the institution which to this day bears his name. It is ironic that a man who spent only the first three years of his life in America and was associated with commerce and exploitation rather than education should have given his name to one of America's leading academic institutions.

Another irony is that New Haven's state of Connecticut was given the unofficial nickname 'the Nutmeg State'. Nutmeg never grew there and almost certainly first reached America through Salem, Massachusetts. The nickname derived from the practice of local traders passing off wooden nutmegs as the real thing, which shows there was a demand for nutmeg in Connecticut at the time and probably alludes to sharp business practices in general, what today we would call 'scams'.

A product from south-east Asia that did come ashore in Connecticut was rubber. In 1911 the United States Rubber Company – the forerunner of Uniroyal – was founded near New Haven. By 1917 it had planted

The inset added later to the 1656 Jansson/Visscher map (page 243) shows the 1673 restitutio view of lower Manhattan, which was briefly renamed Nieuw Amsterdam.

100,000 acres of rubber trees in Sumatra, a lead that other large US rubber companies would follow in the race to meet demand for tyres and other rubber goods.

NEW YORK MISCELLANY

Views of New York's skyline over time, especially views of its Manhattan core, are the best way of demonstrating the evolution of the city. The inset from the previous Amsterdam-published Jansson/Visscher map can be seen at larger scale depicting the settlement with around 1,500 inhabitants. A tall flagpole stands over Fort Amsterdam, as it was then known. One of the houses facing the East River belonged to Petrus Stuyvesant. At the centre is the wharf, with a device for unloading vessels known to the Dutch as Schreyers Hoek, which could also be used as gallows.

The image opposite the chapter opening, from *Valentine's Manual* of 1766–7, shows the city a decade before independence. It comprises both a map based on that by Bernard Ratzer, and below it an onshore view from Governor's Island, a similar perspective to that of the 1656 image. With a city population of around 20,000, we see that the upper part of Manhattan Island was still largely farmland (with the name of Stuyvesant prominent), as was the adjoining area of Long Island, present-day Brooklyn. Both images show how much the city had expanded from its humble and sparsely-populated origins, yet it had a long way to go. In 1746 London had a population of 700,000, whereas that of New York was around 7,000, one hundredth.

Then 80 years later an 'aerial view', which appeared in the *Illustrated London News*, shows an even more developed city with a mass of ships on either side at both river mouths. All vestiges of the fort at the southern point of Manhattan have disappeared, leaving tree-covered Battery Park. Broadway remains the main link to the north of the island, with Trinity Church opposite Wall Street and St Paul's Chapel opposite City Hall both prominent. Text accompanying the view declares the rise of the commercial metropolis as 'one of the marvels of modern history' and gives its population

in 1855 as over 600,000. New York, it goes on, 'has become the emporium of trade between Europe and America', and mentions the packet-ships sailing to and from Liverpool on England's west coast.

In 1869, the year the Suez Canal opened, connecting the Mediterranean Sea to the Indian Ocean and greatly shortening the sea journey between Europe and Asia, a start was made was made on Brooklyn Bridge. It opened fourteen years later, providing the first solid link between Manhattan and Long Island. The official seal of the city of New York, featuring a beaver, reflects the origins of the European colony.

The European competition for spices played a significant role in the rise of New York. It was on a voyage in search of the sources of cinnamon, clove and nutmeg that Christopher Columbus accidentally 'discovered' the Americas. He was followed by Ferdinand Magellan, Francis Drake, Giovanni da Verrazzano, John Cabot and Henry Hudson, all set on reaching and then crossing the Pacific to find spices – but the American continent blocked their way. The Spanish then settled the south and centre of the continent, leaving it to religiously focused emigrés from France, the Netherlands and England to settle in the north. Where European tastes started the competition for global trade, so those of American settlers followed: not just for spices but for tea, sugar and coffee, none of which grew in America.

The only spices native to the Americas are allspice, chillies and vanilla – all plants which have migrated westwards to Africa and Asia – so it is logical that spice migration in the opposite direction also took place, with Grenada in the West Indies (or Caribbean) a particularly rich source of nutmeg, cinnamon, ginger and cloves. After the Revolution ended with American independence, New York became an important hub between industrialising Europe and agricultural America, shipping commodities like cotton produced by slave labour in the southern states to Europe.

American tastes also drove the lively import trade, given the fondness of its people in modern times for adding cinnamon to pastries and using nutmeg in recipes for puddings and cakes. Nutmeg is also believed to be an ingredient for America's (and the world's) favourite beverages, Coca-Cola, whose recipe is a closely guarded secret. (The Coca-Cola corporation would not confirm its use.) New York remains the coffee-drinking capital of the world.

American growth also gave rise to massive demand for another crop which, following another episode of transplantation, came to grow most prolifically in south-east Asia: rubber. This commodity will be the focus of our final chapter.

(previous spread) Bird's-eye view of New York with Battery Park in the foreground and Brooklyn Bridge on the right (built 1869–83.) Colour lithograph by G. Schiegel, published c.1873.

(opposite top) New York's East River quay with Brooklyn Bridge beyond in a photomechanical print, c.1901.

(opposite bottom) Mulberry Street, New York, in an early photomechanical print.

12/ SINGAPORE, LION CITY

A 1578 map by Sebastian Münster marks Cingapolo on the mainland, while also showing the large number of islands clustered around the base of the peninsula.

We have already noted that Singapore, under its former name of Temasek, was colonised by the Srivijaya dynasty in the late fourteenth century and was an active settlement engaging in trade for at least a hundred years. Its last ruler during that period, Parameswara, fled an invasion by the Java-based Majapahit sultanate at the end of the fifteenth century and went on to establish the sultanate of Malacca, taking the title Sultan Iskandar Shah. There is no further record of activity on the island at the foot of the Malay peninsula until the early nineteenth century, possibly because the neighbouring sultanate of Johore was growing in strength.

Archaeological excavations on Singapore have revealed coins and porcelain, suggesting it was a trading port from the time of the Sung dynasty which ruled China from the tenth to thirteenth centuries. It may have been that vessels varied their routes in an effort to evade attacks from pirates for, as the fourteenth-century Chinese trader Wang Dayuan noted, the inhabitants of the islands off the Malay peninsula were 'addicted to piracy'. Nor do we know which route was taken by Zheng He's treasure fleet on its way from Nanjing to Malacca in the early fifteenth century. It would certainly have sailed past Singapore and may have entered Keppel harbour, based on a reference to 'Dragon's Teeth straits' which is thought to refer to twin granite outcrops on Sentosa, an island south of Singapore.

Singapura is mentioned in the *Sejarah Melayu* or Malay Annals written around 1535. The island's name was based on an alleged sighting of a lion there: *singa* means 'lion' in Sanskrit and Malay whilst *pura* means 'town'. Lions are not found anywhere in south-east Asia, so it is likely to have been a false sighting. At any rate it stuck, and to this day Singapore rejoices in the nickname 'Lion City'. The Portuguese traveller and historian João de Barros, writing in 1553, called Cingapura 'anciently the most celebrated settlement in this region', while the Portuguese poet Luiz Vaz de Camões referred to Singapore 'at the peninsula's tip ... where the straits are at their narrowest' in his epic poem the *Lusíads* of 1572.

The name first appears on maps in the works of Giacomo Gastaldi, who in 1548 published a revised edition of Ptolemy's *Geographia* using information from European voyagers, and in 1598 on maps of his fellow Venetian Girolamo Ruscelli. Both used the spelling *Cinca Pula*, suggesting an alternative origin to its name, as *pulau* means 'island' in the Malay language. We see a different spelling, *Cingapolo*, on the map of Sebastian Münster of 1578 facing the chapter opening, though it indicates a settlement on the southern mainland in the sultanate of Johore. It can be compared with two maps in Chapter 5: that by Bertius and Wright of 1612 (page 103), which uses the spelling Sincapura, as does Linschoten's of 1596 (page 133).

The Scottish doctor Alexander Hamilton records that the island was bequeathed to him during a call he made on the sultan of Johore in 1703 saying: 'I told him it could be of no use to a private Person, though a proper place for a Company to settle a colony, lying in the Centre of Trade ... with good Rivers and safe Harbours, so conveniently situated that all Winds served Shipping both to go out and come in.'[1] Given these early references to Singapore's suitability as a trading port and reference to it on maps, it is surprising that it was not until the nineteenth century that any maritime power made a 'land grab' for this chunk of real estate.

THE FOUNDATION OF MODERN SINGAPORE

The island's modern history is all about British trading ambitions and empire building. The East India Company had already founded a port for trading in pepper and other spices at Prince of Wales Island (Penang) and had taken control of Malacca, both ports on the western coast of the Malay peninsula. The Dutch success in taking control of Java and islands of the Malay archipelago encouraged East India Company traders to look for a port better suited than Penang to reach the Spice Islands. Stamford Raffles, the company's administrator at Malacca and then lieutenant-governor of Java, had not wanted to return Batavia to the Dutch when the threat from Napoleon-ruled France disappeared. He was keen to keep a foothold in the archipelago. The west Sumatra port of Bencoolen, where he became lieutenant-governor after the return of Java, was well located for the pepper trade, but less so for the more valuable trade in 'Eastern' spices.

Raffles made a habit of acting on his own authority without awaiting
a response from the company's governor-general in Calcutta, let alone its
headquarters in London. He started searching for another port that would
rival Batavia, by then the most successful trading base in the region. His first
choice was somewhere in the Rhio (now Riau) archipelago, which straddles
the Equator between Sumatra and the Malay peninsula. Discovering that it
was already under Dutch control, he and the company's chief hydrographer,
Captain Daniel Ross (like Raffles a fellow of the Royal Society), turned their
attention to Singapore island, which Raffles had briefly visited some years
earlier on his way to take control of Java. It lay just north of the Equator,
close to the peninsula and near the wide mouth of the Johore River, as
portrayed in the 1753 map by the French cartographer Jacques-Nicolas
Bellin; the image also marks Bencoolen (Bancoulo) in south-west Sumatra
where Raffles was then based.

The company was sensitive about settling an island knowing the Dutch
regarded the entire archipelago as its property. Yet when Raffles and his

company colleague, William Farquhar, landed at Singapore island in January 1819, they felt that the mouth of the Singapore River on the south side of the island just north of the Equator was an ideal location for their chief port. Bugis sailors from the eastern islands were already bringing spices there. It was an ideal transit stop on the route between London or Bombay and China. Raffles set about negotiating with the sultan of Johore and his local representative, the *Temenggong*, a complicated business since the old sultan had recently died and two brothers had rival claims to succeed him, the younger of the two having already been recognised as the new sultan by the Dutch.

Fortunately for the British, the elder brother, Tunku Long, won the argument allowing Raffles, acting at this stage on behalf of the East India Company's Calcutta based governor-general, to sign a rental agreement and treaty of alliance with him on 6 February 1819. The new sultan was fearful of Dutch repercussions, and so were the British. Pending resolution of the issue between London and Amsterdam, it was company policy for vessels sailing from London not to call at Singapore. That did not prevent it developing

By 1753, when Jacques-Nicolas Bellin created this detailed map, it was the Straits (Detroit) of Singapore that were of more interest than the island itself.

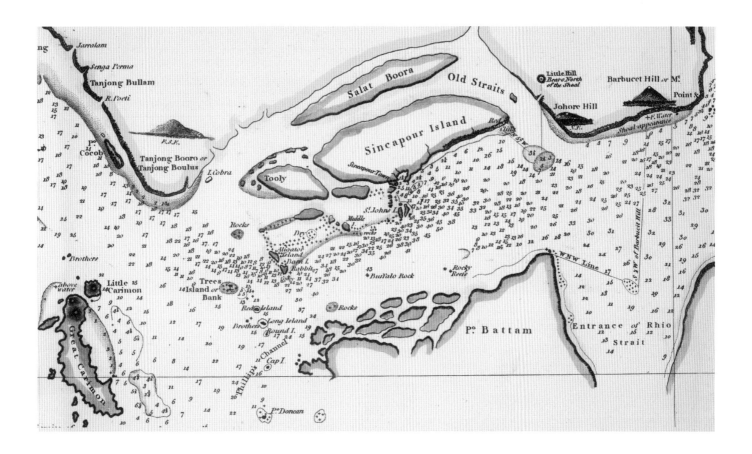

This sea chart of the waterways around Singapore prepared by James Horburgh in 1823 shows that the 'old straits' to the north of Singapore have given way to the southern route which leads to the harbour.

into a busy entrepôt for ships sailing between Asian ports in what was known as the 'country trade'. The handover to the East India Company was remarkably civil, since it suited both parties well; according to one of Raffles' biographers, 'It was not a conquest. It was more like a leasehold purchase.'[2]

It appealed to Raffles' sense of history that the company and country he represented were resettling the long abandoned 'Lion City', which he described in a letter to a friend as 'the site of the ancient maritime capital of the Malays'.[3] There were a few hundred people living on the island at the time: Malays, Chinese who had migrated from Johore or Malacca and a small community of Bugis traders from Sulawesi. It seemed that neither the Portuguese nor the Dutch had even visited the island, let alone settled there. They may have been discouraged by the island's size, which at 42 km (26 miles) long by about 22 km (14 miles) from north to south offered little scope for establishing plantations. But the British felt they had a good deal. A consequence of the foundation of Singapore was that Malacca went into decline as a port, as did Johore. Raffles insisted that the company's 'object is not territory but trade' and compared Singapore's potential as a trade fulcrum with that of Malta in the Mediterranean: 'What Malta is in the West, that may Singapore be in the East.' The chart of the waters around the island in 1823 shows the benefit of the port's position, but also how close it was to islands like Great Carimon and Battam, which were nominally under Dutch control.

Raffles left the island soon after the signing, having made it clear that Farquhar, the company-appointed resident administrator, should report to him in Bencoolen as he held the more senior rank of lieutenant-governor in the company's hierarchy. This effectively made Singapore a dependency of Bencoolen. Raffles' ambition did not end there, since he had plans (which were not necessarily endorsed by the company) to set up a trading post in the Acheen region of northern Sumatra where American traders from Salem had a virtual monopoly on the export of pepper. Also he was expecting the company to make him governor of Prince of Wales Island or Penang, which was on the peninsula opposite Acheen, as a reward for ruling Java and 'acquiring' Singapore.

In all those respects he was unsuccessful; so he returned to Singapore in October 1822, once again pulling rank on Farquhar who had clearly made a success of the settlement. Raffles was pleasantly surprised to find how rapidly the island had developed and that its population after three years now exceeded 10,000. A key attraction was its status as a 'free port' – no import duties were collected. It was also developing as a testing ground for new plantation crops, to which Raffles had contributed by sending potato and nutmeg plants, a further sign of how the British had almost unwittingly breached the Dutch-claimed spice monopoly.

Despite Singapore's evident prosperity as a trading port, Raffles lost no opportunity to countermand Farquhar's instructions, taking over the planning role himself and belittling the achievements of his junior. They did not get on and Raffles (who had never been able to make Bencoolen pay its way) set out to reverse Farquhar's arrangements for the accommodation of company officials. Raffles may have felt undermined; at any rate he was coping with the loss through disease of three of his young children. Having not won the promotion he felt he deserved, he was planning to end his

An 1841 drawing of the Singapore Institute, proposed by Raffles in 1823 for the teaching of Asian languages and education of the sons of Malay sultans. It was later renamed the Raffles Institute.

service with the company and return to London. But firstly he set himself two important duties. One was to set up an English-style school for the children of company officials, the Singapore Institution. The other was to dismiss Farquhar, who had settled in Singapore with his Malay common law wife by whom he had six children. It may have been his lifestyle to which Raffles took exception, or he may have been set on replacing him with his own favoured candidate.

Raffles' biographer Victoria Glendinning writes: 'Farquhar was connected with the people in a way Raffles could never be, and was therefore tolerant of traditional practices such as gaming and opium-farming, and of course slavery.' And despite Raffles' earlier assertion that the company's objective was not territory but trade, it was Farquhar who never lost sight of the fact that the land was vested in the *Temenggong* and the sultan and the port was 'a native port' which to Raffles was 'an extraordinary principle'.[4]

Farquhar's dismissal in May 1823 was ugly, a resounding vote of no confidence by Raffles in the man who in three years had made Singapore a success story, something recognised by parliament in London. Raffles waited only for Farquhar's replacement to arrive from Calcutta before himself departing for London via Bencoolen, having first seen the foundation stone laid for the Singapore Institution, which survives to this day as the Raffles Institute. Raffles and Farquhar laid the groundwork of what would become

a thriving metropolis, as seen in the image of Government Hill in the 1830s, with Singapore harbour beyond amid well-constructed houses for the European population.

It took longer for the territorial and spice-based issues between the Dutch and the British to be resolved, with missives exchanged between respective company headquarters in Amsterdam and London. After Britain returned Java, the Dutch regarded the British presence at Bencoolen and elsewhere in Sumatra and continuing interest in the Spice Islands as an irritant, a hindrance to its own claim on the entire East Indies archipelago. Similarly, the British regarded Dutch control of Malacca as an annoyance – not that the British wanted it themselves, but its occupation by the Dutch detracted from Britain's development of Singapore as a major entrepôt, which the Dutch in turn regarded as an unwanted commercial challenge to Batavia. Agreement was eventually reached and formulated into the Treaty of London of March 1824. It amounted to a sharing out of territory to which neither nation had any intrinsic right. The treaty provided for Britain to cede to the Netherlands 'the Factory of Fort Marlborough [at Bencoolen] and all the English possessions on the Island of Sumatra'. In return, the treaty laid down that 'the Town and Fort of Malacca, and its dependencies, are hereby ceded to his Britannick Majesty'. In other words, a swap of territory tied up the respective 'possessions' (in the treaty's word) of the Dutch and British in south-east Asia. Additionally, the British agreed to respect the Dutch 'Monopoly of Spices' and the Dutch agreed to 'withdraw the objections ... to the occupation of the Island of Singapore, by the Subjects of His Brittanick Majesty'. The treaty also formalised the return of Java to the Dutch.

This view from Government Hill (later Fort Canning) looks towards Singapore harbour (right) and out to 'the roads' where vessels waited their turn to enter the harbour to unload. Coloured lithograph by W.C. Smith, London c.1830.

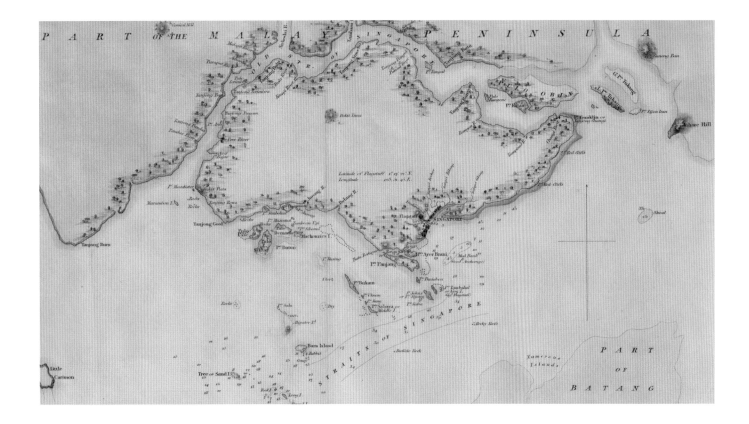

It was the most significant agreement between the two nations since the Treaty of Breda of 1667, which endorsed an earlier territorial exchange involving the Spice Islands and New York. The 1824 treaty divided the Malay world, giving Britain rights to the Malay peninsula and Singapore island, while the Dutch were granted exclusive trading rights over all the islands variously known as the East Indies or the Malay archipelago, including the whole of Sumatra and islands such as Bintang, Battam and Great Carimon that lay within sight of Singapore. Both nations agreed to give up challenges to control exercised by the other. There was no evidence of consultation with the many sultans who exercised authority over much of the territory being shared between London and Amsterdam. One oddity was no mention of the large island of Borneo, which straddles the Equator to the north of Java, possibly because agreement on its status could not be reached.

The treaty came into force on 1 March 1825; although it was not evident at the time, this was the foundation of the modern nation states of Malaysia, Singapore and Indonesia when both European powers withdrew from south-east Asia in the mid-twentieth century. Borneo was by then split between the two powers: the Dutch having taken control of the larger two-thirds part of the island (known as Kalimantan), and Britain the northern third consisting of Sarawak and Sabah, now part of the Malaysian federation, and the separate Malay-speaking Islamic sultanate of Brunei. The Sultan of Brunei is the only south-east Asian sultan still exercising absolute rule over his territory. Malaysia adopted an unusual constitutional system under which its eleven sultans take turns to occupy the throne as 'king' of the federated nation while a democratically elected government rules. Singapore and Brunei both toyed with joining the federation before opting for independent statehood.

By the time of the 1830 sketch of the mouth of the Singapore River, Singapore island appears to have grown in size, though this was probably a result of more accurate survey work rather than the reclamation of land which took place later. The main settlement was, and remains, close to the point where the short Singapore River enters the sea. When ships grew too big to enter the harbour, they anchored offshore and 'lightermen' from the Singapore River transferred cargoes in smaller boats from the 'roads' (as offshore anchorages were known) to warehouses lining the lower reaches of the river.

Raffles is regarded as the founder of modern Singapore, and the date of his landing at the mouth of the Singapore River – 28 January 1819 – marks the birth of one of the world's most successful trading ports. It was the year of Princess Victoria's birth; she would one day rule as queen of Britain and empress of India and other British-ruled territories.

Raffles' role as Singapore's founder needs to be qualified with credit to William Farquhar, who contributed a great deal to the island's success. Indeed, many regard Farquhar as the true founder. The role of map-makers who first charted a shipping route from Malacca to Macao through the straits north of Singapore needs to be acknowledged too. The route is depicted as 'the old straits' on many maps, while the route south of the island was depicted in a 1798 chart as the 'Governor's Straits', after a Spanish governor of the Philippines apparently ran aground there when leading his fleet this way to Malacca in 1616.

Raffles also had a role in planting spices. Not long after Pierre Poivre's success in Mauritius, the British also succeeded with the spice plants they had 'stolen' from under Dutch eyes. They planted seedlings at Bencoolen and Penang, the fruits of which reached Europe around 1815, and Raffles planted more in the experimental botanical gardens he created overlooking the harbour in Singapore. However, a fearful disease made its appearance in the 1840s, which caused the nutmeg fruits to wither before they ripened. By the end of the 1850s, it had spread to every plantation with 'ruin staring the proprietors of the plantation in the face'.[5] A local observer wrote in 1865: 'Most of these plantations are now abandoned, the [nutmeg] trees being dead or dying, and it is a somewhat melancholy sight to see acre upon acre of these skeleton trees, upon which many enterprising men have lost fortunes.'[6]

THE RUBBER CROP

Singapore was key to another transplantation which would have an even greater impact on global trade and power: *Hevea Brasiliensis*, the plant that produces rubber. Native to the Amazon rainforest, the tree produces sap which when dried is good for erasing writing or making a ball bounce, properties discovered in the late nineteenth century. The eraser was called an 'Indian rubber' not for any true connection with India but from the Amazon natives that drained or 'tapped' the liquid rubber or latex from the *Hevea* tree, another confusion based on Columbus thinking he had reached India.

Rubber tapping in Sumatra,
photographed by C. J.
Kleingrothe c.1905.

In the 1880s, the bicycle was becoming popular in Europe and rubber tyres made for a much softer ride than on earlier 'bone-shaker' versions. Also in the 1880s, when American inventor Thomas Edison discovered electricity, rubber was found to be an effective insulator allowing electricity to be transmitted through cables. Demand for rubber grew rapidly when the first internal combustion engine car was invented in the same decade. That was when the big rubber tyre manufacturers came into being: Goodrich, Goodyear and Firestone in the United States and Dunlop, Michelin and Pirelli in Europe.

There were not enough rubber trees in the Amazon to meet the heightened demand, so botanists experimented with cultivating the plant elsewhere. In an episode reminiscent of how spices spread, the British explorer Henry Wickham in 1876 smuggled 70,000 rubber seeds from Brazil to Britain where they were cultivated under glass at the Royal Botanical Gardens at Kew. For reasons of climate, only a small number germinated. Seedlings produced were sent to India, Ceylon and, most successfully, to the Singapore Botanic Gardens at Tanglin, successor to the experimental gardens Raffles created on Government Hill in the heart of the European settlement, where nutmeg and cloves were planted.

Plants cultivated in Singapore under the supervision of another British botanist, Henry Ridley, provided the seed stock for plantations on the Malay peninsula, which became a main source of rubber as rainforest was cleared and rubber trees planted. One of the earliest estates was created by the Tan family in Malacca. Botanist Tan Teck Guan corresponded with experts at Kew, and in 1896 his son, Tan Chay An, planted 48 acres at Malacca using seed provided by Henry Ridley from the Singapore Botanic Gardens. Ridley subsequently sold seedlings to many other planters and, according to rubber historian Henry Hobhouse, by 1901 nearly a million young *Hevea* trees were growing on the Malay peninsula.[7] Malaya became the world's major source of natural rubber, providing half the world's total production; the prosperity of Malaya and Singapore, the main port of export, was founded on rubber. Cultivation spread with American tyre manufacturers creating vast rubber plantations in Sumatra in the Dutch-ruled East Indies, while Michelin did the same in French-ruled Cochin China (south Vietnam). The *Hevea* tree was also cultivated successfully in Thailand, Ceylon and India.

Expansion of the car industry in the twentieth century ensured a constant demand for south-east Asian rubber, especially in the US, and though synthetic versions of rubber have been developed, demand continues for natural rubber for use in motor cars, aircraft, domestic appliances, footwear, electrical insulation, as a waterproofer in clothing and in sports equipment for tennis, football and billiards among others. Rubber was one of the commodities to which the Japanese wanted access when they captured much of south-east Asia in the Second World War.

LIEUTENANT-GOVERNOR MEETS EMPEROR

An extraordinary encounter took place as Raffles sailed back to Britain in 1816 after his period in control of Java – before the foundation of Singapore. His ship made a 36-hour stop at the East India Company-controlled island of St Helena in the Atlantic Ocean. Seven months earlier, Napoleon Bonaparte had arrived there after his defeat at the Battle of Waterloo. The island was chosen for its remoteness.

Napoleon lived in seclusion at Longwood House, near the centre of the island, where he kept a sort of 'royal court' more befitting his former status as emperor of France than that of the prisoner he had become, and he was choosy about whom he saw. East India Company officials returning from the East were in the habit of visiting Longwood in the hope of catching a glimpse of the 'colossus' who once bestrode Europe, their country's adversary over many years. Raffles, however, asked for and was granted an audience of sorts. It seemed Napoleon was interested in meeting this officer of the English East India Company. They had a curious connection: when France annexed the Dutch Republic in 1810, Napoleon became overlord of that country as well as its colonies including Java, until the British invaded the latter in 1811 and Raffles became the island's lieutenant-governor.

Napoleon had dreamed of presiding over an Eastern empire: 'If it had not been for the English I should have been emperor of the East, but wherever there is water to float a ship we are sure to find them in our way.' Napoleon and Raffles had much in common: both thought it a mistake that Britain had returned Java to the Dutch, as it allowed them once more to control supplies of coffee reaching Europe. Napoleon even criticised Britain for allowing the French 'to put their nose beyond the Cape', securing control of the Indian Ocean island of Bourbon (Réunion) and of Pondicherry in southern India, saying they should have maintained a commercial monopoly of the seas of India and China. Both opposed slavery, Raffles having been shocked to learn there were 12,000 enslaved people serving the Dutch in Batavia. (He ended the slave trade on Java and would in due course draft laws to end the practice of slavery in Singapore.) Napoleon had a similar reaction to finding British enslaved workers on St Helena, and criticised the British for not forcing the Portuguese to give up the slave trade (as described in Chapter 8).[8]

During their brief meeting in the grounds of Longwood, the former emperor asked the former lieutenant-governor intelligent questions: about the British invasion of Java and whether Raffles had taken part in it; whether Batavia was as unhealthy as ever; and whether the spice plantations in Ambon were doing well. He was keen to know whether the Spice Islands were being restored to the Dutch, as Java was. His questions came in a quick-fire manner, not waiting for a response before asking his next question. Though Napoleon never set foot east of Egypt, he could have pointed out all these places on a map. He was aware too of their strategic significance and the price-boosting impact of monopoly trade; he may

also have known that it was a Frenchman who first broke the Dutch spice monopoly by planting nutmeg at Mauritius.

Napoleon wanted to know what cargo was being carried in Raffles' ship, and asked the Englishman his view as to whether Bourbon or Java coffee was better. Napoleon was partial to coffee and knew of its power as an energiser and as a soldier's drink useful in alleviating hunger pangs.[9] During his Egyptian campaign he wrote: 'I always had seven coffee-pots on the boil while I was discussing with the Turks, or I had to stay awake all night talking over religious matters with them.' He knew that France had been instrumental in spreading the cultivation of coffee to central America and the Caribbean, and blamed the British for depriving France of its supplies from Haiti, though it had been his own ban on British ships entering continental ports that prevented coffee – and sugar, indigo, cotton and other commodities – from reaching France. Countries no longer supplied by France developed alternatives, extracting sugar from beet and roasting chicory roots as a coffee substitute, albeit without its energising effect.

Napoleon regarded India as the source of Britain's power and believed that control of Java gave power to the Netherlands. By asking what cargo Raffles' ship carried, he may have been hoping the former lieutenant-governor would

make him a present of Java coffee. Perhaps he knew already that Java coffee was superior to that produced on the French island of Bourbon. At any rate, he did not wait for an answer – and did not receive a present.

As it happened, Raffles was something of an expert on coffee cultivation, which he expanded during his rule of Java. To meet an anticipated increase in demand from Europe and America, he ordered that output be increased fivefold, removing a restriction limiting output to ten million pounds' weight. During his final two and a half years as lieutenant-governor, an additional eleven million coffee trees were planted on Java. Later he cultivated coffee in his garden at Bencoolen, as well as cloves and probably nutmeg too. Sadly, two of Europe's most infamous imperialists did not converse for long; they would probably have found other interests in common.

Raffles initially felt well-disposed towards this figure he regarded as 'the greatest man of the age', but afterwards he wrote to a friend: 'This man is a monster, who has none of the feelings of the heart which constitute the real man.' This may have been because of his haughty manner and the fact that he did not put his visitor at ease or invite him to sit. Raffles wrote that he was as 'determined and vindictive, without one spark of soul ... he looked down on all mankind as his inferiors ... as a wild animal caught but not tamed'.[10] History does not record Napoleon's impression of Raffles who,

Sketch of the Singapore River with boats and warehouses, by Sir Henry Yule, 1853.

Singapore today, now one of the world's busiest ports.

with his secretary Captain Thomas Travers, took leave when the fallen emperor indicated the meeting was over.

Had Napoleon lived later in the century he would have taken satisfaction from France's colonisation of Indo-China – Cambodia, Vietnam and Laos – which was in line with Raffles' vision for the development of trade outlined in a document for the East India Company three years after his meeting with Napoleon.[11] The deposed emperor would have relished the fact that spices and coffee flourished in Vietnam, which is now a significant coffee exporter; and also rubber, the key driver of industrialisation in the West and another example of a monopoly being broken through transplantation.

EPILOGUE

I t is appropriate that this history of the spice trade and its role in the development of global trade should conclude with Singapore, the last of these ports to be founded and one of the first to transform itself to serve the age of shipping containerisation. In the first chapter we heard of Venice being dubbed 'a medieval Singapore', so we may think of Singapore as 'a technological Venice', a port for the twenty-first century and now one of the world's busiest. Neither Venice nor Singapore could provide for its own population, which led them both to trade: initially for their inhabitants' sustenance, but ultimately for their prosperity.

As ships grew bigger and heavier, the geographical requirements for a port changed: deeper berths became more important than protection from wind and waves, so inland and river mouth ports like Goa, Malacca and Amsterdam lost their advantage; or else – as with London – the port moved downriver to accommodate larger vessels. Boston, Massachusetts, replaced Salem because it had deeper berths and onward river transportation enabling goods to be carried inland on smaller vessels.

The economics of trade changed significantly in the nineteenth century when steam power took over from wind as the means of propelling ships, giving way in turn to oil in the twentieth century. Those developments kick-started trade in the fuels – coal, oil and gas – needed to drive trains and cars on land and ships at sea. Coal was the driver of Europe's industrial revolution, coalfields replacing spice gardens as creators of wealth; to be supplanted in due course by the oil wells of the Middle East. Specialised tankers were developed to transport oil, and then compressed and refrigerated gas in liquid form.[1] Traditional wharfs gave way to purpose-built tanker terminals, specialising in loading and unloading a particular commodity and located for easy onward transportation.

From the mid-1900s seaborne shipping containers and the vessels that carry them further changed the nature of international trade, with goods packed away at the factory into large sealed crates. Container ships today, which can hold up to 24,000 TEUs or Twenty-foot Equivalent Units,[2] are the new main vehicles of international trade traversing the proverbial 'Seven

Seas' once sailed by galleys, caravels, *fluyts*, clippers and schooners. The entire pepper cargo of a 120-ton Salem schooner, for example, would fit into three modern 20-foot containers.

So next time you enjoy sitting with a coffee, reflect on the trading process that brought you the coffee and accompanying cinnamon pastry, the pepper and mace that went into a later 'curry' meal, perhaps washed down with a glass of clove-infused mulled wine or ginger ale or cup of tea, all products of the East. And consider the ingredients you might include in making a fruit cake, such as cinnamon or nutmeg; how deficient a modern kitchen would be without these valued spices, not to mention chilli powder, vanilla, mustard, seasoning transported from different parts of the world. You may even have need of that most popular of remedies to staunch toothache, oil of cloves. Demand for such spices to make our cuisine more appetising inaugurated long-distance global trade while coffee and tea changed our life styles, coffee with its invigorating effect, tea as a relaxant or sedative.

Reflect too on how the *reasons* for trade have changed. The Venetians sought the sustenance of human life, salt and wheat, from the nearby mainland; spices came from further afield. Later, trade was their means for acquiring the luxuries of life, including different types of cloth and precious stones, perfumes and ceramic tableware. In the modern age it is hard to think of anything that is not transported by ship, including all varieties of manufactured goods including, for example, vehicles and electronic devices.

Our ancestors' appetite for spices gave rise to many human inventions, such as the measurement of distance using time, and the grid of latitude and longitude which enabled map-making; and the use of wind power to cut wood to build ships and then speed their passage. This urge also provided the contacts, inspiration and wealth which generated great art and literature. The trade in spices fuelled economic concepts, like supply and demand and

A liquefied natural gas (LNG) container in the Straits of Singapore.

monopoly power; it gave rise to banking, stock market trading and the futures market.

On the negative side, the contest for control of the market in spices and other goods gave rise to wars, including over the supplying of opium; to the colonisation of other people's lands; and – most iniquitous of all – the enslavement of peoples, a trade in human beings, all for the want of tea, coffee, sugar and spices. The spice trade without doubt widened the economic gap between the colonising and colonised nations; though since then their relative prosperity has changed again to some extent. For example, the islands of Indonesia which once gave the world spices now provide coal, oil and gas and are the world's foremost source of nickel. There is an endless shifting of profit and loss account in world trade; but never can the satisfying of human appetites for taste be balanced against the terrible toll of human suffering that it entailed.

In terms of demand balanced against limited supply, the modern-day spice equivalents are probably the so-called 'green minerals' – like lithium, cobalt, nickel and gallium – all in limited supply yet needed to support alternative energy in combatting climate change. Like the spices of old these largely originate from the East. Nowadays aircraft provide another means of long-distance trade, to transport fresh fruit and vegetables and pharmaceutical products, for example; while that nineteenth-century invention, the railway, brings cars and computers from China to Europe in less time and at lower cost than the long journey by ship, avoiding the always congested Suez Canal as well as the Malacca Straits through which, it is said, passes 25 per cent of all world trade.

If there is a key element that made the trade in spices possible, with all its associated benefits, it is surely the wind and our human ability to harness it; the 'sciences' of map-making and navigation take the next places in the roll of honour of developments that enabled international trade.

Container ships carry far more than the ships of old and easily congest shipping lanes. In 2021, the Ever Given *ran aground, blocking the Suez Canal for six days.*

NOTES

INTRODUCTION

1   Quotations from Abraham Ortelius are from the English translation of *Theatrum Orbis Terrarum* by William Bedwell, published in 1606.

CHAPTER 1

1   Author of *Cità Excelentissima*, quoted in Michelle Lovric, *Venice: Tales of the City*, p. 51.
2   Herodotus, *The Histories*, 5.9.
3   Jan Morris, *Venice*, p. 11.
4   Roger Crowley, *City of Fortune – How Venice Ruled the Seas*, p. 286.
5   Roger Crowley, ibid., pp. 117–18.
6   Ibid., p. 253.
7   Adam Smith, *The Wealth of Nations*, 1776, p. 138.
8   Quoted in Michael Krondl, *The Taste of Conquest*, p. 33. See also Throwley, pp. 372–3.
9   For example, by Michael Krondl in *The Taste of Conquest*, p. 20.
10 Braun and Hogenberg's atlas eventually contained 546 bird's-eye views of important cities.
11 Venetian Jacob de' Barbari is credited with being the first to 'imagine' Venice from the air in 1500. Braun and Hogenberg would have used detail from his 3-metre-long image.
12 Dante Alighieri, *Inferno*, Canto XXI, 7–11.
13 The term 'Silk Road' was coined in 1877 by German scientist and traveller Ferdinand von Richthofen.
14 Probably because the book was initially regarded as being full of 'a million lies'.
15 In an introduction to a 1926 edition of *The Travels of Marco Polo, the Venetian*, pp. ix–x.
16 William Shakespeare, *The Merchant of Venice*, Act 1, Scene 1, lines 177–85 and Act IV, Scene 1, line 180 ff.
17 By Paolo Galluzi, director of the Galileo Museum in Florence.
18 Bertolt Brecht, *Life of Galileo*, Scene 14.

CHAPTER 2

1   Traditional wooden sailing boats used on the Red Sea and River Nile.
2   Known in French as Rosette – hence Rue Rosette – and in English as Rosetta. Rashid is where the Rosetta Stone was discovered, whose text in three ancient Egyptian languages led to the deciphering of hieroglyphics.
3   The Street of Soma became Shariya Horreya and, in the twentieth century, Gamel Abdel Nasser Street. The Canopic Way is now called Tariq al-Hurriyyah.
4   Ptolemy I, otherwise known as Ptolemy Soter.
5   Strabo, *Geographica*, XVII.I.54.
6   E. M. Forster, *Alexandria: A History and a Guide*, Michael Haag edn, 1982, p. 18. The quotation at the chapter heading is from pp. 40–1.
7   This and the subsequent quotation are from *Napoleon, The Last Phase* by Lord Rosebery, a former foreign secretary and prime minister of Britain, 1900, pp. 298–302.
8   From *A Diary of St Helena, The Journal of Lady Malcolm (1816–17)*, 1929, pp. 83–84.
9   Aristotle was writing in the fourth century BC. Other writers who contribute to our understanding of canal building in Egypt include the Roman Pliny the Elder and the Greeks Strabo and Herodotus.
10 Lord Rosebery, p. 299.
11 In Greek, *Periplus Maris Erythræi*. Periplus, literally 'a sailing around', is a Greek word for a nautical almanac, a meaning similar to *navigatio* in Latin and 'navigation' in English.
12 It also gives its name to the nation state of Eritrea, which commands the western coastline of the southern Red Sea.
13 In Sanskrit, the classical language of India, the ocean was known as Ratnakar meaning 'rich in jewels and shells'. The term Indian Ocean was imposed later by European mariners.
14 In Greek *eudaimôn* means blessed, lucky or prosperous, which may have been the origin of the Roman name for the entire peninsula, *Arabia Felix*.
15 Like most early Greeks – Plato, Aristotle, Homer and Strabo, for example – Hippalus is known by a single name.
16 Another version says that this first leg took 20 days, and the last part of the journey was along the Kalizene (or Khalij) canal between Cairo and Alexandria.
17 *Marco Polo's Travels*, Penguin Classics edn, pp. 307–8.
18 *The Travels of Ibn Battutah*, edited by Tim Mackintosh-Smith, p. 87.
19 H. E. Jacob's *The Saga of Coffee* was published in German in 1934. The author calls himself the biographer 'of a hero who for more than a thousand years has been the faithful and vigorous companion of mankind'. Quotations are from the 1935 English edition, pp. 7, 46.

CHAPTER 3

1   Strabo, *Geographica*, 2.5.12.
2   This claim is based on a biblical reference at I Kings 9–10 to almug or sandalwood, of which Kerala is a principal producer. It could have been a source for gold, silver, ivory, apes and peacocks which are also mentioned in those biblical verses.
3   Pliny, *Natural History*, Book VI, chapter 23.
4   *The Periplus of the Erythræan Sea*, # 54.
5   *Kerala Coast: A Byway in History*, by V. Sankaran Nair, pp. 10, 16.
6   *The Travels of Marco Polo*, Penguin Classics edn, 1958, pp. 287–90.
7   *The Travels of Ibn Battuttah*, edited by Tim Mackintosh-Smith, pp. 217–28.
8   From the indigenous word *mala* meaning hill and the Arab word *bar* meaning country.
9   Later Portuguese 'possessions' on India's west coast would include the islands that would merge to form Bombay (from 1534), Daman (or Damão) north of Bombay (1523) and Diu (1535–8) on the coast of Gujarat, the closest part of India to the Red Sea trading ports.
10 Attributed to the English mariner, Sir Walter Raleigh (1554–1618).
11 These are collected as *The Suma Oriental*, a summary of knowledge of the East by Tomé Pires. Quotations are from pp. 53–60 and 516 of the AES two-volume edition.
12 In *Goa, Rome of the Orient*, English edn, pp. 17–18. Subsequent quotations and words attributed to Francis Xavier are from pp. 110–11 of the same book.
13 *Mandelslo's Travels 1603–1671*, edited by Adam Olearius, p. 82.
14 Their canonisation took place during the

reign of Urban VIII, the pope presiding when Galileo was found guilty of heresy for having advanced the theory that the Earth and other planets revolved around the Sun.

15 Quoted by C. R. *Boxer in Portuguese India in the Mid-Seventeenth Century*, p. 19.

16 Goan journalist Frederick Noronha writes in an essay, 'On the Abbé's Trail', that Faria is little remembered in Goa today, his international fame resting on the work he did in France.

17 The sonnet is included in the introduction to da Orta's *Colloquies*.

18 Quotations are from the English version of Linschoten's *Itinerario, The Voyage to the East Indies*, Elibron Classics edn, volume 1, pp. 70, 178–9, 183–4, 214, 236–7. Minor adjustments have been made to the original spelling.

19 Mandelso, p. 80.

20 P. A. Tiele of the University of Utrecht in an introduction to the English edition, dated 1883.

21 From the Sanskrit word *dakhin*, meaning the south, which Europeans mispronounced as 'deccan'.

22 In Malayalam, the language of Kerala, the cashew nut's origin is acknowledged as the tree from which the nut comes: *parangi mavu* translates as 'Portuguese mango'.

CHAPTER 4

1 Herodotus, *The Histories*, 1.205. The Pillars of Hercules are the promontories that flank the entrance to the Mediterranean: the rock of Gibraltar on the northern side and rocky Ceuta to the south.

2 The main source for the 1291 expedition of Vandino and Ugolino Vivaldi is the Genoese annals of Jacopo d'Oria (1294) as translated by Francis M. Rogers in 'The Vivaldi Expedition', in *Annual Reports of the Dante Society*, no. 73, 1955, from which the quote is taken. Rogers argues that 'the expansion of Christendom overseas' was started by the Norman conquest of England and expeditions into the Atlantic Ocean were a logical follow-up to the crusades in the eastern Mediterranean.

3 The Canary island of Alegranza is believed to have been named after one of the Vivaldi brothers' ships, while the large island of Lanzarote was named after the Genoese Lancelotto Malocello, who in 1312 searched unsuccessfully for the Vivaldi brothers.

4 Cristoforo Colombo in his native Genoese; Cristóbal Colón in Spanish.

5 The Oxford academic Sir Peter Russell did much to revise how the world regards Prince Henry, adding inverted commas to Henry's soubriquet – which was coined only in 1854 – in his authoritative 2000 biography, *Prince Henry 'the Navigator': A Life*.

6 King João sought help for this crusader mission from Henry V of England, nephew of his wife, and Charles VI of France, but they were gearing up for a battle of their own against each other at Agincourt.

7 Quoted by Peter Russell in his book *Prince Henry 'the Navigator': A Life* (2000), pp. 225 ff.

8 Peter Russell, ibid., pp. 237–8.

9 According to Sanjay Subrahmanyam in *The Career and Legend of Vasco da Gama*, p. 46, Dias's discrete return to Lisbon was witnessed by Christopher Columbus.

10 Quoted by Sanjay Subrahmanyam, ibid., pp. 149–50.

11 *Journal of the First Voyage of Vasco da Gama, 1497–1499*, Hakluyt Society, 1898, pp. 113–14.

12 Michael Krondl, *The Taste of Conquest, The Rise and Fall of the Three Great Cities of Spice*, pp. 162 ff.

13 Adoption of the word 'turkey' into English is more curious: it was apparently originally applied to the guinea fowl, which comes from the Guinea coast of Africa and was imported to Britain through Turkey, and later misapplied to the entirely different bird. Gold brought to England from the Guinea coast was used to mint a coin, 'the guinea'.

14 According to Subramanyam, ibid., there is some doubt as to whether the bones interred at Belém are those of da Gama.

15 Barry Hatton, *Queen of the Sea, a History of Lisbon*, pp. 2–3.

16 Michael Krondl, ibid., p. 137.

17 Like Lisbon, Seville is some distance from the open sea, on the River Guadalquivir.

18 Luíz Vaz de Camões, *The Lusíads*, canto 2, v 51, canto 9, v 14.

19 Herodotus, at Book 4.42 ff. of *The Histories*, in a discourse about the relationship between the three continents of Libya [Africa], Asia and Europe.

20 Made by Gavin Menzies in his book *1421, The Year China Discovered the World.*

21 Named after the leaden seal, or *bulla*, appended to the end of an official document to authenticate it.

22 C. R. Boxer, *The Portuguese Seaborne Empire 1415–1825*, pp. 20–3.

23 Adam Smith, *The Wealth of Nations*, Book IV, pp. 209 and 25–6.

24 Belém is Portuguese for Bethlehem.

25 Known in Portugal as Filipe I and in Spain as Felipe II.

CHAPTER 5

1 Pliny, *Natural History*, Book 6, chapter 23.

2 *The Travels of Marco Polo*, Penguin Classics edn, 1958, p. 252.

3 Undang-Undang Laut Malacca (Laws of the Malaccan Sea) came into force during the reign of the third sultan, Muhammad Shah, 1424–44.

4 The claim, recorded in *Sejarah Melayu* (Malay Annals), is unlikely to be true since Alexander's conquest of Asia halted at the River Indus.

5 Sarnia Hayes Hoyt in her book *Old Malacca* in the Images of Asia series, Oxford University Press, 2001, p. 14.

6 There is some dispute as to whether he first set foot in Malacca in 1405 or 1408.

7 The seven voyages of China's treasure fleet between 1405 and 1433 are well documented in Chinese and other literature, though accounts differ as to the dimensions of the vessels.

8 Tan Ta Sen in *Cheng Ho and Malacca* published by the International Zheng He Society.

9 From *Commentaries* published in 1557 by Albuquerque's son, Braz, reproduced in English in H. Morse Stephens' *Albuquerque – The Early Portuguese Settlement in India*, 1897, pp. 103–4.

10 This and the headline quotation are from the AES edition of *The Suma Oriental*, a summary of knowledge of the East by Tomé Pires, 1512–15, pp. 286–7.

11 H. Morse Stephens, ibid., p. 95.

12 D. J. M. Tate in *The Making of Modern South-East Asia*, volume 1, p. 45.

13 Also known by his Holy Roman Emperor title as Charles V.

14 As related by Antonio Pigafetta, the Venice-born chronicler of the circumnavigation, in the Dover Publication's edition of *Magellan's Voyage*, 1969, pp. 120–47, translated by R. A. Skelton, formerly superintendent of the Map Room at the British Museum (now British Library).

15 In *Rulers of the Indian Ocean*, 1927, p. 147.

16 The analysis is by C. R. Boxer in *The Portuguese Seaborne Empire 1415–1825*, 1969, from which the subsequent quotation is taken, pp. 110–14.

17 Ballard, ibid., p. 149.

18 In *The Portuguese Seaborne Empire 1415–1825*, C. R. Boxer argues that the Portuguese–Dutch War, which began with Dutch attacks off the coast of west Africa in 1598–9, involved the estuary of the Amazon River and the hinterland of Angola, before concluding with the capture of Dutch settlements on the Malabar coast in 1663, deserves to be regarded as the First World War since it was spread across three continents and lasted far longer than the 1914–18 war. It was a war for control of the oceans and trade.

19 In the case of Timor, the Dutch eventually captured the western part of the island, while the Portuguese retained the eastern half.

20 According to D. J. M. Tate, *The Making of Modern South-East Asia*, 1971, volume 1, p. 316.

21 Known as *Reys-gheschrift vande navigatien der Portugaloysers in Orienten* or Description of the sea journeys undertaken by the Portuguese in the Orient.

CHAPTER 6

1 Pronounced in Dutch as a single vowel sound ('aye') with, in this instance, both characters capitalised.

2 *The Philosopher without Eyes* by Cees Nooteboom, 1997, translated by Manfred Wolf and Virginie M. Kortekaas, from City-Pick Amsterdam, p. 34.

3 The Dutch make no distinction between towns and cities, using the word stad for both.

4 Known in Spain as Felipe II, in Portugal as

Filipe I and elsewhere as Philip II of Spain.

5 The Union of Utrecht of 23 January 1579, which brought together Zeeland, Holland and parts of Utrecht and Groningen, is considered the foundation document of the Dutch Republic. The other northern provinces joined within months.

6 A wind-driven heavy wood cutter has been brought back into service at Zaanse Schans to show how *fluyts* were constructed in the sixteenth century.

7 Roughly equivalent to US$4 million in modern times.

8 This view of Amsterdam will have been based on that by Cornelis Anthonisz dated 1538 which hangs in the Amsterdam Museum.

9 Jan Huygen van Linschoten in the English version of *Itinerario, The Voyage to the East Indies*, Elibron Classics (1885), volume 1, pp. 104, 67.

10 *Oud en Nieuw Oost-Indiën.*

11 Invention of the globe, at least in modern times, is attributed to the German cosmographer Martin Behaim, employed by King João II of Portugal. He produced his first globe in 1492, the year Columbus first sailed to the Americas.

12 Translation is taken from the Taschen edition of *Civitates Orbis Terrarum*, 2008, p. 447.

13 English translation from *The Japanese Discovery of Europe* by Donald Keene, 1952, p. 3.

14 Baruch Spinoza in the English version of his *Theological-Political Treatise*, 1670/1979, translated by R. H. M. Elwes, Preface #20.

15 *The History of Western Philosophy* by Bertrand Russell, 1946, p. 543 in the George Allen and Unwin 1961 edn.

16 William III in the Dutch and English lineage (William II of Scotland) was a grandson of the executed monarch Charles I, so had his own claim to the British throne as well as through his marriage to Mary II, the eldest daughter of James II, Britain's last Catholic monarch.

17 The quotation at the chapter heading is from Voltaire, *Letters (1714–1743)*; that of Montesquieu is from *Voyages*, 1719, both translated by Erica King and extracted from pp. 11–12 in City-Pick Amsterdam; that of Descartes is taken from Russel Shorto's *Amsterdam: A History of the World's Most Liberal City*, p. 144; Onslow Burrish was writing in *Batavia Illustrata, a View of the Policy, and Commerce, of the United Provinces*, 1728, consulted at the British Library.

CHAPTER 7

1 *The Suma Oriental of Tomé Pires*, AES edn, p. 204.

2 The title 'sultan' applies to Muslim rulers, hence the use of 'king' to describe the equivalent ruler of the Hindu Sunda kingdom.

3 A version of this plan of the city was first published in 1657.

4 Quoted in C. R. Boxer, *The Dutch Seaborne Empire 1600–1800*, 1977, p. 96.

5 Jan Huygen van Linschoten, *The Voyage to the East Indies*, volume 2, pp. 83–4.

6 *The Suma Oriental* by Tomé Pires, AES edn, pp. 213–21.

7 Alfred Russel Wallace, *The Malay Archipelago*, 1869, p. 221 in the 1962 Dover edn.

8 Bartholomew Leonardo de Argensola, *The Discovery and Conquest of the Molucco and Philippine Islands*, 1708.

9 The story of Anglo-Dutch rivalry in the Spice Islands is told in *Indonesian Banda – Colonialism and its Aftermath in the Nutmeg Islands*, by Willard A. Hanna.

10 This and the quotation at the chapter head are from Adam Smith, *The Wealth of Nations*, 1776, Books IV–V, Penguin edn, p. 220.

11 In *The Saga of Coffee*, 1935 English version, p. 161. It was Jacob who compared the discovery of coffee with the invention of the telescope and microscope for its beneficial impact on the human brain; see chapter 2.

12 *Max Havelaar – The Coffee Auctions of the Dutch Trading Company*, by Multatuli, Penguin English edn, p. 73.

13 *The Malay Archipelago* by Alfred Russel Wallace, 1962, p. 220.

14 Andrea Wulf's *The Invention of Nature – The Adventures of Alexander von Humboldt, the Lost Hero of Science*, p. 171, tells how von Humboldt, who worked mainly in South America, was refused permission to travel to India by its 'colonial administrators', the English East India Company.

15 Raffles, *History of Java*, 2 vols, 1817, reprinted Kuala Lumpur: Oxford University Press, 1965, Book I, p. 353.

16 Paul Pelliot, *Mémoires sur les coutumes du Cambodge de Tcheou Ta-Kouan*, Paris: Maisonneuve, 1951, p. 20.

17 Ester Boserup, *Woman's Role in Agricultural Development*, Allen & Unwin, 1970, pp. 87–9.

18 Earl wrote: 'By adopting the Greek word for "islands" as a terminal, for which we have a precedent in the term "Polynesia", the inhabitants of the "Indian Archipelago" or "Malayan Archipelago" would become respectively Indu-nesians or Malayu-nesians.'

CHAPTER 8

1 *An Account of the Cape of Good Hope* by C. P. Thunberg, 1772, reproduced in *Voyages and Travels* by John Pinkerton, 1814, volume 16, p. 46.

2 In Voyage to the *Isle of France, the Isle of Bourbon and Cape of Good Hope 1768–1771.*

3 *The Voyage to the East Indies* by J. H. van Linschoten, Elibron edn, pp. 254–7.

4 One of Napoleon's biographers wrote that 'the island would long ago have lapsed into oblivion had it not been for his enforced presence there': Johannes Willms, in *Napoleon and St Helena: On the Island of Exile* (London, 2007), p. 1.

5 In 1804 he issued orders that St Helena be captured from the British, but this never came about. (Willms, ibid., p. 48.)

6 Recorded in *A Diary of St Helena: The Journal of Lady Malcolm, 1816–1817*, edited by Sir Arthur Wilson, p. 53.

7 Linschoten tells us it was actually discovered two years earlier by João de Nova, so it is more accurate to say Albuquerque 'rediscovered' the island.

8 The alternative theories are discussed in Denis Piat's *Mauritius 1598–1810, on the Spice Route.*

9 Maurits finished what his father had started by pushing the Spanish out of the Dutch Republic. Frederik Henrik succeeded him as *stadhouder*.

10 The route was pioneered by Henrik Brouwer in 1611 as a faster way of reaching the East Indies than the more northerly 'monsoon' route via India.

11 The Dutch may have been deterred from moving their settlement to the more suitable Moluccas harbour by the wreck off the port of a fleet of fully laden ships which cost the life of the first governor-general of the Dutch East Indies, Pieter Both. The mountain overlooking Port Louis harbour is named after Admiral Both.

12 *La Compagnie des Indes Orientales* was formed in 1664 and granted a monopoly on trade east of the Cape. After it was dissolved, the French government took over administration of Mauritius, Bourbon and other French colonies.

13 The area was named Pamplemousses, 'grapefruits' in French, because of the large number that grew in the area.

14 Quoted in Piat, Mauritius 1598–1810, on the Spice Route, pp. 57,78.

15 Quoted in Charles Grant, *The History of Mauritius or the Isle of France and the Neighbouring Islands* (London, 1801), p. 519.

16 *Poivre* means 'pepper' in French, but Poivre is remembered for his propagation of cloves and nutmeg rather than pepper.

17 The Pitt quotation is taken from Denis Piat's book, p. 15.

18 Stephen Taylor, *Storm and Conquest*, p. 197.

19 Quotations are from *The Voyage of the Beagle* and *On the Origin of Species by Means of Natural Selection, or the Preservation of Favoured Races in the Struggle for Life.*

CHAPTER 9

1 Salman Rushdie, *Midnight's Children*, 1981, Picador edn, p. 92.

2 Tristram Hunt in *Ten Cities that Made an Empire*, 2014, p. 299.

3 Claudius Ptolemy, *Geographia*, Book 7, chapter 1.95; Wilfred H Schoff, *The Periplus of the Erythræan Sea*, 1911, para 53.

4 There are people of African origin, known as Sidis, in many Indian west coast cities.

5 Stiff linen or cotton used to stiffen clothing and later for bookbinding.

6 Marco Polo, *The Travels*, Penguin Classics edn, p. 292.

7 J. Gerson da Cunha, *The Origin of Bombay*, 1900, p. 68.

8 Bahadur Shah of Gujarat should not be confused with the last Mughal emperor of the same name who ruled in the nineteenth

century. Nuno da Cunha, the tenth governor of Portuguese India, was the son of the first nominated viceroy, Tristão da Cunha.

9 De Castro acceded to the post of viceroy in 1666, too late to influence the transfer of the islands to the British. The quotation is from J. Gerson da Cunha, ibid., p. 5.

10 The map is in the Sloane manuscript *Livro do Estado da India Oriental*, 1646, at the British Library.

11 As recorded by John Fryer in *A New Account of East India and Persia, Being Nine Years Travel 1672–1681*, pp. 219–20. Calico was first produced in Calicut.

12 Published in *A New and Universal System of Geography*, by George Millar, 1782.

13 Her father, King João IV, acceded to the throne of Portugal in 1640 when Portugal regained its independence from Spain.

14 The treaty also gave King Charles II the port of Tangier in north Africa, close to Portugal's first overseas conquest of Ceuta.

15 Anjediva was where Vasco da Gama's ships were becalmed when returning from his first voyage to India.

16 Da Cunha, ibid., pp. 258–9.

17 *The Diary of Samuel Pepys*, Saturday 5 September 1663.

18 Edward Ives in *A Voyage from England to India in the year 1754*, p. 31.

19 Quoted by John Keay in *The Honourable Company*, 1993, p. 136.

20 *The Bombay Dockyard and the Wadia Master Builders* by R. A. Wadia, first published in 1955, tells of the development of the docks at Bombay. Subsequent quotations are taken from pp. 45, 115–16, 120, 159. The family name Wadia derives from the Gujarati word *vadia* meaning carpenter or boat builder.

21 The others were Church Gate and Bazaar Gate.

22 Sharada Dwivedi and Rahul Mehrotra, *Bombay: The Cities Within*, p. 28.

23 According to *Hobson-Jobson*, Salsette takes its name from the Marathi word for 66, *shashashti*, the number of villages on the island.

24 'Dungarees' are trousers made from that cloth, usually with a bib or pinafore top.

25 For an account of how an employee of the East India Company brought seeds and cuttings of the tea plant from China to plant in India, see *For All the Tea in China* by Sarah Rose.

26 The Opium Wars, triggered by Britain's trade in opium and China's clampdown on smugglers evading the dynasty's trading rules, took place in 1839–42 and 1856–60.

27 Quoted in *Ten Cities that Made an Empire* by Tristram Hunt, 2014, p. 269.

28 Jains belong to an indigenous Indian religion which rejects both the polytheism and the caste system of Hindus. Its followers have a strong entrepreneurial tradition.

29 'Bungalow' is another word of Indian origin, meaning a house built in Bengali style or simple dwelling place. The connotation of a single-storey residence came later.

30 'Colloquies' meaning dialogue or conversations; 'simples' here means medicine made from a plant, or the process of gathering such plants. Quotations are from the 1913 Henry Sotheran edn in English, republished by Curato of Mumbai, pp. 111, 132, 121, 225, 423, 372, 215–18, 272–7.

31 Gillian Tindall, *City of Gold*, p. 27.

32 Letters and despatches of Horatio Nelson, including this one dated 9 August 1798, were viewed at www.wtj.com/archives/nelson/1798_08b.htm

CHAPTER 10

1 Tacitus, *The Annals*, 14.33, c.AD 116.

2 Fitzstephen's 'Description of the Most Noble City of London', part of a tribute to his master, the London-born archbishop, is reproduced in *A Survey of London* written in the year 1598 by John Stow, Sutton Publishing, from which quotations are taken, pp. 31–3, 347.

3 Philip II of Spain was the eldest son of Charles V of Spain and Queen Isabella of Portugal. The marriage took place at Winchester Cathedral in a mixture of Spanish, French and Latin.

4 *A Treatise on Money* by John Maynard Keynes, 1930, volume 2, p. 157, in a discussion on Spanish treasure. He estimated that the initial investment in the EIC was worth several billion pounds by 1930 values.

5 *A Discourse on the invention of Ships, Anchors, Compass, &c.* by Walter Raleigh, c.1615.

6 *The Road to Wigan Pier* by George Orwell, 1936, Penguin 1963 edn, p. 140.

7 The two parliaments would merge in 1707 to create the United Kingdom of Great Britain.

8 According to Simon Schama in *The Embarrassment of Riches: An Interpretation of Dutch Culture in the Golden Age*, 1987, p. 96 and endnote chapter 2, 80.

9 *Philosophie Naturalis Principia Mathematica* by Isaac Newton, Royal Society, 1687.

10 The first verse of Masefield's poem 'Cargoes' is included in Chapter 1.

CHAPTER 11

1 The book *Gotham, A History of New York City to 1898*, by E. G. Burrows and Mike Wallace, draws comparison with the 15 million *guilders*' worth of gold, silver, sugar, pearls, spices and hides that the Dutch made in booty plundered from a Spanish fleet off Cuba two years after the alleged purchase of Manhattan (p. 28); also the 5,000 *guilders* collected to build a wall to protect New Amsterdam from the English (p. 64).

2 A point made by Raanan Geberer in his detailed account of the English takeover of New Amsterdam in 'New York's History and Culture Based on Four Centuries of Dutch Treats', https://www.historynet.com/going-dutch/ accessed on 28 February 2021.

3 Of the 700 enslaved Africans brought to New Netherland during the Stuyvesant era, 300 lived in New Amsterdam.

4 It was given the name 'the Duke's Plan' in 1858 by New York Historical Society librarian George H. Moore on discovering the map in the King's Library. It is now held at the British Library in London.

5 The language spoken by the Abenkai people. Naumkeag translates loosely as 'fishing place'.

6 Jerusalem means 'city of peace'.

7 Pepper was introduced to Sumatra from India. By the time traders from Salem arrived, Sumatra had overtaken India as its major source.

8 Originally named Richter, they took on the family name Crowninshield, a reference to the family crest, on their arrival in Massachusetts Bay in 1688.

9 *Antony and Cleopatra*, Act 2, Scene 2. The spirit and prosperity of first-century Alexandria reached America by the nineteenth century.

10 The four largest American cities in 1790 were New York, Philadelphia, Baltimore and Charleston.

11 *Salem and the Indies* by James Duncan Phillips, Houghton Mifflin, 1947, pp. 2, 7, 99.

12 *Pepper and Pirates* by James Duncan Phillips, Houghton Mifflin, 1949, p. xi.

13 *The House of the Seven Gables* by Nathaniel Hawthorne, 1848, chapter VII, p. 86 in the Modern Library edn.

CHAPTER 12

1 Quotations by João de Barros and Dr Alexander Hamilton are from *Hobson-Jobson*, Routledge and Kegan Paul edn, pp. 839–40.

2 *Raffles and the Golden Opportunity* by Victoria Glendinning, Profile Books, 2012, pp. 1–2, 226.

3 Quoted in Noel Barber's *The Singapore Story*, p. 32.

4 Glendinning, ibid., p. 260.

5 A. T. Jaffrey, 'On disease of the nutmeg trees in Singapore', *Transactions and Proceedings of the Botanical Society of Edinburgh*, 6 (1860, March), p. 368.

6 J. Cameron, *Our tropical possessions in Malayan India*, Smith, Elder, 1865, p. 82.

7 Rubber is one of the plants featured in *Seeds of Wealth* by Henry Hobhouse, 2003.

8 *A Diary of St Helena*, by Lady Malcolm, p. 53.

9 *The Saga of Coffee*, by H. E. Jacob, 1935 edn, p. 263.

10 *Raffles of the Eastern Isles* by C. E. Wurtzburg, 1954, pp. 407–8.

11 *Substance of a Memoir on the Administration of the Eastern Isles*, Stamford Raffles, 1819.

EPILOGUE

1 Transporting gas as Liquefied Natural Gas (LNG) reduces its volume to 1/600th of its gas form; and as Liquefied Petroleum Gas (LPG) up to 1/250th. A fleet of over 1,000 specially constructed ships transport gas around the world in liquid form.

2 I.e. containers 20 feet (6.1 metres) in length.

SELECTIVE
BIBLIOGRAPHY

Dates given are the original publication/ edition consulted.

Abeyasekere, Susan, *Jakarta: A History*, OUP, 1987

Aldersley-Williams, Hugh, *Dutch Light – Christian Huygens and the Making of Science in Europe*, Picador, 2020

Aslet, Clive, *Greenwich Millennium*, Fourth Estate, 1999

Balcombe, Betsy, *To Befriend an Emperor – Memoirs of Napoleon on St Helena*, Ravenhall Books, 2005

Ballard, G. A., *Rulers of the Indian Ocean*, Asian Educational Services,1927/1998

Barley, Nigel, *The Duke of Puddle Dock – In the Footsteps of Stamford Raffles*, Penguin, 1991

Beekman, E. M. (ed./trans.), *The Poison Tree: Selected Writings of Rumphius on the Natural History of the Indies*, University of Massachusetts Press, 1981

Bergreen, Laurence, *Over the Edge of the World – Magellan's Terrifying Circumnavigation of the Globe*, Harper Collins, 2003

—, *Marco Polo – From Venice to Xanadu*, Quercus, 2008

Boserup, Ester, *Woman's Role in Agricultural Development*, Allen & Unwin, 1970

Boulger, Demetrius Charles, *The Life of Sir Stamford Raffles*, Pepin Press, Amsterdam, 1897/1999

Boxer, C. R., *The Dutch Seaborne Empire 1600–1800*, Hutchinson, 1965

—, *The Portuguese Seaborne Empire 1415–1825*, Hutchinson, 1969

—, *Portuguese India in the Mid-Seventeenth Century*, OUP, 1980

Bracciolini, Poggio, *The travels of Nicolò Conti in the East, in the early part of the fifteenth century*, 1857, consulted at the British Library

Brecht, Bertolt, *Life of Galileo*, Methuen Drama, 1955/1988

Brierly, Joanna Hall, *Spices: The Story of Indonesia's Spice Trade*, OUP, 1994

Buck, Paul, *Lisbon – A Cultural and Literary Companion*, Signal Books, 2002

Buisseret, David, *The Mapmakers' Quest – Depicting New Worlds in Renaissance Europe*, OUP, 2003

Burrish, Onslow, *Batavia Illustrata, a View of the Policy and Commerce of the United Provinces*, 1728, consulted at the British Library

Burrows, E. G. and Wallace, Mike, *Gotham: A History of New York City to 1898*, OUP, 1999

Camões, Luiz Vaz de, *The Lusíads*, Oxford World's Classics, 1997

Collis, Maurice, *Raffles*, Faber and Faber, 1966

Commissariat, M. S., *Mandelslo's Travels in Western India, 1638–1639*, Asian Educational Services, 1931/1995

Corm, Charles, *The Scents of Eden – A History of the Spice Trade*, Kodansha, 1999

Cottineau de Kloguen, Denis L., *An Historical Sketch of Goa*, Asian Educational Services, 1831/1995

Crane, Nicholas, *Mercator: The Man who Mapped the Planet*, Weidenfeld and Nicolson, 2002

Crawfurd, John, *History of the Indian Archipelago*, Frank Cass & Co., 1820/1967

Crowley, Roger, *City of Fortune – How Venice Ruled the Seas*, Random House, 2011

da Cunha, Gerson, *The Origin of Bombay*, Asian Educational Services, 1900/1993

da Orta, Garcia, *Colloquies on the Simples and Drugs of India*, Sotheran/Curato of Mumbai, 1563/1913

Darwin, Charles, *The Voyage of the Beagle*, Penguin Classics, 1839/1989

—, *On the Origin of Species by Means of Natural Selection*, John Murray, 1860

Dash, Mike, *Tulipomania*, Indigo, 1999

de Argensola, Bartholomew, *The Discovery and Conquest of the Molucco and Philippine Islands*, 1708, consulted at Project Gutenberg

de Saint Pierre, J. H. B., *Voyage to the Isle of France, Isle of Bourbon and the Cape of Good Hope*, Asian Educational Services, 1800/1999

Dryden, John, *Amboyna or the Cruelties of the Dutch to the English Merchants*, Amazon Reprint, 1673

Dwivedi, S. and Mehrotra, R., *Bombay – The Cities Within*, Eminence Designs, 1995/2001

Earl, G. W., *The Eastern Seas*, OUP, 1837/1971

Ellis, Markman, *The Coffee House – A Cultural History*, Weidenfeld and Nicolson, 2004

Empereur, Jean-Yves, *Alexandria Rediscovered*, British Museum Press, 1998

Fara, Patricia, *Sex, Botany and Empire*, Icon Books, 2003

—, *Life after Gravity*, OUP, 2021

Fell, R. T., *Early Maps of South-East Asia*, OUP, 1988

Forster, E. M., *Alexandria: A History and a Guide*, Michael Haag, 1982

Fryer, John, *A New Account of East India and Persia, 1672–1681*, Asian Educational Services, 1909/1992

Gale Ecco Editions, *A Description of the Port and Island of Bombay and an historical account of the transactions between the English and Portugueze concerning it, from the year 1661 to this present time*, 1724, consulted at the British Library

Glendinning, Victoria, *Raffles and the Golden Opportunity*, Profile Books, 2012

Goss, K. David and others, *Salem Cornerstones of a Historical City*, Commonwealth Editions, 1999

Grabsky, Phil, *The Lost Temple of Java*, Seven Dials, 2000

Grant, Charles, *The History of Mauritius or the Isle of France and the Neighbouring Islands*, Asian Educational Services, 1801/1995

Griffiths, John, *Tea – A history of the drink that changed the world*, André Deutsch, 2011

Hakluyt, *Journal of the First Voyage of Vasco da Gama, 1497–1499*, Hakluyt Society, 1898

Hall, Richard, *Empires of the Monsoon*, HarperCollins, 1996

Hanna, Willard A., *Indonesian Banda - Colonialism and its Aftermath in the Nutmeg Islands*, Yayasan Warisan dan Budaya, Banda Naira, 1991

Hanna, Willard and Alwi, Des, *Turbulent Times Past in Ternate and Tidore*, Yayasan Warisan dan Budaya, Banda Naira, 1990

Hatton, Barry, *Queen of the Sea – A History of Lisbon*, Hurst, 2018

Herodotus, *The Histories*, Penguin Classics, 1954

Heuken SJ, A., *Historical Sites of Jakarta*, Yayasan Cipta Loka Caraka, 2000

—, *The Earliest Portuguese Sources for the History of Jakarta*, Yayasan Cipta Loka Caraka, 2002

Hobhouse, Henry, *Seeds of Change*, Papermac, 1985

—, *Seeds of Wealth*, Macmillan/Pan, 2003

Hoyt, Sarnia Hayes, *Old Malacca*, OUP, 1993

Hunt, Tristram, *Ten Cities that Made an Empire*, Penguin, 2014

Hutton, Wendy, *Tropical Herbs and Spices*, Periplus Editions, 1997

Ivens, Edward, *A Voyage from England to India in the year 1754*, 1754, consulted at the British Library

Jackson, Kevin, *The Queen's Pirate – Sir Francis Drake and the Golden Hind*, TS Books, 2020

Jacob, H. E., *The Saga of Coffee, the Biography of an Economic Product*, Unwin, 1935

Jayne, K. G., *Vasco da Gama and his Successors 1460–1580*, Asian Educational Services, 1910/1997

Jaypal, Maya, *Old Singapore*, OUP, 1992

—, *Old Jakarta*, OUP, 1993

Keay, John, *The Honourable Company – A History of the English East India Company*, HarperCollins, 1991

—, *The Spice Route*, John Murray, 2005

Keene, Donald, *The Japanese Discovery of Europe, 1720–1830*, Routledge & Kegan Paul, 1952

Keynes, John Maynard, *A Treatise on Money*, 1930, consulted at the British Library

Knighton, C. S., *Pepys and the Navy*, Sutton Publishing, 2003

Krondl, Michael, *The Taste of Conquest*, Ballantine Books, 2007

le Comte, Christian, *Mauritius from its Origin*, Christian le Comte, 2004

Lim, Irene, *Sketches in the Straits, the watercolours and manuscript of Charles Dyce*, National University of Singapore, 2003

Linschoten, Jan Huygen van, *The Voyage to the East Indies (Itinerario)*, Hakluyt Society/Elibron Classics, 1596/2005

—, *Voyage to Goa and Back, 1583–1592, with his account of the East Indies*, Asian Educational Services, 1903/2004

—, *Jan Huygen van Linschoten and the moral map of Asia*, 1999, consulted at the British Library

Mackintosh-Smith, Tim (ed.), *The Travels of Ibn Battutah*, Picador, 2002

Macleod, Roy (ed.), *The Library of Alexandria – Centre of Learning of the Ancient World*, I. B. Tauris, 2000

Madan, K. D., *Life and Times of Vasco da Gama*, Asian Educational Services, 1998

Menzies, Gavin, *1421, The Year China Discovered the World*, Bantam Books, 2002

Miksic, J. and Gek, C.-A. L. M., *Early Singapore 1300s-1819*, Singapore History Museum, 2004

Millar, George, *A New and Universal System of Geography*, 1782, consulted at the British Library

Milton, Giles, *Nathaniel's Nutmeg*, Hodder and Stoughton, 1999

Mir, Moin, *Surat – Fall of a Port, Rise of a Prince*, Roli Books, 2018

Morris, Jan, *The Venetian Empire – A Sea Voyage*, Penguin, 1980

—, *Venice*, Faber and Faber, 1993

Motley, John Lothrop, *The Rise of the Dutch Republic*, Ward Lock, 1890

Multatuli, *Max Havelaar or the Coffee Auctions of the Dutch Trading Company*, Penguin Classics, 1860/1987

Nieuhof, Johannes, *Voyages into Brazil and the East Indies, 1640–1649*, 1703, consulted at the British Library

Norrington, Ruth, *My dearest Minette – Letters between Charles II and his sister, the Duchesse d'Orléans*, Peter Owen, 1996

Olearius, Adam (ed.), *Mandelso's Travels 1603–1671*, 1669, consulted at the British Library

Orwell, George, *The Road to Wigan Pier*, Penguin, 1937/1963

Padfield, Peter, *Maritime Supremacy and the Opening of the Western Mind*, Pimlico, 1999

Parry, Clive (ed.), *Consolidated Treaty Series (237 volumes)*, 1969–1981, consulted at the British Library

Pelliot, Paul, *Mémoires sur les coutumes du Cambodge de Tcheou Ta-Kouan*, Paris: Maisonneuve, 1951

Pepys, Samuel, *The Diary of Samuel Pepys, 1660–1669*, consulted online

Phillips, James Duncan, *Salem in the Seventeenth Century*, Houghton Mifflin, Boston, 1933

—, *Salem in the Eighteenth Century*, Houghton Mifflin, Boston, 1937

—, *Salem and the Indies*, Houghton Mifflin, Boston, 1947

—, *Pepper and Pirates*, Houghton Mifflin, Boston, 1949

Piat, Denis, *Mauritius on the Spice Route*, Editions Didier Millet, 2010

Pigafetta, Antonio, *Magellan's Voyage: A Narrative Account of the First Circumnavigation*, Dover Publications, 1522/1969

Pinto, J. and Fernandes, N. (eds.), *Bombay, meri jaan*, Penguin, 2003

Pires, Tomé, *The Suma Oriental of Tomé Pires*, 1512–15, Asian Educational Services, 1515/1990

Pliny the Elder, *Natural History*, Penguin Classics, 77/1991

Polo, Marco, *The Travels of Marco Polo*, Penguin Classics, 1958

Ptolemy, Claudius, *Geography of Claudius Ptolemy*, Cosimo Classics, 1932/2011

Raffles, Sophia, *Memoir of the Life and Public Service of Sir Thomas Stamford Raffles*, 1830, consulted at the British Library

Raffles, Stamford, *Substance of a Memoir on the Administration of the Eastern Islands*, 1819, consulted at the British Library

—, *History of Java*, 2 vols, 1817, reprinted Kuala Lumpur: Oxford University Press, 1965

Reid, Anthony and Brewster, Jennifer (eds.), *Slavery, Bondage, and Dependency in Southeast Asia*, University of Queensland Press, 1983

Rémy, Colonel, *Goa: Rome of the Orient*, Arthur Barker, 1957

Reyes, H. and Schiferli, V. (eds.), *City Picks: Amsterdam*, Oxygen Books, 2010

Robins, Nick, *The Corporation that Changed the World*, Pluto Press, 2006

Roegholt, Richter, *A Short History of Amsterdam*, Bekking and Blitz, 2004

Rohatgi, P. and others (eds.), *Bombay to Mumbai*, Marg Publications, 1997/2001

Rose, Sarah, *For All the Tea in China: Espionage, Empire and the Secret Formula for the World's Favourite Drink*, Arrow, 2010

Roseberry, Archibald, *Napoleon: The Last Phase*, Thomas Nelson, 1916

Roy, Tirthankar, *The East India Company – The World's Most Powerful Corporation*, Portfolio Penguin, 2012

Sanghera, Sathnam, *Empireland – How Imperialism Shaped Modern Britain*, Penguin, 2021

Sankaran Nair, V., *Kerala Coast: A Byway in History*, Folio, Trivandrum, 2008

Sanyal, Sangeev, *The Ocean of Churn How the Indian Ocean shaped Human History*, Penguin, 2016

Schama, Simon, *The Embarrassment of Riches, An Interpretation of Dutch Culture in the Golden Age*, Collins, 1987

Schoff, Wilfred H., *The Periplus of the Erythræan Sea – Travel and trade in the Indian Ocean by a merchant of the first century*, Munshiram Manoharlal Publishers, 1911/2011

Shorto, Russell, *The Island at the Center of the World*, Doubleday, 2004

—, *Amsterdam, A History of the World's Most Liberal City*, Little Brown, 2013

Smith, Adam, *The Wealth of Nations*, Penguin Classics, 1776/1999

Sobel, Dava, *Longitude – The True Story of a Lone Genius who solved the Greatest Scientific Problem of his Time*, Fourth Estate, 1996

—, *Galileo's Daughter – A Drama of Science, Faith and Love*, Fourth Estate, 1999

—, *A More Perfect Heaven – How Copernicus Revolutionised the Cosmos*, Bloomsbury, 2011

Spinoza, Baruch, *A Treatise partly Theological and partly Political,* 1670/1979, translated by R. H. M. Elwes, consulted at Project Gutenberg

Stephens, H. Morse, *Albuquerque – The Early Portuguese Settlement in India,* Asian Educational Services, 1897/2000

Stow, John, *A Survey of London written in the year 1598,* Sutton Publishing, 1598/2005

Strabo, *The Geography of Strabo (Geographica)*, CUP, 1st C AD/2014

Suárez, Thomas, *Early Mapping of South-East Asia,* Periplus Editions, 1999

Subrahmanyam, Sanjay, *The Career and Legend of Vasco da Gama*, CUP, 1997

Tan Ta Sen, *Cheng Ho and Malacca*, International Zheng He Society

Tate, D. J. M., *The Making of Modern South-east Asia,* 2 vols, OUP, 1969, 1979

Taylor, Stephen, *Storm and Conquest – The Battle for the Indian Ocean, 1809*, Faber and Faber, 2007

Thunberg, C. P., *An Account of the Cape of Good Hope and some parts of the Interior of Southern Africa*, 1814, consulted at the British Library

Tindall, Gillian, *City of Gold – The Biography of Bombay*, Penguin,1982

Tomalin, Claire, *Samuel Pepys – The Unrivalled Self*, Penguin, 2002

Turner, Jack, *Spice – The History of a Temptation*, Harper Perennial, 2004

Turner, Sarah et al., *Fragrant Frontier*, NIAS Press, 2022

Valentijn, François, *Oud en Nieuw Oost-Indien*, 1726, consulted at the British Library

Virga, Vincent, *Historic Maps and Views of New York*, Black Dog and Levanthall, 2008

Vlekke, Bernard H. M., *Nusantara: A History of Indonesia*, W. Van Hoeve, 1965

Wadia, Ruttonjee Ardeshir, *The Bombay Dockyard and the Wadia Master Builders*, Bombay Parsi Pachayat, 1955/2004

Wallace, Alfred Russel, *The Malay Archipelago*, Dover Publications, 1869/1962

Welsh, Frank, *A History of South Africa*, HarperCollins, 2000

Wilford, John Noble, *The Mapmakers – The Story of the Great Pioneers in Cartography from Antiquity to the Space Age*, Vintage Books, 1982

Willms, Johannes, *Napoleon and St Helena: On the Island of Exile*, Haus Publishing, 2008

Wills, John E., *1688, A Global History*, Granta Books, 2001

Wilson, Sir Arthur (ed.), *A Diary of St Helena: The Journal of Lady Malcolm, 1816–17,* 1817, consulted at the British Library

Wolff, Anne, *How Many Miles to Babylon?* Liverpool University Press, 2003

Worden, N. et al., *Cape Town: The Making of a City*, David Philip, 1998

Wurtzberg, C. E., *Raffles of the Eastern Isles*, Hodder and Stoughton, 1954

Yule, H. and Burnell, A. C., *Hobson-Jobson – A Glossary of Colloquial Anglo-Indian Words and Phrases*, Routledge & Kegan Paul, 1886/1986

Zumthor, Paul, *Daily Life in Rembrandt's Holland*, Weidenfeld and Nicolson, 1962

PICTURE CREDITS

C. Decker fc.

INDEX

Holland 122–7, 134–5, 137–9, 144, 155, 169, 240, 274
Holmes, Admiral Robert 221, 225
Holy Roman Empire 122–3, 274
Hondius, Jodocus 102, 133
Hoorn 125, 127, 130, 139
Horburgh, James 259
Hormuz 66–8, 90, 106, 115, 132
Hudson, Henry 131, 133, 233–4, 252
Hudson River 234, 238–40
Huguenots 124, 169, 235
Huygens, Christiaan 136–7, 223, 225, 277
Hypatia 42

I.
IJ River 121–2
Île de France 175, 178, 180, 182–4, 218; see also Mauritius
Illustrated London News 228, 230, 249
indentured labour 8, 169, 176, 180, 184, 217
India
    and Americans 244, 248
    and British 43, 46, 116, 173, 179, 183, 183, 216–20, 223, 231, 264
    and Egypt 57
    and French 37, 46, 172, 178–80, 184, 266–7
    and Greeks 38, 46
    and Portuguese 14, 25, 28, 58–77, 80, 84–7, 90–2, 94
    cartography 9, 87–90
    coast of Goa 58–77
    port of Bombay 186–207
    spices 7, 11, 14, 21, 30, 91, 154
    see also East India Company
Indian Ocean
    and Dutch 168
    and French 11, 266
    and Portuguese 60, 66, 68, 75, 92, 106
    cartography 9, 15–16, 37, 42, 45, 50–1, 61, 65, 79, 87–9, 102, 175–6
    islands 175–6, 184
    navigation 17, 48–50, 52, 64, 87, 111, 242, 252
    winds 24, 50, 102
indigo 50, 178, 192, 216, 267
Indo-China 108, 269
Indonesia 7, 11, 63, 102, 104, 157–8, 160, 163–5, 263, 272
Indonesian language 7, 117, 142, 149–50, 164
Indus, River 38, 61–2, 67, 274
Inquisition
    in Portugal 72, 97
    in Rome 33–4, 135
    in Spain 122
Isaacsz, Pieter 137
Isabella, Queen 8, 80, 94, 122, 228, 276
Italy 14, 19–20, 28, 93, 223
Itinerario 11, 72, 75, 87–9, 118, 131, 133, 147, 273; see also Linschoten
ivory 30, 50, 63, 83, 92, 197, 273

J.
Jacob, H. E. 56–7, 156, 273, 275
Jains 199, 203, 276
Jakarta 8, 114, 139, 141, 143, 164–5, 277–8; see also Batavia
James I of England, VI of Scotland 218–19
James II of England, VII of Scotland 220–1, 237–8, 275
Jamestown, St Helena 172, 185
Jansson, Jan 50–1, 102–3, 133, 241–3, 248–9
Jerusalem 22, 63, 86, 276
João I 79, 82, 194
João II 80, 84–5, 275
João III 60, 69–70, 91, 148
João IV 97, 115, 194, 276
Japan 35, 70, 107, 139, 154–5, 164, 266
Java 141–65
    and British 116, 262, 266
    and Chinese 104
    and Dutch 114–16, 127, 132, 169, 177, 256, 262, 266
    and French 266–7
    and Portuguese 108
    and Spanish 110
    botany 72
    cartography 19, 118, 131, 133
    cloves 30
    coffee 57, 267–8
    Dekker 11, 157–8
    Demak 107–8, 143–4
    Majapahit 102, 104, 107, 255
    nutmeg 30
    pepper 30
    Raffles 256–7, 260, 266, 268, 279
    rice 117, 169
    sugar 176, 178, 192
    traders 102
Jews
    in Aden 53
    in Alexandria 39, 42
    in Amsterdam 124, 134
    in England 231
    in India 65, 72, 199, 203
    in New York 235
    in Portugal 72, 97
    in Spain 72, 97, 124
    in Venice 32
junks 17, 64, 105

K.
Karachi 198
Kerala 60, 63–6, 72, 77, 131, 273
Kew, Royal Botanical Gardens 185, 226, 265
Khoikhoi 169
Kipling, Rudyard 206, 228
Kolis 187, 191
Kublai Khan 30

L.
La Bourdonnais, Comte de 178–81, 183
Langren, Arnoldus van 88–9, 131
Laplace, Cyrille 267
Latin 19, 46, 50, 64, 71, 117, 131, 157, 273, 276

Leiden 34, 134–5, 236
Leizelt, Balthazar Frederic 247
Leopold, Joseph Friedrich 58–9, 74, 211–13
Libya 41, 80, 274
Linnaeus, Carl 162, 226
Linschoten, Jan Huygen van 72–5, 118–19
    author 11, 87, 131–2, 147
    cartographer 10, 36–7, 87–9, 117, 131–3, 174, 256
    mariner 10, 52, 143–4, 149, 171
Lisbon 8, 17, 23, 59–60, 68–9, 72, 75, 78–99, 106, 110, 112, 118, 125, 130, 146, 192, 206, 209, 274
Lombardy 19–20, 23
London 8, 23, 68, 136, 162–4, 169, 172, 188, 193, 197, 202, 208–31, 238, 244, 247–9, 257–8, 261–3, 270, 276
longitude 41, 111, 136, 147, 158, 177, 223–6, 230, 271, 279
Lonthor 149–50, 152, 154
Louis XIV 178, 225
Louis XVIII 184
Luxembourg 122–3

M.
mace
    the fruit 7–8, 14, 111, 126, 149–50, 206, 228, 271
    the habitat 142, 146
    the trade 19, 67, 90, 93, 109, 114–15, 152–4, 156, 165, 240–1, 243,
Madagascar 169, 175, 178, 181, 183, 191
Madeira 76, 83, 94, 244
Madras 64, 70, 116, 178–9, 193, 197, 216–17, 223, 244, 248
Magellan, Ferdinand 11, 15, 94, 100–1, 110–12, 122, 146, 148, 205, 214, 234, 252
Majapahit 102–5, 107, 255
Makassar 154, 156, 164
Malabar 30, 59, 63–70, 74–7, 87, 112, 114–15, 131–2, 178, 192, 197, 199, 274
Malabar Hill 202–3
Malacca 100–19; also
    and British 163, 256, 262
    and Chinese 255, 259
    and Dutch 146, 169, 262
    and Portuguese 66–7, 72, 92, 142, 144
    botany 205, 265
    cartography 131, 264
    ginger 244
    trade 8, 148, 270
Malacca Straits 102–3, 107, 111–12, 114, 117–18, 133, 144, 272
Malay archipelago 114, 141–2, 146, 149, 158, 160, 256, 263
Malaya 103, 105, 119, 227, 265
Malaysia 105, 118–19, 263
Malcolm, Sir Pulteney 163
Malcolm, Lady 163, 273, 275, 276
Malindi 59, 85, 87, 89, 175–6
Mallet, Alain 167, 192
Mamluks 25, 43, 46, 66–7

Mandovi River 58–9, 67, 73–5
Manhattan 131, 155, 220, 232–41, 248–52
Manhattan Transfer 240–2, 276
Manila 148, 181, 244
Manuel I 59–60, 66–7, 69, 72, 79, 85–6, 89–93, 97–8, 106, 108, 110, 122
Marco Polo 10–11, 14–15, 30, 52, 61, 64, 80, 101, 142, 181
Mary, Queen, wife of Philip II of Spain 214,
Mary, Queen, wife of William III of England 221–2
Mascarene Islands 175–85
Masefield, John 30, 227
Mauritius 11, 150, 167–8, 174–85, 191, 218, 226–7, 244, 264, 267, 278–9; see also Île de France
Mauro, Fra 16–19, 64
Max Havelaar 11, 157–8, 163, 279
Mediterranean Sea
    and cartography 15
    and navigation 14, 252
    and trade 125, 130, 220, 259
    from Alexandria 37–8, 42–9, 52, 55, 94
    from Lisbon 79–84
    from Venice 21–5, 28,
Meisner, Daniel 29
Mercator, Gerardus 133, 277
Merchant of Venice 30, 32, 95, 227
microscope 57, 136, 275
Mocha 55–7, 178, 245
Moluccas 7, 93, 109–11, 132–3, 142–50, 153–5, 158, 161, 205; see also Spice Islands
Mombasa 87, 175
Mongolia 14
monsoon 50–2, 61, 63, 87, 102, 187, 193, 275, 278
Montesquieu, Charles de 138, 275
Moors 68, 81, 87, 106, 112
Morris, Jan 20, 273, 278
Mozambique 87, 90, 115, 131, 167–8, 175–6
Multatuli 11, 157–8, 218; see also Dekker, E. D.
Münster, Sebastian 9, 16–17, 20, 59–61, 80–1, 87, 109, 121, 255–6
Muslims
    in Africa 25, 87, 89, 94
    in Asia 9, 25, 50, 53, 66–8, 90, 93, 101, 104–8, 143, 191, 199, 231
    in Europe 21–2, 25, 82, 122
Muziris 51, 62–4
myrrh 50, 52–4, 62, 92

N.
Naples 25
Napoleon Bonaparte
    aspirations for East Indies 162, 169, 256, 267, 269
    in Egypt 37–8, 43, 46–9, 57, 206
    in France 28, 116
    in Indian Ocean 183–4
    in Venice 23, 29
    on St Helena 172–4, 185, 266–8

ACKNOWLEDGEMENTS

I have drawn heavily on contemporary sources such as Marco Polo, Jan Huygen van Linschoten, Tomé Pires, Antonio Pigafetta, Luís Vaz de Camões, Garcia da Orta and the unknown author of *The Periplus of the Erythræan Sea*. My thanks to the Hakluyt Society, Dover Publications, Elibron Classics, Curato, Cosimo Classics and Asian Educational Services for making old texts available and to the British Library for connecting me to these and other works. The British Library Map Room have helped illustrate the history, as have map dealers in several countries – of which Massimo De Martini of Altea in London deserves my special appreciation. Geoffrey Allibone, John Carroll, C. S. Knighton, Helga Lehmann, Ashok Mahadevan, Sue Ross, Steve Woodhouse and Andrew Whitehead all contributed in different ways, some by translating map inscriptions. My thanks too to Philippa Glanville for pointing me towards the British Library and to Brenda Stones for her support in building the original idea into a book; also to the British Library publications team under John Lee for projecting this history towards a wide audience on several continents.

First published in Great Britain in 2024 by
The British Library
96 Euston Road
London NW1 2DB
www.bl.uk

ISBN 978-0-7123-5595-7

British Library Cataloguing in Publication Data
A catalogue record for this publication is
available from the British Library

First published in North America in 2024 by
Brandeis University Press
415 South Street, MS 046
Waltham MA 02453
brandeisuniversitypress.com

ISBN 978-1-68458-244-0

Library of Congress Control Number: 2024936601

Edited by Brenda Stones
Picture Research by Sally Nicholls
Designed by Ocky Murray

Printed in the Czech Republic by Finidr